Ken Barlow was born in Manchester Cyril, which made for a very ind childhood. His class was the first intake in Infant One at the new post-war Barton Clough County Primary School, leaving after the 11+ for Great Stone Park, then entering printing at 15. He spent several years in his early 20's travelling Europe and working in restaurants. After arriving back in the UK and suffering a broken neck in a freak motor accident, before returning to printing at The Reading Evening Post. More recently he was the landlord of the Swan at Wycombe Marsh, where his son, Christopher, was born: then the Castle Public House in Basingstoke for over 12 years, with Christopher and his two stepdaughters, Louise and Nicola. Afterwards he set up his print company, before embarking on this journey.

Sue Cooper (nee Bradford) was born and educated in Liverpool at Heatherlea and Belvedere Schools. On leaving, she gained experience as a secretary at Sefton General Hospital before moving to Switzerland with The World Health Organisation. She returned to London and was employed as personnel assistant for a firm of Management Consultants, married and moved to Kingswood, Surrey, where her two daughters, Lucy and Mary, were born. After working at an international agricultural company for a number of years, the office was re-located to Berkshire. She met Ken two years later before moving out to Portugal.

Ken and Sue now live happily together in Portugal on 5 ½ acres of land, and split their time between tending the fields, gardens and vegetable patch, the two holiday apartments, printing business, writing, and in their spare time they produce home made chutneys, jams, wine and Jeropiga. They share a mutual enthusiasm for life, as well as a finely honed passion for entertaining and cooking, especially Indian curries.

THE EUCALYPTUS DANCE

Ken Barlow

Colin Helen and Rachel

We hope you enjoy our adventure.

With love

Ken & Sue

xxx

The names of some of the characters and businesses have been changed to protect their identities. The facts are as seen and understood by the authors at the time and are open to interpretation.

Published in conjunction with Trafford Publishing
TEL Print
Casa Sulo, Alombada
Macinhata do Vouga
Águeda, 3750 – 581
Portugal
Tel: +351 9123 18287

Order this book online at www.trafford.com/07-2557
or email orders@trafford.com

Most Trafford titles are also available at major online book retailers.

© Copyright 2007 Ken Barlow.
All rights reserved. No part of this publication may be reproduced, stored in a retrieval system, or transmitted, in any form or by any means, electronic, mechanical, photocopying, recording, or otherwise, without the written prior permission of the author.

Note for Librarians: A cataloguing record for this book is available from Library and Archives Canada at www.collectionscanada.ca/amicus/index-e.html

Printed in Victoria, BC, Canada.

ISBN: 978-1-4251-5694-7

We at Trafford believe that it is the responsibility of us all, as both individuals and corporations, to make choices that are environmentally and socially sound. You, in turn, are supporting this responsible conduct each time you purchase a Trafford book, or make use of our publishing services. To find out how you are helping, please visit www.trafford.com/responsiblepublishing.html

Our mission is to efficiently provide the world's finest, most comprehensive book publishing service, enabling every author to experience success. To find out how to publish your book, your way, and have it available worldwide, visit us online at www.trafford.com/10510

 www.trafford.com

North America & international
toll-free: 1 888 232 4444 (USA & Canada)
phone: 250 383 6864 ♦ fax: 250 383 6804 ♦ email: info@trafford.com

The United Kingdom & Europe
phone: +44 (0)1865 722 113 ♦ local rate: 0845 230 9601
facsimile: +44 (0)1865 722 868 ♦ email: info.uk@trafford.com

10 9 8 7 6 5 4 3 2 1

ACKNOWLEDGEMENTS

To Sue, for hours of patiently correcting my grammatical gaffs, burning the midnight oil, and for allowing this book to be published in the first person singular. But above all, for being my best friend and partner in life.

Ken

There are far too many people who have assisted us over the last few years to thank individually, but our special appreciation goes to:

Terry, wherever you are, thank you for setting us on this adventure.

All family, friends and visitors for their encouragement, advice and help.

The people of Portugal, especially Alombada, without whom our lives would have been more difficult and certainly a lot less fun.

To Rui and Cláudia who have acted as translators, interpreters, computer repair people, information officers and, in particular, for always being there for us.
Ken and Sue

Chapter 1

The single track road from the house where Sue and I were staying wound lazily through the village of Alombada, paused at the top of the valley beside an ominously sited cross, and swung right to plunge down the side of its steep slope into the tree-shaded depths below. It was the second day of our first holiday together.

I had guided the hire car gingerly past a pair of comatose dogs stretching out in the noon sun in the middle of the road and was now testing that the brakes were working fully before braving the descent. We were off exploring armed with our trusty Portuguese phrase book, an almost reliable map and what seemed to us a great sense of adventure. As I drove slowly downhill out of the village, we glanced at each other and I brought the car to a halt on the edge of one of the dizzying curves. The sun was flickering through the trees and the light danced on the surface of the road.

Whatever was in the air – eucalyptus, mainly – I turned to Sue and quietly said: "I could, what about you?"

Sue's reply was instantaneous. "Yes, so could I, if you mean what I think you mean?"

"Live here?"

"Yes," she said, and from that moment the die was cast.

It was hard to explain, because we had no obvious reason to leave the UK. Things were going well and we had certainly never considered so drastic a change. But it just felt right. Our holiday altered completely and, before we knew it, so did our lives. The holiday became a search for a house we could buy and convert or just a plot of land we could build on. All that day as we motored around, we discussed possibilities: how we could disengage from England, what we'd have to give up, whether I could keep my printing business going, could we make a business out of tourism here – you know the sort of stuff, planning a future.

Anyway, as we chattered merrily on about our ideal home, the real Portugal and its people seemed very far away. You could say they were incidental to our distant dreams, although we weren't going to kid ourselves forever. We both knew that without the help and goodwill of the local Portuguese, we would not be offered anything worth having.

So what were we doing here in the first place? Like the most important incident that had brought us together, it had started with an innocent newspaper advertisement.

Four months earlier – it must have been February – Sue had asked me a question out of the blue. "What are you going to do this summer?"

I'm the type who likes to keep myself busy and I'd been working hard establishing my business for the last few years, so I had an answer ready. "Same as usual."

"Which is...?"

"Nothing much – just working and the odd long weekend away."

"Don't you feel like a proper holiday for a change – a complete break?"

And, when I thought about it, I did. We all need one now and again. Besides, Sue and I had been together for a little while by that time, and everything was great. Taking a holiday with her seemed the logical next step.

"Why not?"

We chatted a bit about what we might like to do and for even longer about places we definitely didn't want to see. Basically we were both being far too polite – neither of us was saying flat out where we actually wanted to go. Within reason, of course: we had very little money to spare so it was never going to be an exotic trip to the South American rainforests or a month's backpacking Down Under. But we needed a way out of our impasse.

So we agreed we'd each write down our ideal holiday destination independently. We'd argue about it a little more once we knew where we stood. Sue cut up a piece of paper and we both scribbled down our choices after less than half a minute. With due solemnity, we each folded our fragments and passed them across the table.

On opening them, there was a stunned silence.

"Sure you've given me the right one?" I asked.

"Of course I have. I wrote mine in red biro and nobody else has your scribble," she pointed out.

And that was how we discovered we'd both written 'Portugal.'

"Well, that's settled." I lobbed the papers in the bin.

"When I say Portugal, you realise I mean northern Portugal, don't you? You know, the undiscovered part." Sue was definitely excited about it, no question.

"Get away! I was going to put down the same, but I thought it'd look a bit fussy."

"Because I used to go there as a teenager, you see – I loved it and it's always stuck in my mind."

"Great – let's go and have fun."

The northern bit was an extra bonus because, when we thought about it, neither of us wanted to go to the Algarve. Let's be honest, the southern Atlantic coastline of Portugal is a beautiful place, where we could undoubtedly have had a great time but it might err on the side of over development. And everybody seems to speak English or German there. What we were looking for was a slice of the real, old-fashioned Portugal, where the hills and mountains had kept the foreign tourists in reasonable check, local customs remained and the people spoke their own language. In some ways we were looking for the land we remembered from thirty or forty years earlier.

However, although picking a general region had been fairly easy, translating it into specifics proved a bit harder. Having checked a few brochures with no luck, I was downing a cup of coffee with Terry and Val a few days later. They were friends who did a lot of our artwork for the printing business. Anyway, the subject of holidays came up and I let slip our plans. They smiled at each other and told me that they had been to a delightful cottage a few years earlier in Portugal.

"How did you find it?"

"You're not going to believe this." Terry was grinning conspiratorially.

Blimey! What was he going to say? They'd been abducted by aliens, and put down to land at some villa in the mountains, cannily avoiding air fares? I wouldn't put it past them.

"Try me."

"Dalton's Weekly."

Come to think of it, that was even less likely.

"You're right – I don't believe it."

"Seriously. The place was fantastic, rustic and exactly what we wanted."

I can honestly say I had never given a thought to this particular publication, thinking it was similar to 'Exchange & Mart' – I'd certainly never dreamed of finding a holiday through it.

"Back to the drawing board," I moped later.

"Well, we sort of found each other through a newspaper ad." Sue reminded me. "Why not give it a go?"

"Yes, but that was for a local culture group. Hardly the same thing."

"And we mustn't forget that the Newbury Weekly News is a highly prestigious rag..."

Her teasing masked a truth. Granted, joining a local social group is rather less of a gamble than planning for a holiday, but I'd met Sue through it and, suddenly, after over fifty years of my life, I'd hooked up with my soul mate. What's more, she showed every sign of thinking the same way about me. It was worth a look – what had we got to lose?

Fortified by such musings, I went into a number of newsagents, all beautifully laid out in the modern style and unencumbered by Dalton's Weekly, until finally, in a little corner shop, I saw a copy on the newsstands. However, just as I was about to pick it up, a man with a pencil-thin moustache snatched it off the shelf and began to walk away hurriedly towards the counter.

"Oh," I said, with just that touch of self-pitying despair. Maybe it was fate.

The man turned around: "Why? Were you going to buy this?" His tone was brusque yet not unfriendly.

"Yes, but don't worry, I'll find one elsewhere."

He obviously knew I'd have a job. "No problem, squire. I get it every week so help yourself, you've just saved me some money." He handed it over with a hasty smile.

I brought it back to Sue and we scoured it for holidays in Portugal. Plenty on the Algarve, but anywhere else was thin on the ground. Anorexic, in fact. There was only one advert relating loosely to northern Portugal.

'Full board, near Porto. Country location. Please phone.' Here it gave a telephone number which our STD dialling code book told us was in Somerset.

"No-one can say we're spoilt for choice."

"Are you going to call them, or shall I?"

"Toss you for it," I said.

"Heads." It landed on its side against a chair leg, but she generously declared it tails.

So Sue called the number and it turned out to be a travel agent who acted for an English couple. They had bought the place as a 'four walls & a roof' some years earlier and added a huge extension. They weren't ABTA registered but, in four years of dealing with them, the agent said she hadn't had any problems.

We discussed possible dates and decided to let the travel company do the complete holiday for us, sorting out flights and car rental as well as booking the accommodation. At this point she gave us the phone number and names of the owners, Lynne and Jeremy.

A few minutes later, I was speaking directly to Jeremy in Portugal, asking him all the usual questions about somewhere one hasn't been before:

"Do we need to bring towels, what's the weather like and how far are you from the airport?"

He answered them in strict order.

"If possible, please – you'll find it very pleasantly warm at just about any time of year – depends whether you drive like the English or the Portuguese."

"Oh, really? How long if you're English?"

"About an hour and a half."

"And for the Portuguese?"

"Roughly half that."

Gulp. We also asked if we had to book Saturday – Saturday.

"No, if it's out of season, you can book any dates you like."

"When's your season?"

"July and August – maybe a bit of September. Much like anywhere else."

We settled on Friday – Monday. This gave us two complete weekends but meant that my business was effectively only closed for one full week. So, as long as I remembered to take my mobile phone any problems could easily be overcome.

"By the way, whereabouts exactly are you?"

"A little village called Alombada – it's nicely out of the way. More in the northern part of central Portugal than the north, but I assure you it's no less remote. It's in the Beiras Litoral, handy for the Silver Coast, you see."

I hung up and Sue and I raced each other to the atlas. It was off the beaten track, all right. So far off that it didn't exist. We scoured every millimetre before Sue rang back.

"We can't find it."

There was a weary sigh. "Don't worry, I'll send you a local map."

It arrived a few days later. Alombada was not typed on

the page but had been hand-written, all of which conspired to elevate the place to almost mythical proportions. Appropriately, the contours showed that we were going to be in a mountainous region. The nearest villages were Chãs, Sernada and Macinhata do Vouga, whilst the closest market town was Albergaria-a-Velha, a few kilometres to the north. Twice the distance to the south lay the provincial town of Águeda, the regional administrative centre.

Communications seemed pretty good. Three main roads criss-crossed each other quite near the village, two running from north to south and one from east to west. Side by side were the main auto-route from Porto to Lisbon and the old trunk road between the same cities, which it had largely replaced. Bisecting them was the main road between Viseu, almost halfway from the Atlantic to the Spanish border, and Aveiro, the beautiful coastal city that nestled in broad lagoons separating it from the sea. Aveiro, the epicentre of the area, was less than half an hour away by road, assuming one didn't get lost, with vast swathes of beaches stretching away along the coastline in both directions. So we were going to combine the pleasures of seclusion with the ability to nip around much of central and northern Portugal whenever we wanted.

"We're going on 'oliday to Portugal." I danced lithely around the kitchen, singing like a modern Stanley Holloway in a slightly lower budget My Fair Lady.

Sue glanced at me quizzically. "Getting your daily exercise?"

"You didn't know I could sing, did you?"

"I still don't – best to keep your day job."

Anyway, whatever her opinion of my musical talents, it became the happy refrain we greeted each other with over the next few months. We were both looking forward to our trip with a certain amount of trepidation, as we had never been away together but, at the same time, with an air of thrilled expectancy. I don't think I'd anticipated any holiday so much since I was a schoolboy.

Plans were put in place throughout the next three months

with military precision. We made some vital holiday purchases, sun cream, summer wear, sandals and sunglasses, whilst lists were endlessly prepared and rewritten, then copied in triplicate until we had almost run out of things to panic about.

Finally, the day before our June departure came.

Sue packed all her stuff and came over to my house, where we spent the evening re-packing things into the inside suitcase, (we took two, one inside the other for a reason which now escapes me), including CD player, CDs and car converter, mosquito repellent, spare shorts, radio and a cooler bag. Despite Sue persuading me to leave my elephant trapping net at home, we still had the usual excess.

I awoke with a start on the hour every hour throughout the night, which soothed my nerves no end. Then, just as I was thinking about lugging the suitcases into the hall, the taxi arrived to take us to Heathrow for our 14.50 TAP Airways flight. Being one of those people who have a pathological fear of missing aeroplanes or being late, I had booked the cab for around 10.00, anxious about the prospect of one of those M4 pile-ups that strand motorists for hours and generally disrupt civilised life. It arrived early at 9.00 as we were finishing breakfast, which meant we reached Heathrow by 10.15. This in turn gave us a wait of an hour and a half before we could even check in our luggage. Sue's silence spoke volumes. We wandered around moodily, watched the planes and chatted, me brightly, her somewhat less so. She was, however, very good on the whole about the wait and only mentioned the early arrival every five minutes. The time soon passed though (as I told her every ten minutes) and we checked in and went for a coffee.

Once on board, Sue took the window seat and a meal helped the short flight zip by. She had a white wine and I had a cool lager. Well, two actually. The air hostesses were very persuasive – somehow if you're visiting a place and you fly by its national airline, you seem to start your holiday earlier – although we didn't have much time to reflect on this. The nub was we were going back to Portugal and we were by now like colts (or fillies) off the leash.

There's nothing like changing your mode of transport to slow you down.

After collecting our luggage at Porto, we went to the car hire desk. There appeared to be an awful amount of red tape when hiring a car in Portugal but the bilingual girl at the desk eventually got it all sorted and both Sue and I were on the drivers' list. Although apparently reasonably priced, the 'swipe through visa deposit' suddenly seemed enormously expensive with all the obligatory extras.

She took us to the car park to collect the vehicle, which turned out to be a Clio, just like Sue's back home. Naturally, I decided to drive and Sue, despite rolling her eyes at my presumption, did not openly object. Our girl was very helpful and did her best to explain how to get out of the airport with all the building works taking place. Lynne and Jeremy had sent a hand drawn map with directions to Alombada after leaving Porto on the motorway south towards Lisbon. We soon had another map though showing us the route onto the motorway in the first place.

Unfortunately, it wasn't the easiest drawing to read.

"Is it next left?" I shouted above the roar of the traffic – it was so hot we'd kept the windows open.

"I'm not sure. Have we passed the bank yet?"

"Which one?"

"Hang on. I can't read this writing." Another car zoomed past, cutting in centimetres ahead of us.

First, I was reluctantly compelled to concede that Jeremy's view of Portuguese drivers had been, on the whole, correct: we have since likened it to Place de la Concorde, Paris, Piazza Venezia, Rome, and the Brazilian Grand Prix all rolled into one. Secondly, we had to admit it would be very handy to have eyes in the back of our heads to tick off the roads and check that those we ended up on were the right ones out of Porto. The EEC appeared to have been funnelling every bit of its loose change into upgrading the Portuguese road transport network – the upshot was that all the access points into and out of Porto, including the riverside area and the airport, were at that time one huge construction disaster.

It was fun being back in Portugal (discounting dangers to life and limb) and, although neither of us said it at the time, we both felt this odd sensation that we were not so much here on vacation but returning home. Our language skills did not necessarily bear this out. My Portuguese was non-existent whereas Sue's was basic in the extreme but the odd word was at least understandable. That's if the girl at the car hire desk was to be believed.

"Does that say Lisbon?"

I squinted at the blue and white signs. "Lisboa."

"Take it, Ken – this is no time to split hairs." So I did, and miraculously we were free of the roadworks and onto the motorway.

Apart from the struggle to get in the best lane for the toll booth and find the correct change, the journey to Alombada went easily after that until the last 5km. We turned off the main highway correctly and went over the bridge, preening ourselves on our sang froid, carrying straight on and missing completely the turn towards Chãs and Alombada. A few minutes later I began to get suspicious.

"We've missed it."

"What do you mean we've missed it?"

"The turning. Look, give me the map."

"Now that was obviously the church and that thing there must definitely have been the water tower."

"So where did we go wrong? You see that field on the right is clearly a football pitch…"

And so it went on, because we were determined not to call our hosts (that would have been cheating) until at last a convenient roadside café proprietor obliged us, despite his complete lack of English, by showing us the error of our ways with the universal language of hand signals. He seemed to be suggesting it was a very clearly marked road.

"I bet it's not clear. You've seen what these Portuguese signs are like."

But apparently we hadn't. We retraced the last 5km and found the right road – obvious when you know where to look – that took us into the village of Chãs. Turning right near the end of the village just past the wall painted with a dolphin and a chinaman (what?), we plunged down the road from Chãs through towering eucalyptus trees, going ever deeper into the valley until we reached a small stone bridge over a tiny river, with a clearing for picnickers and fishermen. Suddenly we were faced with a very steep right hand bend and wound our way up through glorious shards of light to the village. Once there, it was only one road (and not very wide at that) so without any further adventures we arrived at our holiday home in Alombada – this was to be our base for the next ten days. After sorting ourselves out in our room and admiring the view, which was absolutely stunning, getting our breath back by inhaling the fragrance of the eucalyptus trees, everything just felt right, including the weather, about which Jeremy had been spot on, not too hot, not too cold. The temperature throughout our stay remained pretty constant at 25-30º.

We unpacked and joined our hosts who informed us the other guests would be back later – they were in Porto at a dog show. Jeremy was amiable, despite having the air of a man who thinks he knows what's best for everyone, rather like an older version of Mr Brittas from the 'Brittas Empire,' whilst Lynne had the brisk efficiency of a Cornish Landlady without the accent. They gave us a crash course in the delights of local society, which appeared to be refreshingly casual and un-snobbish.

Then we took a stroll around Alombada. Frankly, we were amazed the other visitors had needed to visit the 'big city' for a Portuguese Cruft's. The village might be small but it had plenty of varieties of dog. Meanwhile above us stretched a cloudless blue sky; to the west, the sun starting to set with the promise of the sea not far beyond the forest; to the east, the delicate echoes of mountains.

And all around us, peace.

We wandered back down the street to find that the sole car which had passed us on our walk had indeed been carrying our fellow guests. Everybody sat down for dinner together round one big table and enjoyed a fine English stew (the cooking, as advertised, was designed to make us feel at home – thank you, Marjorie Pattern), good Portuguese wine and enthusiastic conversation, a fair proportion of it concerning dogs. The other guests were three English women, from different age groups, one of 30 plus wearing a mini skirt, one of 60 plus who couldn't drive but certainly had opinions about how one should, and the third who didn't do mornings, evenings or any other particular time of day. Their only connection appeared to be dogs and Spanish water dogs in particular.

After a really sound night's sleep (the sort you have when you're not disturbed by traffic of any kind, merely the barking of a few dogs, church bells every quarter of an hour and the roosters crowing) we awoke to the promise of a full English breakfast. Soon this became something of a tradition, only broken occasionally when Sue rang the changes with toast and pure Alombada honey, which had (you've probably guessed) a hint of eucalyptus. We didn't like to tell Lynne and Jeremy but we would have preferred some traditional Portuguese food but we certainly made up for it when we dined in the local cafés. Starting that lunchtime.

And this, more or less, is where we came in, hooked instantly on the dream of moving here. When we returned to Alombada that evening, we discussed it with Lynne and Jeremy who, although they were openly sympathetic to our ideas, poured cold water on them rather morosely.

"We've actually recommended other people to the locals before and we've been let down," reminisced Jeremy.

"I think, after their return to England, reality has just set in," Lynne echoed.

I agreed, in part: "This may well have been the case for them…"

"But it's quite different for us," finished Sue.

However, Jeremy continued to look very doubtful: "We don't even know of anywhere in the area, let alone the village."

We asked them to keep their ears open and if they did

hear of anywhere to let us know. They promised to do this in a manner that held out scant hope for success. That, we thought, was that.

Maybe miracles do exist. A couple of days later they approached us and hinted that a local family, who no longer lived in the village, had a large property that was up for sale. It had been occupied until about two years previously and if we wanted they would make arrangements for us to view it. It was a Quinta (farmhouse) and we had passed it every day as we meandered through Alombada towards the gorge. Naturally we jumped at this and so, with remarkably little fuss (no estate agents) a viewing was arranged and the key miraculously appeared via a cousin who happened to live in the village.

Armed with the key next morning, we went exploring. The Quinta was huge, sprawling along one side of the street, with an enormous barn, a wine cellar with its own wine press, various outhouses and living quarters, all arranged around three sides of a flagstone courtyard, complete with hand pump and grapes dripping by the thousand above our heads. It was rustic Portugal all right. We fell in love instantly with not just the building, but with our ideas for the renovations. It didn't need to be sold – we just knew it was right for us.

The next thing to do was to return the key. João and Elena, who had provided it, made us so welcome in their house – here we were, just a couple of English tourists they'd never met before, being fêted and entertained in true Portuguese style. Although Elena didn't drink and João was recuperating from an abdominal operation so couldn't, whisky was the order of the day (at 10.00 in the morning), complete with cheese, bread, pickles and other nibbles.

João had grown up in Alombada and had the rolling gait and sunburned skin of the countryman. He was still deeply attached to village life – nothing made him happier than looking after his sheep and chickens on his smallholding. To look at her, Elena would have made the classic well proportioned farmer's wife, but she found the village too remote and was much more at ease in the nearby township of Albergaria-a-Velha, where they had their marital home. Both, although superficially of indeterminate age, were in their mid 60s.

We shuddered to think how hospitable they'd have been if they could have imbibed with us. Anyway, Lynne and Jeremy, who had enjoyed our exclamations of delight at the Quinta, did their best to remedy any shortfall.

Our halting linguistic skills enabled us to discover that there were three languages spoken in Portugal as a rule: Portuguese (not surprisingly), Portuguese and English (fortunately), or (as in this case) Portuguese and French. Sue and I are proficient in French and João and Elena had lived in Quebec, the French speaking area of Canada. Lynne and Jeremy had lived in Portugal for several years now yet he couldn't speak Portuguese and she didn't.

As an illustration of this Sue, much later after we moved here, went to a Portuguese class with Lynne. On the way back they called into a supermarket. Lynne went to the delicatessen counter and asked: "Please may I have a meio kilo de bacon?"

Having been given the bacon, she said, "Thank you."

Sue turned to her in disbelief. "Lynne, you've just been to a Portuguese lesson!"

"Oh, yes I know, but I never think I have thanked someone unless I say it in English."

But I digress. Elena, rather on the large side and suffering from various medical problems, mainly to do with her feet and hips, kept heroically waddling out with drinks for us all. Seizing her moment after about three large whiskies, Lynne begged us to interpret an elaborate anecdote about a horse that had been vexing her. We asked João to tell us in French, which we were then able to translate for her and Jeremy.

Lynne used to go to a local riding school each week and ride this particular horse. One day, its owner asked if Lynne could take the horse back to her field in Alombada and keep it there (as a gift – or so she thought).

It transpired that the horse had got into the owner's

neighbour's field and totally destroyed his vegetable crop. The owner of the vegetable patch was none too happy and was demanding payment from the owner of the horse for this loss. He, in turn, had cunningly eliminated the horse from the equation by lending it to Lynne.

A few weeks later the owner of the horse, having resolved his differences with his neighbour over the vegetables, came up to the village looking for his horse and, finding Lynne wasn't there, just took it back. There had been no impropriety on his part but Lynne didn't see things that way. It had upset her quite a lot because, believing the horse had been a present, in typical fashion she had gone out buying all the expensive gear and fodder which had ultimately proved a waste of money. It still rankled with her.

There was a clear moral to this story: learn the language and try to understand local customs and the people. You will never be 100% proficient but it certainly helps to be able to communicate. Diplomatically, we decided not to point this out to Lynne.

After this 2 $^{1}/_{2}$ hour session in the blazing heat on Elena and João's patio, all four of us began merrily weaving our short way back to our lodgings. Before we left, we had contacted Francisca, the daughter of the owners of the property, who themselves lived in Venezuela. Happily she was nearer at hand and spoke really good English.

Lynne and Jeremy suggested we go down the following evening to the recently renovated local club to meet her and discuss prices and terms. First we took a trip down to Albergaria-a-Velha market. It was a joyous throwback, an open air market held twice a week, where everyone was friendly, the produce was traditional, fresh and local, and the atmosphere was certainly colourful. It sold everything: fruit, vegetables, dairy products, live poultry, along with plants and clothing. After an invigorating time wandering around, we were taken by our hosts to their club.

Francisca, a woman in her late 30's, typically for Portuguese women on the short side, with a bubbly personality and figure to match, was waiting for us and placed very few obstacles in our path. We soon agreed the price of the Quinta, including the land by the side which was large enough to keep as part orchard and part car park for our guests, this being one of the many reasons for buying a property in Portugal. We had discussed the project in great detail during the week and realised that we would have to obtain an income from a couple of self-contained letting apartments for holidaymakers. Even we had worked out that we couldn't leap from barely affording a holiday here to buying a property without some swift returns.

So we were on the verge of becoming Portuguese home owners. Surely it couldn't be that easy?

Apparently it was. Nevertheless, we were aware that we were making a huge leap into the unknown. Neither of us was in the first flush of youth, and it was clear to us that if we didn't make the jump soon, it might well be too late. In the not too distant future when we were in our 60's, we might not feel quite so ready to make the effort. And subconsciously, we knew that a big effort would be necessary.

The next day we went back into Albergaria-a-Velha to open a bank account. Firstly, we had to register for social security numbers (número de contribuinte) because without these we couldn't open a bank account, buy land or indeed do anything official. We entered the local council offices and were soon struggling to answer a raft of questions. Lynne and Jeremy were no use of course. Fortunately, the man next to us in the queue saw our plight, introduced himself (he was from Angola) and volunteered his services.

The brisk female official had to take multiple photocopies of our passports, birth certificates, death certificates, driving licences, milk tokens and anything else that seemed of even passing interest, but the actual procedure was fairly straightforward. Considering this is a third world country (as many of our Portuguese friends themselves have described it), the computer system in the public sector appeared to work extremely quickly and, having filled out a relatively uncomplicated form, which we did with the help of our Angolan translator, we both soon had our numbers on an official looking piece of paper.

We were now registered in Portugal and just had to wait for our cards to come through. These numbers, she explained, would be our sole references for tax, VAT, medical and every other financial and legal transaction from now on and, she hinted darkly, it would be worthwhile memorising them. As we were leaving she said to us in perfect English: "Goodbye, have a pleasant afternoon and I hope you enjoy your eventual life here in Portugal." Her smile had a trace of wickedness. It was so frustrating knowing that she could have easily translated everything for us in the first place, but a salutary lesson that we must never assume the Portuguese could not speak English.

Next, bolstered by these omnipotent numbers, we moved on to the bank. We had been recommended to a particular bank and because we had no idea whether one was better than the other, we decided to give it a try. This too proved relatively straightforward after the obligatory photocopying session, filling the forms out and giving them some funds to open the account. We were advised that everything was in place and we could make use of the account when we were next in the country.

High on the success of the morning, we wandered around the open market again then went on to Angeja for coffee and a celebratory aguardente. Angeja was fast becoming a favourite local traditional town of ours, complete with narrow streets and cobblestones, where a particular café proprietor introduced us to new local drinks and bar food, such as soft shelled crabs and intestines, the latter being a one-off taste experience. There are two types of aguardente, one called, with faultless logic, Aguardente, which is distilled wine and much smoother than the other, bagaço, which is just distilled fermenting grape skins, and consequently rougher and cheaper. Today though we just had a bottle of house red and proceeded to take stock. We had discussed in great detail over the preceding couple of days the practicalities, some of the problems and many of the advantages of moving en-bloc out to Portugal:

Both our mothers were elderly (in their 80s) and we could only do this if we had their wholehearted blessings.

Sue would have to give up her long term job.

This would have to be supplemented by the income from the proposed letting apartments.

My printing company would have to change out of all recognition from the way it was operating. At that time it was very much a hands-on and face to face business, involving weekly and sometimes daily contact with certain clients. This, over the coming year or eighteen months, had to be changed to run solely by phone, fax and e-mail so that my clients could see that the business was still being run efficiently, personally and cost-effectively. At that point I would take an educated gamble to inform them of my plans and hope that I could retain both their goodwill and, crucially, their business.

The Portuguese system of purchasing land or property required every member of the family to agree the sale. At any point, one or more of the interested parties could halt the process by refusing to sell. It was our understanding, and also interesting to note, that the land, once purchased, remained within the family.

We had agreed to meet Francisca again and by the end of the evening and after many cervejas, the sale and the price were agreed.

"It just so happens," said Francisca, "that my parents are returning from Venezuela next Thursday. My father has to have an operation."

"Nothing serious, I hope?" asked Sue.

"No, no, it is merely a precaution. He will not be distracted for long so we can discuss the matter in full then."

"Good. I shouldn't want to add to his worries." I watched her face for any signals, but she seemed relaxed enough.

"I don't think there will be any problems because we've talked about it over the phone and everybody has been asked about the sale. They all want to get shot of the place. I'll call you when everybody has signed." She clinked her glass against ours confidently.

A day or two later, we returned to England content in the knowledge that we had secured a property – albeit one requiring much renovation – in Alombada. Our dreams were many and our hopes were high.

We even decided on a name for the Quinta. Throwing out our plastic bin liners one day Sue turned to me and said, "That's a good name." I looked back, puzzled, and then it dawned on me what she meant. She had been tipping the rubbish into a large green wheelie bin with the word SULO written in bold capital letters on the side. "Perfect," I said, "The Quinta, building wise, is a load of rubbish at the moment but will become our home." And we both said in unison "Casa Sulo." The name has stuck, through many trials.

Our hopes stayed high for the next month, even though we heard little apart from the occasional bland reassurances from Lynne and Jeremy. Then the delay began to make us fret. What could have gone wrong?

"These things always take their time here in Portugal," soothed Lynne.

Chapter 2

"I'm the bringer of bad news." It was Jeremy, lugubriously unleashing a thunderbolt over the phone to Sue. *"Francisca's brother doesn't want to sell the Quinta."*

In Portugal, as we knew, all the family (which in this case effectively meant the children) had to agree the sale, otherwise there would be complications which might take forever to resolve. Ultimately, one person might not be able to stop a sale going through but it's not really worth the hassle. Also – a new one, this – the people whose property borders the land must be given first refusal before any sale.

We were devastated. All the emotional effort and planning that we had invested in the Quinta had come to nothing. We phoned Francisca to find out the story direct from the horse's mouth, so to speak.

She confirmed the facts and was clearly fed up, presumably because she'd lost out on a fair share of the profits. However, there was an unexpected outcome.

"I have a plot of land for sale in the village about 1 ¼ hectares which I own and will sell only to you. Why don't you come out and see it? It has quite marvellous views facing west, nothing in the way of the horizon at all. You could build a new place with all the old materials. Believe me, it will be cheaper and easier. You know, I was worried about selling the old original house to you because of the cost of putting in a damp course. When you add in the refurbishment of the upstairs, I really think a new build would

be infinitely better for you."

This was quite a turn-up for the books – we spoke to Lynne and Jeremy who assured us that they knew the land in question and it would be perfect for our requirements. So we agreed to travel out to view the plot. It was the first time, needless to say, that we had heard of any complications about the Quinta and that it would have required more extensive renovation than we had planned. Up until this point it had been sold to us, not only by Francisca, but crucially by Lynne and Jeremy, as an extremely attractive, dry property with only modernisation required to bring it up to standard. Had we just had a narrow escape?

It was our first lesson in shifting sands. It was not to be our last.

We flew back to Portugal to see the land which Lynne and Jeremy (as well as Francisca, who clearly had her own motives) told us was ideal for our project. Once bitten, twice shy, but still shining with hope and wanting to start again on the right foot, we arrived in Alombada late on a glorious afternoon – it felt good to be back, despite the suspicious collapse of the Quinta sale.

That bright aspect rapidly darkened as storm clouds rolled in from the Atlantic a few kilometres away. As we unpacked, Lynne and Jeremy once again pontificated on the land's suitability.

"It's got beautiful views across the forests," gushed Lynne.

"Plenty of space – you'll find it's huge," Jeremy rushed to her support.

"Well, can we see it as soon as possible?" asked Sue.

Jeremy gazed out of the window dolefully. "It's looking a bit bleak. Could be a downpour soon."

My patience was not so vast that I was prepared to be delayed by any shilly-shallying. "If you don't mind, we'd like to pop down and give it the once over straightaway."

So, before our evening meal we set off back down the street into the village. Trying not to glance at the original ill-fated Quinta, we turned away from it to the land opposite, nestling down the slope behind an unused house.

"Who owns that?" I queried.

"João," muttered Jeremy.

Lynne continued: "He lets us store our spare furniture in there."

Sue glanced at me as it started to rain. It was not a great omen as we all moved through a five-barred gate onto the land. Immediately it felt wrong: the direction, the sharp slope, the glaringly insufficient size, all capped by a tall blue, rusting, domestic water tower within a few hundred metres and in full view of any building which we might have wanted to construct. Some stray bleats betrayed the current occupants.

"Whose are those?"

"They're João's as well, I'm pretty sure."

This was not looking good.

"What does João use the land for? Just to graze his sheep?"

"I really can't remember much else going on here."

"How about access?"

"Well, there's the gate of course."

"Is there an alternative entrance?"

Jeremy obviously didn't know much about it. "I think it might be between our storage house and the one next door."

This was hardly calculated to reassure us. The house next door was a complete ruin with half a roof and a pile of crumbing old furniture still visible on the first floor, open to the elements because there was no external wall to the rear. A real eyesore, it could have come from any post air-raid photograph.

"Well, who owns that?"

"That's the funny thing. Nobody seems to know."

"It's unlikely to get repaired then."

"Do you mean it would have to remain in that awful condition?" Sue was incredulous.

"Listen, perhaps you'd better wait and get answers direct from Francisca," said Jeremy.

Sue and I looked at each other and nodded our heads.

We'd flown all this way and we didn't want to give up on our dreams on the first evening. We decided, not without trepidation, to leave any further questions for Francisca the next morning, and passed a night that was not interrupted by too much sleep.

Francisca duly arrived around ten o'clock with her husband in tow, a man who managed to negotiate the whole social encounter without a word other than "Olá" and "Adeus." She proceeded to walk us (although squelching was more the operative term after the previous night's rains) around the area of land she was proposing to sell. It was even smaller than we had been shown the preceding evening. Obviously, there was some reason for holding back on the rest of the land, probably so they could make extra money out of us by offering it later on at a 'discount' price. We were becoming more sceptical by the minute.

"I thought the land went down to that fence there," I said.

"No, it stops a little higher up." She blithely waved her hand in the direction of some interested sheep.

"Why's that, then?"

"Oh, some government regulations," she explained vaguely. This horse's mouth was proving unreliable.

"Talk about being taken for a pair of mugs!" Sue whispered.

"So would you like to make an offer for the land?"

I demurred. "Thanks for showing us round but no thanks. It's not quite what we were expecting."

Francisca was breathtakingly insouciant. Not a bit put out by this rejection, she said she would ask her brother again about the Quinta.

"He may sell if you increase your offer." This, after telling us it was not only impossible under Portuguese law, but also that it would be a 'never ending money drain renovating it…'

We declined the opportunity and said our farewells hurriedly. As we walked away, we agreed we had made a dreadful error of judgment in accepting, at face value, the word of a person we didn't really know.

"It all comes from not knowing the country and its inhabitants properly," said Sue.

I couldn't agree more. "We're going to have to learn to distinguish between someone who is honest and others who are going to try it on."

Easier said than done, you may think.

We went back to Lynne and Jeremy's for coffee, to decide what to do.

"Any luck?" Lynne greeted us as we stumped in the entrance.

I was terse. "No. The goalposts kept moving."

"Nothing ventured, nothing gained." Jeremy was philosophical. I could have brained him.

Sue noticed my agitation and suggested we went for a drive so I could cool off.

We drove around chatting in a desultory fashion, but most of all lamenting that we had been let down very badly. There was the deflation of our hopes, the expense of flying back and forth, and the amount of time we'd taken off work. On our meanderings we looked at various houses for sale and plots of land that might offer promising places to build.

In our naivety we just hadn't a clue where to start. What basis did we have to go on? In order to be sure it was worth continuing, Sue and I kept asking each other if we thought it was reality or just a pipe dream. Always the answer was a definite: "It's a reality – let's go for it." Our positive attitude was to be blessed sooner than we thought.

That evening Jeremy told us that on hearing about the lack of progress we had made with Francisca, he had spoken to his neighbour, Natálio. And now Natálio had come up with a solution. He had a plot of land for sale if we wanted and he would be delighted to show us.

Could we go for it? Despite our recent experiences I thought we could and glanced across at Sue.

Sue backed me up. "Well done, Jeremy. What are we waiting for?" We scooted around to Natálio's.

Natálio was a larger than life character, broad shouldered with a piratical moustache and a seemingly limitless store of good humour. He had injured his back through working so hard but still never took a day off. They were long days too – he started at dawn and didn't finish until dusk. Rumour in the village had it that he used to eat sackfuls of potatoes for fuel. All in all, he had a finger in many pies. Between him, his wife and his father-in-law, they owned half the mountain's eucalyptus forest.

"It's good land," Natálio reassured us as we checked it out. Once again, we could feel our hopes building up. Third time lucky, we prayed.

Because he was right – it was perfect for our needs, a sizeable chunk in a T shape so that we could build our home at the top and then construct the tourist apartments lower down on relatively flat or at least gently rolling terrain. Immediately we could see the potential the whole land would give us. There were about three hectares in all, secluded by the sweet-smelling eucalyptus forests. The top of the land was near the entrance to Alombada, separated only by a field from the village.

On returning to Lynne and Jeremy's, we phoned a local surveyor and then alerted our solicitor, Dr Aldina Rainhas, whom we had previously contacted when we still thought we were buying Francisca's family Quinta. We had already spoken to Natálio, having surveyed the land, and discussed the details of the sale, including prices, with him. We passed on all this information to our solicitor. As usual, there was a slight snag.

"This is Friday, you realise," she said.

"I'm aware of that."

"Well, the surveyor and I won't be able to come out until Tuesday – around 10 a.m. if that's okay."

"Er, we only have Monday to conclude any deal because we have to leave at lunchtime on Tuesday for the UK."

"I'm sorry, Ken. It's the best we can do."

"Will you hold on a moment?" I had a hurried conversation with Sue.

"Fine – we're certain there won't be any problems so Tuesday's okay by us." It was a leap of faith and, given everything that had gone on before, a huge one.

Nevertheless, full of thoughts of snatching triumph from the jaws of defeat at the eleventh hour, we took Lynne and Jeremy for leitão at a restaurant in Mealhada, on the road south to Coimbra. Mealhada is famous throughout Portugal for this regional dish and people arrive by the car and bus load to enjoy it – in fact, it's extremely difficult to find a restaurant serving anything else. Leitão is spit roast suckling pig with wafer thin crispy crackling, a delicate and sweet pinkish white meat with a taste to die for, usually served with sliced oranges, game chips and a green salad with vinaigrette sauce, all washed down with a beautiful crisp, clean tasting, chilled vinho verde.

The thing about this town is that it doesn't look particularly special. One could quite easily be forgiven for thinking that it is just a collection of cafés and truck stops on the old trunk road between Porto and Lisbon. Few of the restaurants appear especially inviting from the outside as the lorries roar past, but they all serve great quality food and each has its devoted admirers. It's one of the more unlikely gastronomic centres of the world.

We chugged back to the villa replete. All our frustrations and difficulties now seemed forgotten and we passed a happy weekend, making elaborate plans, sightseeing and relaxing.

We returned to our land (note how we already owned it in our heads) the following day, walked around it, viewed it from every conceivable angle, photographed and videoed it, trying to see how our plans would take shape. We did this knowing that the next day would be a rush to catch the flight back to the UK, leaving all the paperwork to Aldina so, quite understandably, we wanted a record to take home with us. To calm our mounting excitement, we went for a drive and whiled away the rest of the day buying up the supermarket's stock of whisky and brandy to take back – it was extraordinarily good value, about a third the price of the UK.

We got up especially early on our last morning, dressed and breakfasted in a hurry, congratulating ourselves that the final outcome was turning out even better than we could have hoped for. Lynne and Jeremy concurred that the land was exactly the ticket for our life style and adjudicated that, although slightly isolated, it would, in time, have its own place in Alombadian society. We dashed down to the site for a final viewing before Sr. Eng. Leonardo Costas (our architect and surveyor) and Dr. Aldina Rainhas arrived. When they did so, we showed them around the land and explained exactly how we thought the building would look and where it would be sited.

Leonardo, in his mid 40's, of medium height, and slimly built, had brown hair and a moustache. A serious man, he had a warm smile which was the more welcome when it appeared, and a fundamentally generous nature. He was painstaking in his approach and if at times things seemed to be advancing more slowly than we might have wished, that was more a function of the Portuguese system than of any dilatoriness on his part. He was supremely reliable, albeit somewhat inclined to pessimism.

Our solicitor, Aldina, at least ten years younger, pretty, with long dark hair and a comely figure, was in many ways a contradiction. Although perennially smartly dressed, she also contrived to be always flustered, and could remember absolutely nothing without laying her hands on the correct file, which she could rarely find. But despite this, she would invariably come up with the goods. The very opposite of legal restraint, she flirted outrageously with all men (but so charmingly that Sue never took offence), and it was always a genuine delight to see her.

We told them we had already made plans and had high hopes that, even with a bit of movement of the apartments here and there we felt it was just right for us – we had even filmed it in detail.

It was then that the bombshell was dropped.

"I'm afraid it's no use for building on," said Leonardo. "It's ten metres inside the green belt area."

"What's that?" It sounded suspiciously building-free.

It was.

Showing us a very detailed ordinance survey map with a shaded area (we had never seen any map before which included Alombada, let alone green belt areas. Indeed most people as close as our local council town did not even know of its existence), he shrugged: "We can appeal to the Camara Municipal for planning permission but that would incur a tremendous amount of time and money and, of course, it comes with no guarantees."

The Camara Municipal is the city council office not necessarily best known for its speed of response.

We were devastated. If someone up there was testing our desire to move out to Portugal they were doing a great job. Aldina and Leonardo left as all our sale agreements went up in smoke. We stood looking at each other, hugely deflated.

I tried to make light of it: "Well, one or two or even three doors may close but another one opens."

"Let's just forget it – we obviously aren't supposed to move out here at all." Sue, heaving a great sigh and throwing all her toys out of the pram, started to walk away with tears in her eyes.

I caught up with her, gently put my arms around her, looked her in the eyes and asked earnestly: "How much do you really want to live here?"

"Desperately."

"Okay then, we'll go and ask Natálio – see if he has anything else."

"He'll be busy in the fields. We can't interrupt him."

"Watch me."

I took her hand and we went up the hill to see Natálio – as it was grape picking time he was in his back wine cellar getting the barrels ready with his son, Paulo.

Paulo, in his early twenties, a lovely person, with a disarmingly cheeky grin, helped Natálio with the family business. I could see that Sue found him easy on the eye. His roguish good nature and youthful high spirits endeared him to all who met him.

Augusto, his father-in-law, along with Beatriz (Augusto's wife), Isabela (Natálio's wife) and Sandra, (their daughter), were out picking the grapes from their vines. As we were quickly able to gather, it was a real family affair. We explained in pidgin Portuguese and sign language what the problem was.

Natálio appeared crestfallen for a second, but not for long. Immediately he barked out an instruction to Paulo, who hurried off. A few minutes later, he reappeared with the women of the house and their pickings.

First came Isabela, daughter of Augusto and Beatriz. Blessed with a wicked sense of humour, she was a striking woman with long brown hair and high cheekbones. Like Natálio, she was always very helpful and friendly – although rather more reserved than her husband, she could sound caustic, but underneath that she had a heart of gold, and we could tell how much she loved all (especially her own) children. Perpetually industrious like the rest of them, she would spend all day logging alongside Natálio and Paulo, then come home and busy herself with the housework and cooking.

Sandra, the daughter of Natálio and Isabela, is a couple of years older than her brother Paulo, and the more thoughtful of the two, but like him she has a most winning personality. Beaming behind her glasses, she normally worked with handicapped children in Águeda, but was temporarily helping out with the grape harvest.

Behind them rumbled Beatriz, who was certainly the grand old lady, moving through the village in a stately fashion, a toothy smile ever ready to emerge. She was, however, still incredibly active and was always ready to chip in with ideas and practical help, sometimes indeed before she had even been approached.

Ushering the ladies was Augusto, the senior citizen of the village, seemingly frailer than his wife, but a wiry and deceptively resilient character. A few years older than her, he was correspondingly less forward, but was a great one for a convivial party once there was a sniff.

So there we were, in this small hilltop village in temperatures in excess of 30º on a fine autumn day, beside an ox cart loaded with baskets of grapes, while a pack of five excitable village dogs were running around the cart chasing a cunning cat, which always seemed to exploit any situation to its favour and escape them. Chickens, anxious not to be left out, were clucking around in fussy disapproval. Meanwhile Natálio, Isabela, Augusto, Beatriz, Paulo and Sandra were standing in the middle of the road (granted the whole carriageway was merely one cart width and did not see much traffic), waving their arms around discussing our problem in great depth. We tried to grasp a few phrases, but the truth was we were being totally excluded from their conversation until a resolution had been made.

Sue said, "Do you realise they're deciding our future and we haven't a clue what they are talking about!"

At length they broke off from their deliberations and Natálio walked across to us with a big smile on his face. He stood on the curve opposite his home and opened his arms in a sweeping gesture at some land. We thought he meant the top bit so we indicated it was too small. He climbed over the fence and gestured that we do the same. We followed him down the hill, around the plot. Twenty minutes later we had walked the boundary and returned to the road.

The views were spectacular, surging down the mountain into the depths of the forest, with a wonderful view of the nearby range. Balancing this rugged natural aspect, we were positioned right in the heart of the community, and the land was definitely more than big enough. Once again, it appeared we might have landed on our feet. We were overjoyed and highly emotional.

By now it was coming up to 11.30, we still hadn't packed and we had to finalise the price and make a deal, then let Aldina know the change of plans. We explained our dilemma to Natálio but, like everything in this part of Portugal, life has its own pace and rituals.

He grinned. "Come in and we'll sort this out over a drink."

How could we refuse?

Immediately, glasses appeared as if by magic. We were

treated to a couple of drinks from a very old, 'top shelf' dusty and crusty bottle of locally produced port. It was delicious – warming its way down. During the conversations that followed it transpired that they owned most of the land they were selling but that some part was duplicated by family ties. Alarm bells might have been starting to ring, but they assured us that there would be no problem in transferring the registration of land.

"We are a family that knows how to agree on all important things," avowed Natálio. Isabela, Augusto, Beatriz, Paulo and Sandra nodded their heads enthusiastically.

The Portuguese have a system of keeping land registration numbers in a booklet the size and shape of a large cheque book. Each page in the book represented a plot of land – this could be either a few square metres or thousands of hectares. Natálio flicked through their book to the relevant pages.

Jeremy came over during the discussions and attempted to find out what was being paid and how much land we were buying. We were at such a delicate stage that we hadn't the time to explain. Besides, this was private business. Thwarted, he helped himself to a glass of port and then reluctantly went back to report to Lynne. Finally at 12.35 we shook hands on the deal and dashed off to pack.

Lynne and Jeremy professed themselves delighted with our change in fortunes.

"Honestly, you've had a lucky escape – the Quinta would have been a drain on your finances for years to come," said Lynne.

"That first bit of land we saw on your current trip was useless," droned Jeremy.

"And it was a pity about the second plot but it would have been a bit lonely down there," mused Lynne. "Anyway, we are going to be neighbours after all, so hasn't everything ended for the best?"

All we could think was how typically native they had become in their eight or nine years in Portugal – apart from the fact they couldn't speak the language of course. They had never previously expressed any doubts about any of the options we were contemplating. On the contrary, they had positively encouraged us in our pursuit of what were suddenly revealed to be 'inappropriate' projects. But we were now too happy to care overmuch.

We left soon afterwards and raced to Porto, reaching the check-in desk just in time, before phoning Aldina from the airport departure lounge, telling her of our progress and that now we definitely had a 'field in Portugal.' She was overjoyed for us, since she knew how disappointed we had been when she left us. While we were in England, we said we needed her and Leonardo to do the searches and sort out the paperwork for the purchase of the various plots of land. We also insisted we needed outline planning permission for building before we would actually agree to the purchase. Once bitten, twice shy.

The flight back was uneventful and it wasn't until we arrived home that reality kicked in. We unpacked, poured ourselves a pair of very large scotches and drank a toast to us, the land and Portugal. Our whisky had never tasted so good. Sleep was easy that night.

But if we were going to move, what and how should we tell our mothers? We decided the best way to tell them would be on one of our trips up north – which we called 'The Mum Run.' Every six weeks or so we would leave home early on the Saturday, drive up to Manchester, see my mum and then, after having the usual fish and chip lunch, we would drive on to Birkdale, see Sue's mother, Cathy, staying overnight at her flat and returning south the next morning.

The first time Sue was introduced to my mother over lunch, the latter, as so often, put her proverbial foot in it.

"Where do you come from, Susan?"

"Liverpool."

My mother instantly looked horrified, breathed in sharply, but recovered her composure enough to comment, "Oh, that's probably all right then, we already have someone in the family from Liverpool, but then he doesn't have an accent." Sue who, unlike that somebody, has absolutely no trace of any accent, smiled beatifically at her.

"I suppose it's more Southport, really."

My mother, the epitome of middle-class snobbery, enquired: "Whereabouts? Because there are some rough areas of Southport, you know."

"Birkdale," said Sue.

"Royal Birkdale," I underlined, knowing my mum's penchant for all things regal.

"Oh, that's all right then," she said and calmly continued eating her lunch.

Fortunately, telling them we were thinking of moving to Portugal went about as smoothly as it could. At the time they were both in a slightly fragile state and we had feared they might feel deserted, but not a bit of it. We promised to let them know our plans in full after our next trip to Alombada.

At last outline planning permission had been granted and we were ready, flying back out to Portugal with the intention of paying for the land and having it all signed over to us in the notario's (judge's) office.

In the airport we were sitting in the departure lounge when the announcement came over the tannoy: "Will rows No. 16-32 board now." A Portuguese man sitting next to us jumped up and asked what rows they had called. When we told him he sat back down and patiently waited for the next announcement. On boarding the plane he was seated across the aisle to us and we all got chatting.

Rui, who had the looks of a languorous rock star, as Sue never tired of reminding me, was in his mid-thirties, with a friendly, open expression. It turned out that he was a computer whiz kid, that he and his wife, Cláudia, lived in Aveiro, about twenty minutes or so from Alombada, and he was very interested in what we were planning to do. He spoke perfect English – they became very good friends.

During the rest of the flight we discussed many things, one of which was a local eating house, which he said had a very good reputation for leitão. Asking the stewardess for a piece of paper, he drew us a map showing how to get there. He also gave us his phone number, told us to contact him if we were having any difficulties at all, and said it would be great to meet up again (we still have his original map and phone number sellotaped to our office filing cabinet).

There were an awful lot of meetings between our solicitor and us during this trip. Each time Aldina would call with a request that we go down to her office to sign some piece of paper, or answer questions on various aspects of the project. On every visit her office desk appeared ever more chaotic. Finally, we asked when we might get the paperwork signed, pay for the land and complete the purchase.

Aldina emerged from an untidy heap of files on her desk. "You'll need to give the notario three cheques at the completion of the sale of the land."

"Three cheques!" I nearly blew a fuse, but Aldina calmed me down.

"However, it can't possibly be done this week so can you come back next Tuesday?"

"But we're leaving for the UK on Wednesday," said Sue.

"And this is the last time we'll have a chance to be out here before October," I added.

"I'm sorry. It's the earliest we can do." With that, we had to be content.

On Tuesday morning we decided to go to our bank and enquire where our chequebook was, as we still hadn't received one. After much deliberation and checking of records, all concerned agreed we had money in the account but we were politely told there was no way we could have a chequebook. Confused, we asked for an explanation.

"Do we have money in our account with sufficient funds to pay for any cheques we are likely to be presenting?"

"Yes."

"And are our references any good?"

"All seems to be in order."

"Are the specimens of our signatures okay?"

"Yes."

"So can we have a chequebook, please?"

"No."

"We'll pay you for one." We'd found out we had to do this anyway.

"The answer's still no."

Although we had had money in our bank account now for some time, because we hadn't taken money out or put more funds in, it was treated as nominally dead – and until we made use of the account it would continue to be regarded as such.

So no cheques.

"Tell us this. How can we possibly activate the bank account if you won't give us a chequebook?" I thought I might have struck home there.

"I'm sorry, but those are the rules."

No amount of remonstrating would persuade the bank to change its policy, even though we explained that the account would definitely be used more extensively over the coming months because building work would be starting and we would require access to the funds by way of cheques. So, we concluded, it was about to be live. No dice. At the end of about half an hour, we gave up and told the cashier that we must have three cheques to present to the notario the next day.

"No problem. Each cheque will cost you €7."

"Why?"

"Because they are our cheques."

"Yes, but it is our money."

"Ah, yes, but to access it with a cheque your only option now is to use one of our cheques and for that service we charge."

"But it is our money."

And so another chase round the houses took place. Everybody agreed with each other but no-one was making any concessions. If we hadn't needed the cheques so desperately we honestly believe the frustrations caused by this simplistic and single-minded attitude would have forced us into closing the account and opening another one elsewhere. As it was, we had no alternative but to pay the money for the cheques.

Not with the greatest grace in the world, I'll admit.

Having finally decided to buy the cheques it then became even more of a marathon event – apparently not very many people have cheques written by the bank so we tied up the whole counter because the first cashier had to have special clearance and hadn't had sufficient training on this aspect of banking, the second cashier came across to help and the third one came to have a look and see what was going on. Kafka would have had a field day.

The queue behind us grew ever longer – people were wandering out and going for a beer or a coffee and returning only to find we were still there. The bank cheques were all produced on an extremely sophisticated computerised system, in triplicate, each had to be signed and witnessed in full view of everybody, the signatures checked against their card index system, until eventually after about an hour we left the bank with the three cheques. It has to be said that the swelling crowd never became angry, just ever more despairing that the system should take so long. Comments were passed without any reflection on us (as far as we could ascertain) – we doubted whether a British queue would have been as understanding for so long.

Not that long ago people would not be admitted into any Portuguese bank unless they wore formal clothes and a tie…so perhaps we got off lightly. Nevertheless, the rigidity within the structure has not changed even if the dress code has been relaxed.

Aldina had a word with the notaria and, both being practical women, they agreed to rush things through for us so eventually we had a meeting in the notaria's offices at 6.35 on the evening before returning to the UK. Natálio attended in his best suit, beaming at everyone.

The notaria was extremely helpful and fortunately spoke very good English. She explained that all the legal documents had to be in Portuguese but if there were any points we did not understand she would explain them to us in English afterwards. This was dutifully done, before we began the three cheque ceremony. We gave her a cheque which she handed over to Natálio for the amount of the land, then passed her the second cheque, which she gratefully received for her services, and, finally, the third cheque was handed over to pay for the taxes on the land. In case we felt we hadn't done enough, we were then given an invoice for a further cheque to be paid at some stage to Aldina.

Everybody kissed and shook hands and we left the notaria's office and waited for her clerk to make duplicates of all our documents. Finally, we left the building, said goodbye and heartfelt thanks first to Natálio, then to Aldina.

As we lingered by her car, watching Natálio walking away briskly down the street, I glanced at Sue: we were both a little deflated. We had just spent the best part of two hours in the notaria's office buying our future dream and we had absolutely nothing to show for it – not a piece of paper or anything... Natálio had bundles of papers, Aldina had bundles of papers, yet the pieces of paper that we had taken as evidence had all been photocopied and handed over. All we had were our passports and número de contribuinte papers.

Aldina assured us that, if it were paper we wanted, not only would we soon have a copy of the title deeds but plenty more besides.

Chapter 3

We had decided that, if we were going to live in Portugal – and we now knew that, barring acts of God and accidents, we were – we really ought to buy a car.

Lynne and Jeremy shocked us when we enquired innocently about the price of second hand cars in Portugal by saying that it was probably the most expensive car market in Europe. This gave us pause for thought. However, it just so happened a friend of theirs, Arun, an American Baptist Minister, was going back to the States for a year with his wife and had a second hand Ford Escort for sale. They would ask how much he wanted for it and let us know.

Our calculations were based on the fact that, as we would eventually require a car in Portugal, we might as well jump sooner rather than later. At that time, having to hire a vehicle every time we came over for at least five or six days (never the most advantageous rates), the costs were building up. Obviously, we couldn't afford to leave the car parked at Porto Airport for months at a time, but although a taxi to and from the airport would be dear, we felt that to have our own vehicle would outweigh the expense and be cost effective.

Jeremy made enquiries and reported back the price for the car was €800. As you'll see from this e-mail exchange, the final price was a little more – in fact, it rose by 150% – we bought it as seen with no guarantees (trusting or what?).

----- Original Message -----
From: Ken
To: Arun
Subject: Car
Hi Arun,
We didn't have much time to think about your offer of the car for €800. Can you answer a few questions please?
1. What year & mileage?
2. Is it Portuguese registered?
3. How long is its MOT?
4. What is the insurance situation in Portugal? Can we transfer yours to our name and about how much a year?
5. What is the system for re-registering it to us?
6. Can we have first refusal on it?
If all okay we will be over October/November to buy it but, if you required it for a couple of months after that it wouldn't be a problem to us.
Best regards
Ken & Sue

From: "Arun"
To: "Ken"
Subject: Re: Car
Ken & Sue,
The car is a 1991 Ford Escort. Presently 170,000km. Portuguese registration. Insurance cannot be transferred. Insurance would probably be at least €300 per year for basic coverage. I don't know what MOT is, sorry. I am having it inspected now which is required every year. I have owned the car for three years. I have had to do some repairs over that period of time. Front brake rotors and pads most recently, also the computer was replaced about a year ago because of a fault caused by a shorted wire. Other than that the car has been very reliable. It is an eleven year old car and it does have the normal wear. The body is in good shape, tires and such. I replaced the front windscreen a year ago after it was hit by a rock on the highway. I am asking €2,000 for the car. That is a firm price. The car is sold 'as is' with no warranty.

As I do not need to sell the car but am open to sell if someone has the money, first person with my price gets the car. We are leaving the first week of December for a year.

Paperwork transfer is done locally but it takes a couple of months before the papers are back. At least it did the last time I bought a car. They are constantly changing things so it is hard to say. You would be required to sign documents though. I don't think that it costs very much for the transfer.

Hope that answers your questions.

Arun

It all appeared straightforward enough although we were shocked at the price increase from what we had been led to believe by Jeremy. Perhaps we were very naïve, but you need to bear in mind the following factors:

a) we were not mechanically minded;

b) we knew even less about the prices of second hand cars on the forecourts of garages in Portugal;

c) Arun had already been helpful to us and was a man of God. Moreover, Lynne and Jeremy assured us their friend was 'an okay guy' who regularly made trips from Aveiro to Alombada and had had no problems with the vehicle.

There was a very good reason why we didn't know what the forecourt price of second hand cars was. At that time they never advertised one. We had become a bit cynical about this, and grew to believe that if you walk on to the forecourt they assess what you can afford and start off at the highest point and possibly haggle down. We didn't know for sure because we hadn't tried – it was daunting enough just to contemplate.

Anyway, we bought the car from Arun although it needed a couple of minor repairs, which he had told us about, one of which was the driver's seat needed welding back to the floor. He said he would pay for the cost of this repair. Off we drove, having dropped him back at his house after going from office to office in the usual Portuguese merry-go-round. Firstly we had to transfer the insurance from his name to ours (which, amazingly, turned out to be possible) and, secondly and at great length, we had brave the Loja do Cidadão.

This is a huge building in a recently developed part of town. It has the reputation, despite its relatively sunny aspect, of being a bewildering bureaucratic nightmare. It is an administrative complex which, until one has made several visits and became used to the layout and practices, is a busy and intimidating place. However, once we found our way around, we discovered it was a very efficient way for people to conduct all their business under one roof. It houses the majority of the public service departments – telecommunications, electricity company, roadway services including driving licences, registration of immigrants, social security and many others. If we needed to visit two or three different departments, it made things a great deal simpler.

But that lay in the future. On that first visit we went into at least three different sections to complete all the necessaries as, once again, they required copies of all our documentation in triplicate. Eventually we reeled out and drove home, our heads still spinning.

Parking the vehicle back in Alombada, we discovered another problem. I phoned up the Minister.

"Did you know that the driver's window won't close?"

"I forgot to tell you that."

"Yeah! So we found out."

"However, it's easily solved. If you lever the switches out of the console and change them over, you can then close the window, but you might well have to buy a new one for it. Shouldn't cost much."

"Okay, thanks – any more surprises you know of?" I tried to keep the sarcasm out of my voice.

When we enquired about a spare switch, we were told we'd have to buy the complete double rocker switch at a cost of €85.

"Thanks, but no thanks," we said, we'll try a scrap merchant on our return to the UK.

Which is what we did and it cost us £8 for the complete

console.

"So much for buying second hand vehicles from Men of the Cloth," I said to Sue.

Because cars do better when they are used regularly, we asked Lynne to drive it from time to time, this would keep the battery charged and the wheels turning. It was a couple of months before we came back out again, and she told us she had taken it out several times with no trouble. All sounded well.

On our next trip over, Lynne was there to meet us and drove us back to Alombada in her jalopy, a somewhat rickety ride. Jeremy was working in the UK, so she was alone. She told us she had to go back to England next day and asked if we would take her to the airport early in the morning. This obviously meant that we were going to be on our own in their house – not what we were expecting, but no problem. We said we would be happy to take her up to the airport but would take our car.

Lynne told us how she had looked after the Escort in our absence. She said she had filled it up with petrol, had let it idle every day and had driven it once a week so all was okay. We managed to contact Rui who was going to act as translator with Leonardo and the meeting was arranged for the next day at 5.00 p.m. So far, so good.

The alarm clock went off at 6.00 a.m. – a great start to the holiday. Lynne wanted to leave by seven o'clock so we showered, had a quick cup of tea and a bacon butty and out I went to start the car. It ticked over for a minute and died.

As far as I could tell, there was hardly any petrol in it, and both the oil and water warning lights had come on. I went back into the house and called out to Lynne. "There seems to be something the matter with the car."

"Yes, I've noticed that." Now she tells me.

"Why didn't you say something last night?"

"I thought you'd be able to fix it."

"Well, both the oil and water warning lights are flashing."

"I know, I've had the same problems all along. I've been

topping the water up regularly. What do you think it is?"

"Absolutely no idea. We've been in the UK all the time, remember, and we're not mechanics. Tell you one thing – the petrol gauge is showing empty."

"That's never been working anyway." What on earth had we done?

So we ended up taking her car, a 28 year old Volvo Estate, which I soon decreed to be a death trap with its balding tyres, alarmingly vague steering and a tendency to veer off to the right whenever you touched the brakes. Miraculously, we got Lynne to the airport and waved her off, before I drove back in a gingerly fashion.

We stopped off at the local garage and spoke to the only person who understood English to find out if someone could come and examine our car. He said, rather grudgingly, he would see if he could get a mechanic to drive up to Alombada and look at it some time in the afternoon. We mentioned we had a meeting at 5.00. I guided the Volvo back, taking the mountain at record low speed and then we sat and waited.

At last two guys arrived, speaking no English of course, but what they had to tell us required little translation. It transpired there wasn't a drop of petrol in the car. They indicated to us in a mixture of sign language and Portuguese that they would go and pick up a 5ltr can of petrol to at least get us down the mountain. We waited ... and waited.

The bells on the chapel clock struck 4.00 and they still weren't back. We had no choice but to go off to meet Rui in the Volvo and then hitch a ride in his car to meet Leonardo. You can perhaps guess what happened. The warning light for low petrol came on as we were going down the mountain so we had to limp to the garage, stop and put fuel into the old gas guzzler. Our saviour mechanics were nowhere to be seen en-route, although they were supposed to be making their way back to Alombada. Just to be on the safe side, we also bought a 5ltr can of petrol for our own car, which we had now christened Bozo for its hapless qualities.

"Do you know something?" Sue quizzed me in her I've-come-to-a-realisation voice as we approached Rui's house.

"What?"

"I reckon Lynne and Jeremy live in a fantasy bubble. They don't have much of a clue about anything."

I could agree on that. "They certainly don't know much about cars."

"And you know something else?"

"Yes. We bought ours on their say-so."

"Do you think they realised what a heap it was?"

"No. Well, I hope not anyway."

Rui laughed uproariously when we told him the story. "Now I suppose our car will run out of petrol as well," he chortled. "Cláudia has taken it out to see some friends. I must ring and tell her to stop at the next service station. I'll have to come with you."

He wasn't laughing so hard after a few minutes in the Volvo. "I'm not happy in this car," he gasped.

"Prefer that one?" I pointed to a car travelling in the opposite direction, belching smoke.

"No comment." But we made it to Leonardo's office safely.

It was a very good meeting, although not without its tricky moments. We asked Leonardo what we had to do next and how did we go about getting quotations to build.

"It's up to you to decide on the exact floor coverings, such as tiles, the colours of the walls, the bathroom and kitchen fittings."

"What, all of them?" I caught Sue's eye, instantly spotting problems.

"Yes, then we can ask for quotes."

"That's impossible. We don't have time to choose all those before we go back to England."

Leonardo shrugged, and began to examine his cufflinks.

"How about this for a plan?" said Sue. He signalled that she should continue. "Can you go ahead and get quotations on the basis of costing average bits and pieces and if we want to change something at a later stage we can adjust costs accordingly?"

Leonardo thought about it with great deliberation before slowly nodding his head. After that, the sailing was relatively plain.

The result of our hour and a half together was to get most things resolved and leave us feeling more relaxed about the future. Leonardo said he should be able to get three quotes from builders he could trust within four weeks.

"As soon as all the quotations are in, you must return to Portugal, discuss matters with potential builders and choose one."

"That should be fun," I said.

He raised an eyebrow. "Once you've chosen the builders, I'll oversee the project and make sure the work is done to a high standard."

Our plan of campaign was to have the holiday apartments built first (hopefully by September) and then if necessary come back out to supervise the building of our home. It was agreed by all parties and seemed logical.

By this time it was 7.00 p.m. and Cláudia arrived as he refused to get into Lynne's car again. Cláudia is the perfect partner for Rui. A schoolteacher in Aveiro, she is bright and intelligent, lively, with a good sense of humour and terrific company.

"Come on," encouraged Sue, "you must at least let us buy you dinner." So, they followed us back up to Alombada where we demolished two enormous pizzas and three bottles of wine – well, the drinking was done mostly by Rui and us as Cláudia was driving. We felt we'd earned that at the very least. They finally disappeared down the mountain: it was only after we had waved goodbye to them that we noticed a small can of petrol had been left on the doorstep.

There was now petrol in our car, no problem about that. The difficulty was that the battery had now gone flat. We managed to track down some jump leads from Natálio, who was proving to be always generous and reliable, and started it up. I drove it up and down the village and the mountain for 15 minutes or so to charge up the battery and went back to the house for breakfast.

We then had a reasonably leisurely day, recharging our own batteries after Friday's exertions, drifting around the local market, getting some food and drink in, picking oranges from the garden and finding a nice little restaurant for lunch. We spent the evening trying to sort out the building project as we were having lunch with Rui and Cláudia at their home the next day.

Refreshed, we woke up early, and Sue was typing up the to-do list for the building work, when Augusto came round. He grinned at me and indulged in an elaborate mime on the doorstep. Eventually I twigged.

"What does he want?" Sue called from the laptop.

"I think he's going to show us how to tidy and prune our vines."

"Fair enough – they used to be his vines until the field was sold to us."

"I remember I asked him what we should do about them."

It didn't take us long to find out. He pruned them and showed us how to tie them securely with willow (no string used here) and we passed an enjoyable and instructive morning together. I felt I was receiving a crash course in how to become a vintner.

"It's so satisfying to have your own vineyard, however small," I confided to Sue.

"Invite him in for a drink," she whispered, and I did so. Though why we whispered, neither of us knew. Augusto didn't speak any English and was notoriously hard of hearing.

We sat in the kitchen for a few minutes, enjoying a quiet glass of wine, interspersed with satisfied sighs and occasional comments in halting Portuguese, until the clock struck 12 and it was time for Augusto to return home for his midday meal and for us to go to Aveiro.

What was already a very pleasant day just continued to get better and better. Cláudia had cooked bacalhau com natas (traditional Portuguese salt cod, re-hydrated and cooked with cream and sliced potatoes) and rice for lunch.

This went down a treat.

"Have you been to the Costa Nova?" asked Rui.

"Not yet," I admitted.

"Oh, you must, it's just beyond us here in Aveiro, and it looks a picture. All the houses are painted in glorious different-coloured candy stripes," enthused Cláudia.

She was right. With the lagoon on one side and the sea on the other, the long, narrow front of delightfully painted houses appeared as though it were auditioning for the part of the idealised seaside town – it was almost too set-designed to be real. Even though it was so early in the season, there was already a healthy weekend crowd strolling around.

We drifted on to the beach and sat at a little café munching pastries and drinking cups of tea and coffee. Facing due west, the sun was beginning to go down towards the horizon on the Atlantic Ocean and its rays were sparkling on the wave tops. I couldn't believe there was a more idyllic place to be at that moment.

"Would you like to see the fish market?" Cláudia interrupted my reverie.

"On Sunday?" queried Sue.

"It opens every day and has the most amazing selection of fresh fish you'll ever see," said Rui.

We wandered lazily around the market, with its pungent smells of the sea and a large array of seafood – he was right, you'd be hard pushed to find a better choice anywhere. We congratulated ourselves on our good fortune. Perhaps our luck had changed. The weather was perfect all week and now, on Sunday at 6.00 p.m. it was still 22º.

We drove home later in a contented daze.

I awoke in a sudden panic that night. How were we going to get to the airport on Tuesday morning as Lynne was in the UK. After a lot of debate about whether we could catch any trains or buses (our flight was leaving at 10.30 a.m.), we contacted Lydia, a Portuguese friend of Lynne, whose number she had left for emergencies on the fridge door. Lydia said she would book us a taxi for 7.00 on the Tuesday morning and invited us to their house for supper that evening, a friendly gesture above and beyond the call of duty.

Rising early again for our last full day, we called into the garage to see if they could look at the car as it was misfiring – it apparently needed an air filter so we went and had a coffee while they fixed it. After that, we chugged down to the bank to get some money for Leonardo (again we had to wait for about an hour, our statutory banking period), went over to pay him and discuss one or two things. There was no interpreter this time as Rui wasn't able to attend, and we had only gestures, dictionaries, a bit of Portuguese and a fair amount of French between us, but we got there, aided greatly by Leonardo's wife, a petite and lively pharmacist who chanced to drop in while we were there and spoke good English.

We had been trying for an appointment with our solicitor all weekend and finally managed to see her for five minutes at lunch time. Aldina seemed to be even more flustered than usual.

"Um, I appear to have mislaid your file," she confessed.

"You've what?" I tried to keep my cool. We really liked Aldina but this could be a disaster.

"Don't worry, it's in there somewhere." She waved a hand vaguely at the mounds of files and papers.

"Can you find it? It's urgent," Sue pleaded.

"Of course. I've just got a rush job on at the moment. I'll be able to take care of your needs as soon as I've finished that."

It wasn't the most reassuring statement, but it would have to do.

Grabbing a quick bite to eat, we raced back up the mountain, where we started packing before going to Tony and Lydia's for supper. Tony arrived to show us the way to his house. He said he had walked up but he could come back in our car. I'm not sure he'd have agreed if he'd known its history. Nor would we have agreed if we'd known the route. We ended up descending the mountain in Bozo on what could kindly be called a tractor path all the way down to the river. There were branches of eucalyptus trees in the way, the burnt-out wreck of a tractor that hadn't made it, rocks and stones and, just to complicate matters, it was viciously slippery because there had been a recent shower. We slid most of the way down but, amazingly, we got to the foot of the mountain in one piece.

An incredible sight awaited us. In a clearing stood a house built in the style of a castle, turrets glinting in the setting sun as though it were a fairy tale come to life. All it lacked was a moat and a drawbridge. However, beyond the fortification, we could catch glimpses of the river surging by, effectively sealing it from the main road beyond, noise from which provided the only reminder that we were viewing the scene in the 21st century.

We never saw the inside of the castle, however. The Portuguese have this habit of entertaining people either in the garage or a special 'eating house' as was the case this time. Lydia was waiting for us in the entertaining suite amidst a pile of lovely old furnishings and bric-a-brac.

"It's very kind of you to invite us," said Sue.

"Nonsense. You're very welcome." Tony was handing round glasses of wine.

"We lived in London for many years before returning to Portugal," expanded Lydia. "Tony and I still spend quite a lot of time in England each year, going to antique fairs buying up anything that catches our fancy."

Looking around, this was hard to disbelieve, although they presumably ended up selling some of them in Portugal.

Tony showed us round his vast grounds full of orange and lemon trees, kiwis and other fruits, all of which he lovingly tended without using any chemicals – although now in his seventies he was clearly a workaholic. His garage lay on the other side of the river and he had built single-handed four suspension bridges spanning the River Vouga. This might seem excessive until he told us that three of them had fallen into the river over various winters when it had been in flood. He also still logged the eucalyptus trees, had built a summer house, as well as all his bridges, and had a head full of further grand designs. A tiny man, he still went cycling regularly with a club for up to 50km, some off road.

We returned to the eating house, now lit by candles, to enjoy a splendid supper, during which the two of them chattered away about their contrasting lives in Portugal and London. Lydia was wonderful, delightfully mad, highly entertaining and great fun. All in all, they were (and remain) a terrific pair of lovable eccentrics, and we knew instinctively that we were destined to become firm friends with them.

We left there about 9.30 p.m. and after a couple of false starts and with much slipping backwards, we managed to get back up the mud track to Alombada.

The taxi arrived punctually next day (thankfully, because we were a bit worried as the Portuguese aren't the most reliable of people when it comes to timekeeping), allaying my phobia about being late. So, we had another trouble-free trip back to the UK, although there was one last uplifting experience before we left. Going through Duty Free at Porto airport the local port lodges usually each have a stand with samples of their products. Taylors, Sandemans, Warre, Dow – you take your choice. Approaching one of these, the girl behind the counter enquired if we would like to participate in a tasting.

"Is the Pope Catholic?" I enquired. She laughed and poured us out two reasonably sized glasses.

"Where have you been staying?"

"We're not just on holiday," said Sue, and told her about our land purchase and plans for the project.

"That sounds fantastic. It is good for Portugal that people want to invest in the country," she said, promptly vanishing.

We looked at each other, wondering what we had said to make her disappear so abruptly. Finishing our glasses, we were about to leave when she returned carrying another bottle.

"As a celebration, would you like to try a rather special port? It's 50 years old."

"Ooh, yes please," Sue beat me to the punch.

This time though she poured three glasses, lifted hers to ours and proclaimed us the future of Portugal. We felt really warmed by this toast, although we had to admit the effect of the port might have had something to do with it.

Arriving home, we reflected on progress to date.

"Once we get the quotes in," I began, as I turned out the bedside light.

"Hopefully in about three to four weeks," Sue continued.

"Can you get time off to give the builders the once-over and find out when they can start?"

"Have to."

We made our contingency plans to fly back out again for the next stage. That was going to be crunch time.

Chapter 4

As promised, we drove north one weekend to tell our respective mothers more about our decision to buy some land in Portugal, build a home and move out. We were a little apprehensive about how they would react now it was a fact. So it was a pleasant surprise when my mother announced quite candidly:

"I'm getting on anyway and if you leave the decision much longer you'll probably never take the plunge – and regret it. So, good luck to both of you."

"You realise, Mum, if there are any problems they'll have to be left to the rest of the family."

But she merely nodded her head; it wasn't an issue as far as she was concerned.

We then drove over to Cathy's and told her the same news. She had had a fairly major stroke and was unable to live in her flat in Birkdale any longer so she'd moved into a nursing home. She was instantly excited about our plans and although the stroke had impaired her speech, her brain was still as sharp as ever.

Raising both hands towards us she exclaimed, "Azulejos." Pronounced 'urzoolayjosh' it is the Portuguese word for tiles – difficult enough to say at the best of times.

"D'you know" she continued, "we wanted to move there some 30 years ago... often wish we'd done it – so every success and happiness for the future. But where on earth will you go to the opera, and what about the library?"

Sue was happy to disabuse her. "Considering we already

possess a mountain of books, the library won't be an issue and neither of us are devotees of the opera, so I think we'll get by!" Cathy looked doubtful but said no more.

The only other worries we had concerned their health in the future. Sue would be leaving any possible problems with her sister, Judy, in the UK, but this wasn't quite as easily dealt with because she lived in Surrey, whereas Cathy was in the North. Judy suggested her mother might like to move to a nursing home in the south, which was met with a guarded welcome. One of my two sisters and my brother, Bob, on the other hand, both lived within a 40 minute drive of Manchester. So we also had to involve them before a final decision was taken to move out and, thankfully, they all gave us their unconditional blessing.

Even so, the life-changing nature of what we were about to do was really starting to strike home. Whenever we began to get cold feet – which did happen – we would simply recall what Cathy had said to us, that she wished she'd moved out to Portugal in the early '70s, and our resolve was hardened. Unlike so many British couples of our age who moved abroad, this wasn't a case of us taking early retirement. We had no intention of retiring just yet, quite the contrary. We were moving to extend our working lives and we believed that placed us in a minority.

Leonardo had told us all the builders' quotes were in. It was decision time. We were flying from Gatwick first thing on Saturday morning.

Arriving back in Alombada, we unpacked and immediately went to look at our field. The weather was just right, a magnificent day – it was about 28º, bright sunlight and clear blue skies. Natálio saw us wandering around and invited us in for a glass of his wine.

While we were sitting in the kitchen we noticed four huge bowls of something marinating. Apparently, it was a wild boar (Javali); one of Natálio's neighbours had shot it and they were going to celebrate by having a village festa that night. He insisted that we should come along as well.

"That sounds great. We've never tried wild boar, funnily

enough," said Sue.

"You'd probably best get used to it," replied Natálio with a wink. "You never know, there may be another one some time."

He showed us how they were cooking it, which seemed fairly simple, mainly involving drenching it with masses of robust local red wine, and repeated his offer to come back later. We didn't know what to expect so we wandered over in the evening and were amazed to be met by the whole village, friends, friends of friends, children and grandparents – about 40 people in total.

As we mentioned earlier, the Portuguese don't generally invite people into their houses, so there we were, all crammed into a purpose-built barn with a blazing log fire at one end – obviously it was a little cold for them – and two rows of tables and benches. Although we couldn't talk to that many people in depth, there was a great atmosphere with everyone laughing, chatting and drinking litres and litres of locally produced wine.

It was a terrific meal consisting of soup, the wild boar in that rich marinated wine sauce, onions, rice and potatoes, vegetables, salad and desserts – delicious crème caramel and plenty of local cakes. The wild boar was surprisingly good and, after such a long, slow dousing, very tender.

After the evening was over, we meandered back to our lodgings in a very relaxed and happy state.

"Great meal," I said.

"And not one to break the bank," added Sue.

"How do you mean?"

"Well, for the 40 or so guests they had there, they didn't go out frittering away their readies. Apart from their labour, the only thing that had been bought in a shop was the rice."

"They've probably got some paddy fields down by the salt marshes in Aveiro," I joked.

Sue decided to ignore me: "Everything else we ate had been home grown – the salad, potatoes and vegetables were all from their fields, the wine produced from the village grapes..."

"...As we well know, possibly even our grapes," I carried on. "Even the wild boar was a gift from God, I believe they call it."

"And to cap it all, the desserts were made from their own eggs and flour," finished Sue.

There is a tradition in this part of Portugal, certainly here on the mountain, that if you are invited out for a meal you invariably take along a dessert, usually home made, and we have since been to some parties where ten couples have arrived bearing different puddings. As a result the desserts have taken far longer to eat than the main course, especially with them all being washed down with wine and coffee, and the whole meal has taken at least three or four hours instead of two – but what a wonderful way it is to enjoy an evening, nibbling at all those different sweets.

The next morning we awoke, feeling slightly slow, and spent time on the patio trying to sort out colours for the holiday apartments, along with all the bathroom and kitchen equipment. We had brought a load of brochures from the UK and just went through them cutting bits and pieces out and sticking them on to rough plans so we could show the builder exactly what we wanted. This might have been a somewhat unusual technique, but we reckoned it would save a lot of dictionary time. It is surprising how difficult it is choosing colours, kitchen fittings and general fixtures for a building that doesn't yet exist.

In the afternoon we embarked on some research with Bozo and went to visit a couple who ran a bed and breakfast place the other side of the river about 10km away. On arrival at their house we were met at the tall iron-barred, closed gate by the lady of the household, who was petite and, somewhat incongruously, Japanese.

"My husband asleep," she whispered. Plainly, she didn't want to disturb him. We were about to turn away.

At that precise moment, he appeared in the background and hailed us. "There ye are. Why don't ye come in?" He had a broad Scottish accent.

She shot him a rapid glance, but gave in with good grace,

throwing opening the gate.

It was hard to work out why she had been so reluctant. The house was absolutely superb – it had been designed by her most thoughtfully, was spacious and filled with her paintings. Everything was beautifully intricate and perfect; she was obviously a very talented designer as well as an excellent artist. They showed us around the B&B part of it and we stopped and chatted for a while on their patio overlooking their land.

We asked for some general guidelines on building works. "Any good tips you can give us?"

"Aye, things are a bit complicated in Portugal," he said, his brow furrowing slightly. He soon relaxed though: "Realistically and honestly, if ye want to do it, then go ahead. But ye must bear in mind one thing: to the Portuguese, time is like a Highland country mile – it can go on forever."

It was something we'd already discovered in the banks.

This was what we'd come out for; the day came for choosing our builder. Leonardo arrived bang on time, complete with dossiers comprising the rest of our project plans, dealing with electricity, gas, water, telephone lines and all the necessaries.

Rui was working so we had asked Lydia to come over to help out with translation. Having heard about our car from Tony, she decided to walk up the mountain to Alombada from their castle rather than risk a lift in Bozo.

First of all, we went through the various quotations for the building with her help. Finally, it was time to choose. This proved an idiosyncratic affair, which chiefly consisted of Leonardo holding two of the quotes firmly in his hand and pushing the third one towards us, saying:

"It is entirely up to you which one of these three you select. I'm legally not allowed to advise you." He smiled gently.

I checked with Lydia, Leonardo waited patiently. Lydia nodded her head. Sue beamed encouragingly.

I picked up the remaining quote off the table, at which point a big smile broke out on his face and he clapped me on the back, before shaking Sue's hand with great energy.

"Congratulations, you have made a very wise choice."

Quite by chance, we had selected probably the best builder to undertake the construction of our project in the area. Remarkable how we were able to do this on our own...

Leonardo then phoned the chosen builder and arranged for us all to meet at Lydia's castellated house in the late afternoon when she could spare us more time to act as translator.

That afternoon we all bounced down the mountain in Lynne's Volvo, sat in the sun and sorted out the major details of the proposed construction, along with timings. Adrio, the builder we had chosen, turned out to be a most pleasant young man, in appearance quite unlike the prototype of his profession, studious, of average height, and medium build. Behind his glasses lurked a ready disarming smile, and although he was not entirely free from the builder's disease of being everywhere at once, we found him generally at ease with himself and life, and eventually he too became a good friend. Despite, of course, having absolutely no English, he agreed to start fairly quickly and settled for always calling me "Mister Ken."

"He promises to finish the apartments by the end of October," interpreted Lydia.

"Good. When will the main house be ready?" I asked.

There were some rapid exchanges between Adrio and Lydia.

"He thinks that will take until June next year."

"That timescale's no good to us," said Sue. "The house has to be completed by April at the latest."

"So we can capitalise on the Euro 2004 football competition in Portugal next summer," I added. "You like football, don't you?"

Adrio smiled nervously, but said nothing.

A big debate ensued until Adrio eventually backed down and agreed to finish the inside of the house by the end of

April and complete the outside painting by July. At least we could then move in before letting the apartments.

As a guide, we asked if we could see some houses he had built and it was agreed he would meet up with us on Wednesday. Adrio also said he needed to know the exact tiles for the floors and bathroom walls. This was a bit intimidating, as we didn't know where to start finding them. Still, we knew we needed to get the ball rolling.

We chugged back up the hill after thanking Lydia for her Herculean efforts. Over a cold drink, we continued sorting out more colours, bathroom furniture and other details from the brochures. We were, by now, getting used to 14 hour days on our holidays – it was harder graft than work.

We had quite an easy start to the following day with only one meeting with Aldina in the morning where she produced draft contracts for Adrio. It was arranged that she should act as 'go between' for the payment of deposits to Adrio and making all the further stage payments. To this end we gave her our Power of Attorney and a euro cheque to pay in to her account – she could then pay him the money direct. Having fallen foul of the Portuguese banking system once, we weren't going to land in the same trap again.

Shopping is normally fun but not when it's for tiles and eventually we found a factory warehouse by the name of 'Aleluja.'

"God must be smiling on us today," said Sue, looking heavenwards.

"Don't let's count our chickens." I was inclined to be gloomier. It wasn't all done and dusted yet. Have you ever entered a tile manufacturer's warehouse with thousands of tiles of every hue, size and style on display?

No? Well, let me explain. We had this one morning – and this morning only – to select the correct tiles for all the flooring, kitchen areas and four bathrooms in the two apartments, which we'd named Portuguese and Terracotta respectively.

So we walked into this showroom with thousands of different boards glaring at us. Daunting was hardly the word. The first thing we decided was the basic colours and chose blues (Portuguese apartment) and browns/greens (Terracotta apartment). We thought we'd cracked it, but now the real decision-making began. Sometimes there is such a thing as too much choice, and we were facing it.

Frankly, we were floundering in a sea of tiles.

The next hour and a half was more than traumatic until finally, a very sympathetic sales assistant took pity on us.

"Do you need any help?" she enquired.

"Not half," I muttered.

"Yes, please." Sue realised that even the good English of the saleswoman wouldn't necessarily translate all the idiomatic phrases we used.

"There's too much choice?"

We nodded our heads.

"Why don't I take samples of the designs you like from our stockroom and put them on one side for you? Then you can just examine those."

Soon we had a stack of about twenty five samples. From this first pile we spent another hour and a half discarding shapes and designs until we got it down to a more manageable five or six types. The sales assistant came back in to help us from a professional point of view and guided us to the exact ones she reckoned we would require.

So, after about four hours we had successfully completed the design of our tiles for the apartments. We asked if we could order them but this proved to be the next problem. Sadly, the sales assistant shook her head. They could only sell direct to their outlets, so we would now have to take the tile codes and order them via the builder through his stockist (strangely this proved the best solution of all – we phoned Adrio who told us where his supplier's warehouse was and we found this without too much difficulty, giving them our list of tile codes. In fact, we became a regular source of entertainment at Maco Rafael with our oddball requests over the ensuing months during the building project).

We did at least manage to get some samples to take away.

Brain dead by now, we planned to have a quick supper on

the way back up the mountain. The owner of the café remembered us from our last visit, a good sign. There was a group of young people sitting on another table shooting glances at us from time to time and after we had finished our meal they watched the café proprietor give us a glass of wine and pastries on the house. These pastries are only produced in one particular town although there are many similar variations.

Smacking our lips over the last morsels of the pastries, we were preparing to leave when one of the young people leaned over towards us.

"Excuse me, please. Are you English, French or German?"

"English," replied Sue.

Someone had won a bet. The young man turned to his friends, two women and another three men, and a volley of dialogue followed. Smiling, he addressed us again.

"We would like to invite you to join us."

It seemed churlish to refuse, and soon another couple of bottles of wine were ordered and evaporating rapidly.

"Are you local to here?" I asked.

"No. We live in Porto. Most of us are working in a BMW garage there."

"But that's about 50 minutes drive away," cried Sue.

"Sure," he said. "But we drive out to this café because of its reputation for good food."

I dropped my voice, careful not to insult the owners, who were always so friendly to us. "Isn't it rather a scruffy small local café for big city folk?"

"It's not the outside that matters. It's the inside."

We were very pleased that culinary reputations went far deeper than the glossy façades of other establishments. Our 'quick supper' ended up as lengthy as a leisurely dinner, since we spent about 3 ½ hours there instead of the hour we'd planned.

It had been just another example of the many displays of friendliness we met with from the people here.

Wednesday saw us back at the bank so we could draw out money for Leonardo. Incredibly, there were no problems and we escaped in the blink of an eye in banking terms – maybe a quarter of an hour – then drove on to meet up with Leonardo and Adrio. We had a lively discussion in the architect's office over all our choices of tiles and colours, and for once managed to get our points across without anyone translating for us. The language lessons we had embarked on in England were slowly beginning to pay off.

The Portuguese have a healthy disrespect for north European taste and had just expected us to choose bland colours – our schemes appeared to have surprised them. Goodness knows what was going to happen when we finally selected colours for our home. Adrio then took us, as he had promised, to see a couple of houses he was in the process of constructing – one large and one fairly small but both seemed, to our innocent and amateurish eyes, in pretty good condition.

We met Adrio again early the following morning – he took us to Credit Agricole, as we needed public liability insurance for the construction project. We were quite bemused when a small room in an almost ruined house proved to be the insurance company's office. In order to enter we had to go through an outside door and into a sealed and locked lobby. Then an assistant came out, the door closed behind him and we spoke in the lobby without any access to the interior. It was rather like being in one of those James Bond films where 'M' has set up an emergency HQ in disguise.

Anyway, they decided that everybody was busy in the office and it would be better for us to return half an hour later. This being Portugal, off we went round the corner, had a coffee and waited for the revised appointment time.

Returning to the insurance offices, our mobile rang. It was Aldina telling us that the cheque would take at least 20 days to clear. We had a quick chat with Adrio – after all, it was his money, but he didn't seem too fazed and said:

"That's the way of the world – okay, no problem. I'll wait, but I can still start work, Mister Ken."

We concluded our business at the insurance offices and

took out €5,500,000 worth of indemnity for two years at a minimal cost. It seemed a little on the high side to us.

"You never know," muttered Adrio darkly.

Discretion was the better part of valour, we concluded.

We were all due to meet up with Aldina to sign the contracts at midday so, having some time to kill, he took us on a tour around the area, taking us up to a small village in the hills with beautiful, narrow cobbled roads where he had built five new houses (there were only about ten houses in total in the village) – all different but in similar style and each blending well into the surroundings. He showed us the interiors of a couple of these houses so that we could see various styles of doors, shutters, loos, taps and other fittings.

He then gave us the great honour by driving on to his own home where he produced port and biscuits, introduced us to his wife, Teresa, and we all walked round their huge garden in the style of a tropical island with banana plants, pineapples and cactus, lacking only the piercing shrieks of the wildlife. Teresa was obviously a very keen gardener, considering the size of the garden and the amount of watering she had to do each day.

Reluctantly we left this mini-paradise, and arrived back at Aldina's only to find that she was still busy and asked if we could return later still.

"But you did say noon."

"I'm sorry." Papers were fluttering everywhere. "I could see you at three."

It was hard to be annoyed with her, as she was so winningly scatty. Besides, I thought we might be able to put the time to good use.

"We would rather make it later. Then we could do some sightseeing."

"That's fine."

We had negotiated a whole afternoon off and decided to drive to Vouzela, the small town where they made the pastries we had eaten in the café previously. It was a lovely drive inland initially alongside one of the most beautiful rivers in Portugal, the Rio Vouga, the road curving gently in and out of the sun and shade, before leaving the riverside, skirting the mountains of the Serra do Caramulo to our right and climbing towards the foothills of the Serra de Arada. From time to time the road dipped down towards the river's edge and after about an hour of sedate progress, we found Vouzela and, in due course, the pastries. We bought a few for gifts to take back – well, if I'm honest, a few happened to be five boxes as we needed some for ourselves!

As the heat mounted in the mid-afternoon, we wandered into the small tourist office (we'd found they're invariably quite cool if we needed a break).

"What else is there to do around here apart from eat pastries?"

The girl behind the desk smiled brightly and suggested: "You might like to drive up to the highest point in the area. It has wonderful panoramic views and, right at the top, there's a small chapel cut into the side of the rock face."

She gave us a map and pointed out the route.

There was also a small museum in the tourist office so we took advantage of the air conditioning and wandered around that as well. Outside we made straight for the ice cream shop but we decided to keep the panorama for another day.

We returned to Aldina's office to sign the contracts and found that, true to form, she wasn't there. However, after making various amendments to the contracts over the phone via Paula, her assistant, we eventually signed them all, had them copied in triplicate along with passports, número de contribuinte, etc., shook hands all round and went for a beer with Adrio.

As we were strolling to the bar, he pointed out that our car tax was nearly out of date. Sue's lessons were bearing fruit to the point where she could just about understand Adrio when he spoke very deliberately.

"With everything else going on we hadn't noticed."

"You really need to purchase a new one because the fines are very expensive."

"Where do we go for that?"

All was not lost however.

"There is a 'slot' of about five weeks when everyone has to renew their car tax," he explained.

"There's good news as well," said Sue looking at the windscreen, "because, unlike the UK, here it's less than €20."

Adrio took us to the papelaria (similar to a local UK post office) and we bought a new one for display on our windscreen.

As it turned out the café next to the papelaria was a very good choice for a beer halt. The owners' daughter had lived in Australia for many years and spoke 'Australian,' and an elderly man came in, became confused, and chatted to us with every other word in English and the rest in Portuguese! So, after a couple of beers and this bizarre conversation we were all totally flummoxed.

But we were happy that the contracts had finally been signed, the stage payments for the project and the timetable agreed, and the plans had been rubber stamped by the local council. We felt we were finally making progress and Adrio confirmed he was ready to organise the bore hole which we would require for drinking water, domestic and irrigation, as there was no mains water in Alombada.

It was a blisteringly hot morning on Friday. For once, we had no immediate tasks. Bozo could, in theory, take us anywhere.

"We're on holiday – what shall we do?" Sue was in very good spirits.

"Why don't we follow the advice of that tourist office guide from Vouzela and drive up to the little chapel at São Macário?"

"How long will it take?"

"It's probably a 3-4 hour round trip."

"I don't think rain will bother us." Sue did enjoy tempting fate.

We set off driving through a string of picturesque little villages, Paradela, Ribeiradio and Oliveira de Frades, on our partly riverside route, made our way through Vouzela and

São Pedro do Sul and started the climb up the mountains into the Serra de Arada. If the countryside around where we were staying was rugged, then gradually these aspects became even more stark and barren. There were vast areas of scrub and scree on the mountainsides, punctuated by stubborn bushes and, quite frequently, the clustered skeletons of charred trees. As if to lift our spirits, we came across a wonderful sight in the middle of nowhere – there were two old women, probably in their eighties, in temperatures of 40º plus, sitting under a large black umbrella surrounded by about 50 goats and a dog. They must have walked at least 8km with these goats because there was absolutely nothing before or after on the road for that distance. They gave us a cheery wave as we passed.

I suppose we had been pushing our luck with Bozo. We had just arrived at the highest point of São Macário when the car, which had been spluttering on its way uphill, decided to overheat and go on strike. Steam was emerging from every orifice of its engine – there was no way it was moving further. There were no other cars in sight, nor any people, birds nor any sign of the goats, just a solitary road, shimmering in the haze, heading back down the mountain, stretching as far as the eye could see. To the west and north we were ringed by mountains, the Serras of Gralheira, Montemuiro and Biggorne competing to catch our admiration as links in a great natural bowl. At least we had plenty of time to admire these spectacular panoramic views and look at the little chapel built in the rock.

We were though extremely lucky on several counts – we happened to have our fully charged mobiles with us, and, equally important, there were a couple of – what we had up to now considered a rather hideous eyesore – antennae towers which completely spoiled the scenery but saved our bacon and gave us a phone signal. We also still had the leaflet from the tourist office with a contact number.

I called them up.

"Do you remember two English people who came into the tourist office yesterday? You suggested we visited São

Macário. Well, we're here!"

The same lady was on duty. "Of course I remember you. Are you enjoying the view?"

"It's wonderful, most spectacular – slight hitch, we can't get down again."

"Why?"

"Because our car has blown up!"

"Do you have insurance?"

"Yes. It's in the car. Why?"

"Well, stay right there."

"Don't worry. We're going nowhere."

She proved extremely helpful and organised a breakdown truck to come and collect us, although we couldn't understand at the time what significance the insurance for the car had. We also asked if they could bring water for the car just in case a hose had broken. To our relief, we were able to watch from afar as the breakdown truck wound its way up the mountain and it was with us in less than 40 minutes. The driver got out and presented us with two 1ltr bottles of water explaining that he had been asked to bring water for us (not the car). We were very grateful though and enjoyed the drink.

He piggy-backed us back down to his garage in Vouzela where we waited whilst five mechanics scratched their heads and looked at Bozo. They eventually decided that the cylinder head gasket had gone (ouch – that would be expensive) and that they could fix it the following week. This was obviously not an option as we were returning to England in a couple of days and this garage was at least an hour's drive away from Alombada. A huge discussion ensued and eventually we were asked for our insurance papers. It now became apparent why the lady in the tourist board had asked us about them. On our policy, and unbeknown to us, we had paid a small extra sum for breakdown insurance, which saved us over €300 for the tow – it is a legal requirement in Portugal and everybody with car insurance pays it. So we finally had a lift back to our local garage on the back of another breakdown truck.

We had a quote from the local garage for the repair which was €2,500.

"That Bozo is definitely for the scrap yard!" Sue was pretty firm.

"I just wonder if our friendly American Baptist missionary knew about it when he sold us the car," I mused. "Or perhaps Lynne had just been topping Bozo up with water all along, instead of adding antifreeze/coolant." This would have had the same effect, making the engine boil over. It was certainly hot enough to have done that.

Bozo's days were numbered. As a postscript to the story, the next time we returned to Portugal it cost us a further €1,200 to have a reconditioned engine and gearbox installed. We discovered also that the oil was way over the maximum level. Even we knew this was probably worse than too little, so we drained a bit out, leaving it at the normal measurement, rechecked the water and went on our merry way. With hindsight we shouldn't have bothered having it repaired – we should have cut our losses and scrapped it there and then.

Finally, though, we brought our UK registered Peugeot over to Portugal and asked a local car salesman to sell Bozo for us. He put it on his forecourt without much enthusiasm where it remained unsold for over a year. We saw it regularly as we drove past on our frequent trips into Aveiro. One day we asked the salesman to drive it to our local garage who gave us €500 for it – goodbye Bozo, not the best investment we had ever made. We still see the car around sometimes but it's a millstone gone from around our necks.

On the day of our departure, we wandered round the local shopping centre and met up with Lynne for lunch before she drove us to the airport. As we set off the weather suddenly changed, having been perfect all week, and started raining. We were about 15 minutes from the airport, going from one motorway to the other on a slip road when the Volvo skidded. Unfortunately, it didn't come out of the skid so we ended up doing a Torvill and Dean act, spinning round and round, bouncing from one crash barrier to another. We came to a halt, got our breath back (luckily no-one was hurt) and tried to get moving again, only to find that the steering had gone.

We now had more than a few problems – we were stuck on the hard shoulder of a motorway (and didn't know our exact position) – we needed to get to the airport – and we had to get Lynne back home. Lynne's mobile wasn't charged (not unusually) and it was left to us to make a variety of phone calls, at last reaching a friend of hers in Porto who said he would arrange a taxi for us to the airport and a garage to help Lynne back to Alombada.

Standing by the side of the road, Sue felt something blow into her eye and had a rummage for some paper tissues in the glove compartment.

"Guess what I found?" she whispered, when Lynne was distracted.

"Try me."

"The car's documents showing that the MOT (British) and insurance (also British) ran out at the beginning of February and we know that the car hasn't been back there for at least two years."

So, there we had been, driving on a Portuguese motorway through a downpour in a potential death-trap with no insurance or MOT and the usual mad Portuguese drivers for company.

Marvellous.

After a lot of waiting around, with various motorway police and rescue people stopping, seeing we were all right and disappearing again, the taxi at last arrived. We started removing our luggage from the Volvo and putting it in the boot of the taxi when another taxi pulled up immediately behind, whose driver began waving his hands and shouting at us. We had no idea what was going on, until the first taxi driver put both hands up, removed our luggage from his cab, turned to us and apologised in faltering English explaining that he hadn't realised a cab had been booked for us and he had just assumed we needed a taxi. It was all very amicable from then on with our new taxi driver seeing the funny side. Time was running out so we had to leave Lynne waiting for a breakdown vehicle.

Anyway, our taxi hurtled to the airport and we arrived with a few minutes to spare, only to be told that our luggage was 5Kg overweight. We had done our usual trick of putting both our suitcases into one to save on space and having left clothes, brochures, paperwork and other essential items at Lynne and Jeremy's to cut down on luggage on future trips. So all we did was take one suitcase out of the other and re-presented them. Whatever, it worked, but after all our adventures with the car, we weren't too happy with the officious airline staff.

Further insults were to follow. We were told that our flight had been delayed by three hours – bloody BA, we muttered. Then, to compound everything, fog came down over the airport. The plane tried to land three times before it eventually made it to the runway. To be fair to the staff, they turned that plane round with cleaners, catering, luggage, people offloaded and reloaded, and in record time we were off to Gatwick finally getting back home around 1.30 a.m.

Chapter 5

Sue had spotted an advert in the local Newbury paper about 'Is your house a living home?' which intrigued both of us. Coincidentally there was an article in a different newspaper on the same day which I noticed, saying that the Millennium Stadium in Cardiff had had, since being built, a 'good' chi dressing room and a 'bad' chi dressing room and whoever had the use of the 'bad' chi room (the away team) lost. As a result, they had called in a Feng Shui consultant who researched the stadium, took various notes and measurements, looked at all the aspects of the build and came up with a simple and apparently successful solution. Following the consultation and changes, the home and away teams had both won more or less on equal terms.

Having discussed the Cardiff story, and, because neither of us knew anything at all about Feng Shui, I went on to the internet to research it. Sue phoned various specialists, and the one who responded and said she would be interested in our project was a woman called Brenda who, at the time, happened to be in Wantage but was returning to her home in Portugal the next day. It was a happy coincidence. We agreed to send her our plans.

Our project was the biggest thing either of us had ever undertaken and we considered a consultation fee a small price to pay if it made the difference between a harmonious home and a functional building. Life was wonderful between us, we were first and foremost the best of friends and communicated any doubts or worries to each other. So this was definitely worth thinking about.

Before dawn we headed off to Portugal – it was an early start because we had to be at Gatwick by 8.00 a.m.

Collecting the hire car, we negotiated the maze of roads around Porto airport, buzzed down the motorway and went to the supermarket. We were again staying at Lynne's while they were away. As before, we had agreed to keep their cats and dog fed and watered so we stocked up on pet food as well as supplies for ourselves. Arriving in Alombada mid afternoon, we unloaded the car and hot-footed it the few metres down to see our building site.

At first, all seemed well. The building of the apartments looked in great shape and they were progressing very quickly. The foundations had been completed, the supporting pillars were upright and the builders were dashing away with the bricklaying.

There was only one problem. Well, two, if you like.

They were being built in the wrong place and at the wrong angle.

I jumped up and down and swore a bit. Sue just laughed. Then we both went to find the plans to confront the builders. They looked at the plans and scratched their heads and, after much shrugging of shoulders, sort of agreed there was a problem. They phoned Adrio, who said he would come up and have a look at 7.00 p.m. At the same time, we phoned Leonardo, who said there was no problem and they were definitely in the right place. But he said he'd come up anyway.

Adrio and Leonardo duly arrived on time that evening and a big discussion ensued, with the help of an even bigger dictionary.

"When this project is over we will know just about every building term in Portuguese." observed Sue.

Anyway, the long and short of it was that we asked them to stop work on the building until we had seen our solicitor the next morning – Aldina's English would undoubtedly help matters.

In the morning, we set off down the mountain to Aldina's – on the way we saw Adrio going into Leonardo's office so we parked up and piled in there as well. Leonardo was insisting that the building was in the right place and Adrio really didn't care much about that as long as we were happy with the actual building works. We all trooped over to Aldina's to try and sort it out.

"The reason everything appears to be in the wrong place," said Aldina from behind an impressive edifice of papers, "is because everything has to be built a certain distance from the centre of the road."

"Why on earth is that?"

"Just in case the local council decide they want to increase the road's width."

"So they can then steal a bit of our land!"

"Not exactly – to make the road through the village better."

"But there is no road beyond our village," I mentioned.

"That's beside the point."

"It's very much the point for our home."

"So," she said, "the apartments are being built according to the plans."

"Well, why did no-one explain it to us?" I questioned.

Aldina looked at Leonardo. Leonardo looked at Adrio. Adrio looked out of the window. I decided to be conciliatory.

"I suppose to some extent it's our fault because we never asked the questions."

"It is no problem to move the apartments but it would have to go back to the Planning Council," Leonardo explained.

"Portugal more or less shuts down in August, as you know, and it probably would not be approved until October," said Aldina.

"Assuming it is approved," added Leonardo with gloomy relish. "the building would not be re-started until November or December and everything would be delayed by about six months to a year."

"I suppose we'd have to pay Adrio quite a lot more for all his work to date and for demolition."

Adrio perked up at the mention of this and stopped counting the clouds.

Sue and I looked at each other in resignation. "Okay, we'll keep the apartments as they are," I agreed.

"Our guests will now have a much better view of the valley and mountains than we'll have," said Sue.

"But if that's the case, can we make a couple of small changes to the interior of our home?" I changed tack.

"We realise the exterior is a no go," Sue chipped in.

Leonardo indicated he was listening.

"The first is a cellar cut into the mountain. We'd like it running the full length of the house."

Hardly small, but if we were going to give way on the new positions, we might as well extract some concessions. Leonardo glanced at Adrio and pointed out the area on the plans. They were evidently relieved it wasn't something even more arduous. There was a general nodding of heads.

"And the other one is French windows on the lounge wall so that we can see our new view."

Again, a brief nod from Leonardo signalled assent.

We also discussed putting in underfloor heating, adding ceiling points for electric fly zappers and a few other small items – all were graciously conceded.

Adrio reached for his mobile phone.

Work resumed.

Whilst at Aldina's we had to shell out vast sums of money for our bore hole which she and Adrio had organised on our behalf. Apparently you have to pay so much per metre and ours is about 175 metres deep.

"We're going to have to drink bucket loads of the stuff to make it pay," I said.

"Not to mention take thousands of showers," added Sue.

Adrio then took us back to Maco Rafael where we spent a happy hour going through the tiles we had previously chosen. He was able to confirm they were within budget for the project. A trip that had begun disastrously was certainly looking up.

For the evening meal we decided to have a Madras curry,

home made with rice, cooked in that special Portuguese way, and a bottle, or maybe two, of red wine. Meanwhile Sue did her super secretarial bit and went to check our business e-mails.

"Guess what?" she called out.

"Try me."

"Lynne has changed her IPS server."

"So…"

"So she's also changed her password."

"Don't tell me – we can't get on the computer."

"Right. Not until she phones us back. I've left a message."

Clearly, not everything could go right. However, the meal was a great success – I credit the ingredients – and just what we needed. So was the wine. Then it was time for relaxing. We finally turned the television on to see the 10 o'clock news and woke up two hours later on the sofa complete with two contentedly snoring cats asleep on our laps and a dog warming our feet.

We had a fairly leisurely start on Saturday – the weather was a bit iffy, with cloud and threatening rain, although it was still warm. We moseyed down to Albergaria-a-Velha and headed first of all for the local computer shop to try and sort out the internet and e-mails for when we moved out here permanently. The shop assistants were very helpful, and one of them, Carlos, spoke English, having lived in America for 12 years.

We then went into the Portuguese Telecommunications office and talked to them about the difficulties or otherwise of obtaining a phone line. We had been told it might take three or four months. They laughed and said it should take two to three weeks. This was great news. The only drawback was that they professed not to have heard of Alombada, but we were getting used to this by now, and drew them a map.

"I think I should copyright these," I muttered.

It was market day in Albergaria-a-Velha so we wandered round, then went for coffee – well, okay, it might have been a cerveja – before heading into Aveiro.

We had bought a small present for Lydia in England as a thank you for acting as interpreter previously. She had told us she was going to be in Aveiro as there was an antiques market that day. However, by the time we found it, it was pelting down with rain and everyone had gone.

"Plan B," said Sue, sticking our umbrella back in the boot of the car.

We tried to deliver the present at her home but there was no-one there either, so we ended up putting it through their letterbox and never saw her. Calling it a 'letter box' was quite a misnomer. Technically, maybe, but it was on the opposite side of the river from their home and at the far end of the latest bridge which was still standing. The entrance to it was gated and locked.

We took the long way home – no slipping and sliding up the mud track in that torrential rain.

Sunday was a glorious day – beautiful sunshine, hot and clear, the sort of dry heat that makes one feel good to be alive. We had a day off and were just pondering what to do with it when the phone rang – it was Lynne with the password. That took care of the next hour because, unlike other times, I hadn't sent the usual 'I'm away for a few days' e-mail, so my in-box was full.

After business was concluded, we decided to retrace our steps up to the highest point in the mountains, where poor old Bozo had blown up, and complete the trip in our more reliable rented car. Off we set, full of enthusiasm complete with a picnic. Stopping off in Vouzela, we re-filled our petrol tank and called into the Tourist Office.

"We just wanted to say 'thank you' for your help when our car broke down last time."

The woman recognised us instantly and was pleased we had called in to see her.

"Ah yes, the English explorers. How is your car?"

"Not good. We've got a different one this time."

"It's probably best."

We were also able to obtain another route map from her and asked her to show us the topmost point again.

Driving along fantastically empty roads, we started off on our tour, gradually working our way up to the mountains. Stopping by a little stream, we had our picnic in dappled sunlight, it was such a beautiful spot, so quiet and peaceful.

Or rather, almost. We only saw one other vehicle the whole time we were there. Sod's law dictated that, having been on the move for around three hours, eaten lunch, drunk a couple of beers, and being out of the way, nature called. Both of us were in full flow, when we heard the sound first of a horn, then of a car engine. It duly arrived around the corner just as modesty had been rather frenetically restored. Needless to say, those were the only people we saw for the next 40 or so kilometres.

Perhaps flustered by our narrow escape, we missed the turning to the little chapel at São Macário but a short distance further on, we found another signpost to it so took that instead. It seemed to be a red herring. The road became narrower and narrower, and we ended up on a dirt track, just wide enough for a tractor, with a sheer drop down one side to the valley far below. The panorama was wondrous but we were getting worried. I thanked God that we weren't in Bozo.

We crawled along following the contours of the mountain for about an hour. There was nowhere to turn round. I didn't fancy reversing back along this narrow winding mountain path and the track just went on and on. At last, we turned a bend, and came to a fork – one path going back up the mountain and the other continuing along the same contour. We stopped and looked at the map, bemused.

Suddenly, potential salvation arose as from nowhere two 4-wheel drive cars materialised.

"Where are we?" I shouted at their occupants.

The driver of the first car appeared puzzled by the question. I decided to be more precise.

"Does this dirt track lead somewhere?" It obviously did, otherwise these cars wouldn't have been there, unless of course they had driven up the side of the mountain, which didn't seem likely.

"Just keep going and you'll meet up with a road," the driver waved back down the track.

So we did and they were right – we eventually reached a newly tarmac'd road leading straight on from the dirt track. It was as though we were re-entering civilisation. Presumably the tarmac would be extended at some point, although we rather hoped not. Why shouldn't others inch along the same mountain path in boiling temperatures? With these thoughts, we drove along and passed through an outcrop of houses with two cafés and dozens of young people on motorbikes, lounging in or on cars all around. Clouds of smoke were billowing across the road.

"Do you recognise the smell?" I said.

Sue wrinkled her nose. "No."

"It's cannabis!" And it was, or my name's Howard Marks. Everybody must have been smoking joints because the odour was so strong we could smell it from inside the car with the windows open going at about 30km an hour. It was lucky we weren't stationary otherwise we would soon have been pretty high... Sadly, we have never found this village again.

We never did find the top of the mountain but we had loads of fun trying and another splendid (and less costly) adventure with the advertised fantastic views. Sue has often suggested returning to São Macário for a picnic but I have always refused, not wanting to tempt fate a third time.

Before we reached home that evening, we stopped at the café in Angeja. As we walked in, the owner looked across at us in recognition. I held up two fingers and he nodded. We sauntered through to the restaurant to be properly greeted as friends.

"The usual, senhor?"

It was our turn to nod.

After our meal, the patron chatted away happily in French to us whilst we attempted to answer him in Portuguese. The net result as usual was that neither party understood the whole conversation, or much more than half of it, but it was definitely fun – especially when he stuck to his other tradition of introducing us to another delicacy from his food selection, or even better still, a new drink.

"Have you tried this fortified wine?" he enquired.

"Er, no," I responded cautiously.

"It is very similar to port. You will like it."

Of course we did, and the camaraderie really boosted our self-confidence, confirming we were doing the right thing. We felt we were becoming accepted by many of the locals – the proprietor of this café certainly knew us well by now.

When we returned to Alombada, we looked at the gauge: we had travelled 166 kilometres since filling up that morning – at least 80 of which must have been up, down and round that blessed mountain.

Monday, having dropped in at a café for a quick bite, our sitting at the bar seemed to cause a problem since the waiters kept indicating the restaurant to us, but as we only wanted a snack, we stayed put. However, when we ordered what we thought was a small portion of chicken salad and a couple of beers, we received confirmation that 'small' wasn't a word favoured in Portuguese cafés.

A vast oval plate about 50cm appeared, full of freshly barbecued chicken quarters, together with another one of similar gargantuan size, crammed with green salad, tomatoes and onions.

"If this is a snack, I can't wait to see their main course," gasped Sue.

Yet it was the one of the best salads we had ever eaten; It was cool, the dressing light, bringing out the tenderness of the mild, white onions and sliced tomatoes and, with a couple of beers, the whole was a veritable feast.

Our business was almost complete so we went to find another garden centre to compare prices of citrus trees and exotic flowering shrubs like bougainvillaea – we discovered it and now we had somewhere else to buy plants and shrubs. Life for us was one huge learning curve.

It was incredibly hot by this stage so we headed back for an early swim. Driving through Alombada, we noticed a crowd milling about beside the old Quinta we had tried to buy. It was being painted and all the doors had been flung open. An earnest group of Evangelists had taken it over (apparently for free provided they did it up a bit) so we asked if we could take a look around.

The site was still as good as we remembered and our thoughts went back to those early days when this house had seemed our ultimate dream. We remembered our crushing disappointment when the sale broke down and we had watched the Quinta fall further and further into disrepair on our subsequent visits. At least now it wouldn't collapse into utter ruin. We spent a fair amount of time with the Evangelists and eventually the minister accepted that we weren't religious types, relaxed and enjoyed some general conversation with us, although the young lad who spoke English and translated the difficult bits refused to concede that we weren't convert material.

"So you are moving to Alombada?" he quizzed us.

"Very soon now," confirmed Sue.

"But are you not coming to Portugal because you are seeking spiritual fulfilment?"

"Not exactly," she said.

"I think you need to be touched by our faith," he exhorted earnestly, eyes blazing.

"God is always welcome in our home but leave religion outside," I said gently but firmly.

He finally got the message and began to chat more openly, before we made our way back for our long, overdue swim.

Just before the guys finished working for the night we wandered over with some cold beers for them and took another look round – unlike our arrival, there were no problems this time. Once they had left, we returned with the video camera and took a record of progress so far.

It seemed incredible we were leaving so soon. We had had some fantastic times on this trip and, once again, we had overcome any problems and made progress on every front. Any disappointments that we had were by far outweighed by the people, the weather and the pace of life. The downside was that it was very difficult leaving our village. Packing, tidying up and returning to the UK was becoming harder each time.

We were slowly becoming Portuguese in outlook.

Chapter 6

Our plane had arrived late the previous evening but we did our best to rise and shine in the morning. After breakfast, we fed the animals, and hurried to check the internet for work. Surprisingly, there was nothing. Perhaps we'd miscalculated, and people were already writing me off as a business contact. Our projections depended on my printing business continuing to tick over. I brooded about this as the Portuguese sun did its best to inspire me.

We were expecting Adrio at 3.00 on site to discuss doors and windows for the apartments. As it was only 2.45, we reckoned we'd chill out for a while; we had opened a beer each and were sunning ourselves on the veranda when he arrived, bang on time. This was a really strange situation for Portugal – or, we supposed, anywhere – we had engaged a builder who arrived punctually or even a few minutes early every time... Typical luck, as we were trying to become laid back and develop our native concepts of 'amanhã' about life.

"Would you like a beer, Adrio?"

His eyes lit up.

"So where are you taking us this afternoon?" Sue smiled at him.

"Nowhere." Adrio looked puzzled as he unscrewed the bottle top.

"But I thought you were helping us choose our doors and windows?"

"Yes. The man from the company is coming here." On cue, we heard the sound of a car in the lane.

"We thought we were going to a factory or showroom to look at them and say – yes, that's what we'd like," persisted Sue.

"Easier here. May I introduce you to Nuno," Adrio assured us.

Nuno could not have looked less like a company salesman, as he waddled over from his car. Enormously fat, sweating profusely, his appearance was hardly prepossessing. Fortunately, he did at least know his stuff, as far as we could gather. We stood in the apartments with him and Adrio and, with no common language between any of us, we tried to say what we wanted and they tried to tell us what we were getting. At the end of it we shook hands and Nuno, still mopping his brow with a handkerchief, drove off in his shabby van.

"I bet we all have totally different ideas as to what we are getting," I muttered to Sue, as Adrio waved goodbye.

"So it'll be even more interesting than usual to see what turns up," she replied philosophically. Her ability to look on the bright side never ceased to impress me.

Deciding it was too good a day to be indoors, a drive through Aveiro and out to the Costa Nova to take some photographs for our website seemed a great idea. It was absolutely fantastic on the coast that afternoon. There was a light sea breeze blowing from the west; the beach, with its golden sands stretching for miles, was virtually empty and there were wonderful Atlantic rollers coming in on a rising tide. A couple of diehards were surfing. After a walk up and down for half an hour or so we sat at a beach café and reflected on the day's events.

Being a working holiday, we decided that a treat was in order and went to look for a restaurant. We knew exactly which one we wanted to eat in but fate was against us – it was closed until 7 p.m. So we meandered back inland, ending up in Albergaria-a-Velha, where we headed straight for another favourite churrasqueira (grill restaurant). I wolfed down a huge steak whilst Sue munched on a giant prawn and octopus kebab and we shared the obligatory garafe of house wine. Everything was beautifully presented and tasted fantastic. The seaside and meal were just what we needed.

Wandering back up to Alombada we checked e-mails – still nothing. Our whole plan for moving the business to Portugal was in jeopardy. Then I suddenly had this brainwave – I do occasionally – that the e-mails, which should have been coming in on my new address, were not going through the original server. Could that be it? Mad panic; Sue tried to phone our website manager in the UK but she was out. We sent her a text message – oh, the joys of modern communication – and she came back with a suggestion of a site where we might be able to pick up our e-mail. After a lot of playing around we managed to find the site and, lo and behold, there were they were.

The Portuguese project was saved.

We responded to the queries we could immediately, and afterwards relaxed on the terrace looking at the crystal clear starlit canopy with the Milky Way cutting a broad swathe through the centre. It still felt a little strange that we were on the same time zone and night sky as the UK – but without any light pollution here on the mountain it was an entirely different experience. Like a couple of school kids, we competed as to who saw the first and most satellites.

"Here comes the 9.15 from Moscow."

"There goes the 9.35 Washington to London."

In the quiet of the evening we could often make out shapes from the silhouettes of the nearby eucalyptus trees. One looked exactly like King Charles II with his long wig. Another group resembled gorillas following each other and our imaginations boggled at what others suggested! On that especially beautiful moonlit evening, a warm breeze gently blowing from the west, I turned to Sue:

"Have you noticed anything about the eucalyptus trees?"

"What do you mean?"

"They dance, don't they?"

Fortified by coffee and toast in the morning, we were ready for the challenge of updating our bank records. In Portugal every transaction is updated in a passbook, rather like a UK post office savings account book, and is not itemised. As a result, it is an extremely difficult for customers to remember what each entry relates to. The bank was closed so we used our debit card to gain entry into the lobby, after which we updated our passbook. We did this by placing the book open at the appropriate page; the machine then grabbed it, pulled it inside and, after a lot of whirring and hammering, out it popped with lines of dates, figures and codes.

That's not all it can do. If it has been some time since you last updated the book and it fills a page, it then spits it back out at you, tells you to turn the page and re-enter the book. Also, on the last page it hurls the book out to you, instructs you to wait and issues you with a new one.

Neat, huh? We were impressed with the sheer mechanics of the machine – this was very 21st century technology, although sadly saddled with an early 20th century mentality. Nevertheless, we felt that another hurdle in the tortuous banking system had been overcome and it would now be easier having managed it once.

We drove along the road beside the river towards Sever do Vouga looking for anglers to photograph. Unfortunately, the rains had been absent for so long that the water level in most places was too low for fishing. Nice idea, though.

So we gave up and had a beer in the café nearest to Alombada (known by us as the French café because of its patron). He took great delight in telling all the customers in the bar who we were.

"Bonjour, les Anglais," he announced loudly.

Some of the babble in the bar subsided. The patron gesticulated to his flock as though he were a parish priest.

"These are the mad English who are building a home in Alombada."

"Ah, ha," one of them said, examining us with genuine

curiosity: "you must be the ones we have heard about."

There was much laughter, backslapping and handshaking as the patron introduced us.

"Welcome to Portugal. Alombada has the purest air in the region, so we would all love to build our homes and live there, but land is so hard to come by in the village that we can only envy you."

This was solemnly agreed by all assembled and pleased us greatly.

It was time for our introduction into the intricacies of the Portuguese language with regard to drink: we discovered caneca here. This is a wonderful word and should be used every time instead of fino. The difference – a fino is a 20cl. beer but a caneca is ½ litre. Thus at a stroke it eliminated all that getting up and down to order three small beers!

We wandered home, with 'au revoir' ringing in our ears.

As soon as we arrived back at Alombada we had a phone call. It was from Sergio, a holiday home letting agent in northern Portugal, whom we had discovered and contacted whilst looking for the dates of the Euro 2004 football competition on the internet.

"I would like to come and have a look at your place on Sunday late afternoon if that is all right."

"No problem," I put the phone down and told Sue the news.

"Bloody hell, that's tomorrow."

"So it is."

"The quicker the better – that's great." But we both knew it would be a test.

We went for a swim – the water was still lovely and warm and we lazed about in it before nipping out to the local supermarket to buy beers for the topping out ceremony of the apartments later that week. Having heard about their recycling incentives, we brought along with us six crates of empties. This was another wonderfully complicated Portuguese system.

First, we had to go to a small hatch in the wall inside the store, and put one crate of empties on a ledge. The person behind the counter emptied the crates one by one on to a large flat bottle carrier (which took 10 dozen at a time) and gave us the empty crates back. This is all in the interests of conservation and has to be applauded. Then off we went to the aisle where the beers were stacked and re-loaded them individually into the crates. Finally we took the crates, now full, to the check out desk, along with the receipt for our returned bottles. We got €4 back on the transaction and as a crate (24 bottles) was only about €4 we considered this was a very good deal. It would, however, have been simpler to leave the crates of empties, receive a credit note and replace them with full ones. This though is Portugal.

We spent a very pleasant couple of hours on the veranda in the evening, sitting once again watching the satellites go overhead. Oh yes, and drinking some of those beers. After all, we needed the empties.

We had an earlyish breakfast and played around with photos on the computer. Then drove back over the other side of the river to check out other scenic views and ended up in Sever do Vouga, discovering a hill paradox – whichever way we walked it was all uphill (or appeared to be). Even, for some reason, when we were supposedly walking back downhill towards the car. We sat on a bench overlooking the town and the distant mountains making copious notes ready for our meeting with Sergio.

On our way back to Sernada, where we were due to meet him, we saw a sign for ices and stopped for a Magnum ice cream (this being our 'holiday' treat – me almond, Sue double caramel). We enquired if we could use the loo. Candidly, I was expecting a rather primitive set up – bearing in mind this was in the middle of nowhere with local farmer types as clients – but we were both rather desperate. The proprietor looked blank, but a young Portuguese customer said in perfect English:

"Yes, there is one, but I'm afraid it's outside and up the steps. Come, I'll show you."

Sue glanced at me. Evidently she shared my worst fears, and it seemed as though they were about to be confirmed.

But we followed him. He guided us out of the bar, around the corner and announced in Portuguese to an old lady, dressed in black, standing at the top of the stairs, that we wanted to use the 'facilities.' The old lady, doubtless good natured, resembled one of the Witches in Macbeth, and I was preparing myself for a roadside halt as soon as we were out of sight.

She beckoned us forward and I shuddered. We climbed the stairs, she unlocked the door, and... it just goes to show you should never judge a book by its cover. Gratefully, we made use of the facilities, which were spotlessly clean, spacious and a credit to any hotel, let alone a small, remote café.

"What do you think would have happened in England if a foreigner had asked the same question?" I mused as we drove away.

"Told the loo was out of order, probably," said Sue.

"I very much doubt he'd have been answered courteously."

"And certainly not in his own tongue," she added.

We arrived at Sernada early for our meeting so we made a slight diversion down to the riverside and walked along the river bank. It was a hive of merriment and activity. There were hoards of local families parked up for the afternoon, with children and adults alike splashing about in the river along with rubber dinghies, balls and lilos. Many of them had barbecues on the go, making it all great fun and, in temperatures reaching 28°, very inviting. As we were about to order cold drinks from the riverside tent bar our mobile went off. It was Sergio, arriving in 10 minutes and, you've guessed it, early. We despaired of the new generation of Portuguese. So we cancelled our drinks, went to the café by the railway station instead and waited for him.

Sergio was a charming young guy, aged around 35, who spoke good English and arrived with Janis, his Canadian fiancée. We introduced ourselves over a mineral water and talked a bit about our project before driving them up the mountain. Sergio and Janis fell silent on the way up while we kept pointing out various landmarks en route.

Back at Alombada we showed them around the apartments (or rather the building site), bedrooms, shower rooms, lounge/diner area, where the patio area and swimming pool were going to be. Sergio remained silent. Oh God, I thought, he hates it, he thinks we're miles from nowhere and disappearing fast.

His only comment was about the boiler on the inside of the wall of the lounge diner area. He didn't care for it.

"I'd like it outside."

"It's a balanced flue system, perfectly safe, but it's going to be replaced." Sue pointed out.

He nodded slowly, deliberately. This was the acid test, our first business opportunity, and it was going to be thumbs down. We were sure we were doomed – he stood in the doorway, looked out at the view and said:

"Fantastic – what an amazing panorama. I could let these a million times over."

We both breathed a huge sigh of relief. If nothing else, this proved that we were not being foolhardy in our plans – it was a truly memorable moment for us. He'd given the first independent appraisal of our project and it had passed with flying colours.

Now he'd started, Sergio never stopped talking all the way down the mountain. We ended up back at the café and sat around drawing up plans, prices, sales ideas and advertisements before they finally left at seven. They must have been genuinely enthusiastic because they had told us they were due in Porto an hour earlier.

As we waved them off, we were a bit alarmed to see palls of smoke rising in the nearby hills: there was obviously a forest fire of some sort and it was close enough for us to smell. It seemed typical of our project somehow – for every step forward, there was a potential step back.

"I hope Sergio doesn't see that," commented Sue.

"He's Portuguese and must be used to them by now," I deadpanned. But I wasn't Portuguese and I didn't care for it myself.

Brushing away visions of fire sweeping Alombada, we thought we'd celebrate our successful meeting with Sergio with leitão for supper. The proprietor showed us a sorry sight. Arranged on a plate were four pigs' heads, as though they were the remains of a gruesome medieval banquet.

So much for our celebration.

We telephoned Cathy, Sue's mother, who was due to move south to her new nursing home the following morning. This was obviously quite a big adventure for her and somewhat alarming. However she seemed to be coping.

We also phoned our Feng Shui friend, Brenda, in Cascais and had a good chat with her about our plans. She suggested some good ideas on positive colours and alignments before we agreed we all needed late evening drinks in our respective homes. We stargazed and listened to the chapel clock, recently re-wound by Augusto, chiming every quarter of an hour. Funnily enough, we'd only noticed it once or twice, and certainly it never kept us awake – we were now obviously locals.

Our meeting with Aldina and Adrio took two and a half hours of fairly solid concentration the next morning. Money was discussed first as the next stage payment was due.

We then spent a lot of time discussing underfloor heating – we had asked for this in the house from the very early planning stages – everyone had been asked, builder, architect, solicitor, old Uncle Tom Cobley and all. We had pressed repeatedly for a quote.

Adrio decided otherwise. "No, never been mentioned," he insisted.

"I'm sure it was," I said. Sue nodded vigorously.

He thumbed through a notebook. "No record, Mister Ken."

At that point I'd had enough. I told Adrio in no uncertain terms that we did want it in the house but we needed a quote before we placed the order. After many phone calls, a price – well, a very rough ballpark figure – was fixed and we also agreed to the cost of radiators in the apartments. It was a victory of sorts.

The system of building in Portugal is varied as it is in the rest of the world, but we had asked for a 'key in the door' price. However, and this was a difference from the UK, the price may be quoted as key in the door, but that means all the fittings, fixtures, painting, electrics, sanitary ware, walls, doors, roofs and plumbing are included, but only the water pipes up to where the radiators are going to be placed. Everything was priced in the house, apparently – except the radiators. Or so we understood.

We also had another long discussion about aspirators in the walls, which are built-in vacuum cleaners. This was a novel innovation for new build homes whereby the motor and collection sack for the vacuum cleaner are placed strategically out of the way in a cellar or garage, linked throughout the house by tubes in the walls and each outlet has a connection slot which enables the householder to plug in a vacuum hose and attachment rather than lugging around the whole vacuum cleaner.

After this discussion Adrio left and we continued our meeting with Aldina about phones, wills and many other things. But I couldn't let go.

"Are you sure radiators aren't included?" I fretted at Aldina.

"That's Portugal," she shrugged.

In the afternoon, we went into Aveiro and spent a long two hours in PT, continuing our discussions to have the phone connected at Casa Sulo ready for our return in October, so that we could test the system. This was clearly a problem, not exactly to our surprise.

The dilemma was this. Even though we have a Portuguese bank account and our número de contribuinte was given to us three years ago, we will not have our licence to live in Casa Sulo until after it's built. On our part, we required the phone line before we moved in – it appeared to be an impasse. I then uttered the magic words:

"We are setting up a tourist business."

Politically, the Ministry of Tourism has a very powerful pull and if something is slowing down a project then they want to know about it. I used this shamelessly. The PT people hastily decided that they would try and put us on a temporary line but that would only last for a month.

"No good," I said, "we will be needing it for at least six months."

"No problem. We will renew it every month."

"Does that mean we have to come back here and renew it each month and have a different phone number?"

"No, we will do it automatically and by direct debit until the final and permanent line is installed."

"Ah yes, but will we have to change numbers and internet addresses when it goes permanent?" Sue had hit on the crux of the issue.

"No, nothing changes, just the form."

"What's the difference between permanent and temporary?" I added.

"One's called permanent and, er, the other's called temporary."

The bureaucracy was wonderful to behold.

We left with our heads swimming from this bewildering exchange and still unclear whether we had succeeded in having a phone or not. Only time and PT would tell. They had in the meantime taken photocopies of all our relevant papers and said they'd let us know in a few days.

It was by now time to eat as we hadn't had anything since breakfast – we were famished. Rui had recently given us directions to 'The 2 Duques' restaurant in Aveiro. This was one he had taken us to a couple of years back, which we remembered as being extremely high quality and very friendly. We were convinced we'd never find it again without him driving us there so set off more in hope than conviction. Much to our surprise we soon found it (Rui was obviously a dab hand at directions) and had a thoroughly good meal before heading back.

On the way we phoned Cathy who had arrived at the nursing home after an eight hour journey and was exhausted. We knew how she must be feeling, but her next words really cheered us up.

"I like it already," she said. Whether or not she was trying to put our minds at rest, we felt a great surge of relief.

We promptly ran out of whisky on our return – very bad planning on my part, although I pleaded other business.

We went to see Aldina. This turned into another marathon session with a plethora of details about PT, tax, payments, building times and other red tape issues before we could escape and make plans for the festa.

The Topping Out Party was held in the evening and we all trooped down to the site. We had invited Augusto and Beatriz as well as Natálio and Isabela, not forgetting Sandra and Paulo with their respective partners. Adrio arrived with a whole roasted suckling pig, this being traditional for topping out ceremonies, together with crisps, sliced fresh and sweet oranges, wine and more beer. The builders kept themselves to themselves at one end of the trestle table whilst we played it very low key at the other end. It wasn't long though before we were chatting away with them and everyone relaxed, drank and enjoyed the festive board in good company. Beatriz arrived last, having done her hair and put on her best pinny. Like every other good Portuguese female guest, she brought a home made cake and, having had a couple of tumblers of local wine, entertained everyone. She chatted, she sang, she danced: she was the life and soul. The cake was beautiful – it looked rather flat and heavy but was incredibly light and tasty – made with carrots, honey and a chocolate icing. It certainly didn't slow her down.

The holiday apartments were suitably 'topped out' and their interiors could now be started and, we hoped, completed in our absence. This was the first time we had been able to invite our neighbours to a party. It was beginning to feel as though we really belonged.

Another day another early start – we went out to pick some grapes and figs off our vines and trees to take home. Before heading to the airport, we dropped a crate of beer down to the workmen who, still mildly hung over, were very grateful and tucked in straightaway.

On the way I topped up the car with petrol remembering one previous trip when we had filled up the night before and, due to going a long way back to the village, we had used just enough fuel to go down one notch on the fuel gauge. This cost us their tariff of half a tank of petrol at their rates – €18 for about three litres – I wasn't going to get caught like that again.

The flight was made memorable by a wonderful twilight descent over London.

We dropped in to see Cathy on the way back who was really enjoying herself. Wonderful food, people, the room, area, everything was great – it was good to see her happy and content.

By about 9.30 we were home, unpacked and started downloading all the photos we had sent ourselves by e-mail.

We woke up on Thursday not really ready for work.

Especially when we saw it was raining.

Chapter 7

I was starting to get hot flushes on the aeroplane as we took the late flight over. By the time we arrived in Porto about 10.00 p.m., all I could think about was lying down in bed. As we collected a hire car, I thought my luck was changing. We were upgraded to a 1.8 turbo diesel instead of our usual basic 1.2. Needless to say, I surged immediately into Portuguese driver mode and we therefore missed the first three turnings, ending up heading north to the Spanish border instead of south towards Lisbon.

"What on earth are you playing at?" Sue complained.

"They've changed the roads again, I'm sure," I protested unconvincingly.

"You're sweating rather a lot."

"I know. I'm not feeling at all well."

"Why didn't you say so before?"

"I didn't want to bother you, you know me – don't worry, I'll be okay."

"Oh, don't be such a fool. You should have let me drive."

"I'll be fine." But she was probably right.

By the time we approached Sernada, I had a viciously sore throat and, with feverish waves racking my body, I slowed the car to a crawl. A few minutes later when we pulled up in Alombada I had developed a raging temperature, with spasmodic shakes, persistent aching and a load of other lousy symptoms. I knocked back a quick hot toddy and a couple of paracetamol, followed by bed. Unsurprisingly, it was not a very successful night's rest for either of us as I burned up all night restlessly, causing Sue to have a sleepless night as well.

For the past few months I had been seeing a homeopathic practitioner who had been trying – unsuccessfully so far – to sort out my stubborn psoriasis. At my last appointment, I was given a 'kill or cure' treatment of just two very small pills, one to be taken early morning and one in the evening, both at least 15 minutes before or after having anything to eat or drink. This I had done religiously for the previous four days and still I wasn't cured. On the other hand, I wasn't dead either, so perhaps it had something to commend it.

I tried to get up in the morning but it was all too much, so I soon retired leaving Sue to sort out the bluetooth connection.

"I'll drive you darling." I protested feebly.

"Nonsense. You need to rest, I'll be fine."

"Well, call me if you need any help." I flopped back onto the pillows, hoping she wouldn't.

Whilst she was out I answered three business calls, about the only sort of interruption I could take.

The computer people couldn't solve the bluetooth so Sue returned and gave it up as a bad job for the day, deciding to concentrate on our other concern – the building progress.

By now I was feeling a bit better, suitably dosed up to the eyeballs, so I walked down with Sue to look at the progress of our new home and apartments. There were a few minor issues that could be easily resolved (we hoped).

The staircase had been built in with a floor to ceiling wall on either side – we wanted it open plan.

As we had arranged a telephone connection, we required a temporary landline for use after we took up residence in the apartments before the main house was completed. This would be a huge step forward and resolve one of our major concerns.

The tiles on the floor of the apartments looked fantastic but we now decided to have the same colour throughout.

As if by magic Adrio turned up and declared that none of these things would be a problem and suggested a meeting the next day with our solicitor. So we phoned Aldina and arranged a conference for 10.30 on the Friday morning. Lynne had again asked us to take her to the airport for the early flight to England. We were quite happy to do this but each time it was a 2 ½ hour round trip out of our all too short working break in Portugal. The plus side was that we had the place to ourselves and were able to come and go as we pleased.

Adrio also said he would take us to pick some other tiles for the bathrooms because one of the styles we had chosen was no longer in production.

We then went back to Albergaria-a-Velha with the laptop and once again the computer people attempted to get the bluetooth connection working – no joy. However, we did discover the reason our connection hadn't worked on the land line was the cable to the phone – although the connection was okay, the cable itself was deemed a 'crossover' and wouldn't work in Portugal. Not only did we have to learn Portuguese from scratch but we also had to learn new technical gobbledegook for computers and the internet which neither of us had a clue about. We just turned them on and expected them to work.

Apart from being hungry, I felt we were missing out on the Portuguese atmosphere and general ambience so we took ourselves off for lunch. We normally saw the proprietor in this particular café – he was an exceptionally jovial character unlike his wife who, although friendly enough, had always appeared rather aloof. Our spirits fell as we noticed through the window that he was absent and she was holding court.

However when we walked in she greeted us like long lost friends and happily chatted to us in French. In accordance with our established custom, no-one understood more than half of what the other said, but that wasn't really the point. The bonhomie and a beer or two strangely helped my fever to subside.

She even brought out a great big bowl of monkey nuts for us – a great honour because they normally offer a small dish of tromoços. These are a type of lupin seed similar in appearance to small cooked butter beans, where you discard the skins and eat the inners. We always found them pretty tasteless but as they were a local snack, we were prepared to show willing.

Thus boosted, we left to head back up to Alombada. Entering Jafafe we saw two men sitting on the garden wall of a house that we had admired for two years while it was under construction and the gardens subsequently landscaped.

"Ah, let's ask them who their landscape gardener was." I stopped the car, wound the window down and enquired in pidgin Portuguese:

"Is this your property?"

A rather blank stare – perhaps my Portuguese manners were at fault.

"Or are you the gardener?"

The nearest man gave a baffled shake of the head.

I raised my voice a notch. "We are English."

"Ingleses?"

"Living in Alombada."

"Ah, Alombada."

Without further ado, they jumped in their car, pulled out in front of ours and indicated for us to follow, then drove the 7km up the mountain. When we reached Alombada, we pulled up behind, picking up our laptop and some luggage left unpacked from the previous night. Pointing to Lynne and Jeremy's house, the driver said:

"Ingleses live in that house there."

Sue replied in mime, pointing down the road to our building site: "That's going to be our home there."

"That house is not built." He replied in similar fashion.

"We're building it!" Sue indicated.

They saw the funny side of it straightaway because typically the natural character of the Portuguese is to be friendly and helpful. There is a slight flaw to this because they always assume they understand the situation and on this occasion they had guessed incorrectly thinking we needed directions to the English couple's house in Alombada and they had taken off without any explanation, expecting us to follow. He said, when he had understood, that he would definitely try and learn more English for the future. In turn we promised to speak more Portuguese. As they drove off, they asked us to call in at their home any time – just knock on the door. That seemed to be the way of life on the mountain. Out of the blue a chance meeting could swiftly turn into a new contact.

We tried the laptop and it didn't work in the apartments – surprise, surprise, the line still wasn't kicking in. Then we tried at Lynne and Jeremy's again, which didn't function either at first. I changed the connectors and it worked fine. Exhausted, I was in bed by 9.30, and instantly asleep. Sue stayed up reading for a while; anxious to finish a book she'd started on the plane.

She paid for it because at three in the morning I sat up suddenly.

"Roof!" I shouted out, waking her with a start.

Despite her protests, I dragged Sue across to the shell of our new home, stood in the middle, shone a torch up and said:

"What's that?"

"I don't know and I don't care," replied Sue, "can we go back to bed, please?"

"Not until you tell me what it is."

"Go on, you tell me."

"It's a ceiling." This didn't go down well.

"Yes," said Sue, "I can see that."

I explained. "We shouldn't have one there – we asked for exposed beams and a cathedral style roof."

They had laid concrete slabs across the entire length of our home, meaning we would now no longer have exposed beams. Frankly, it would just look ordinary. They would have to be removed before the builder could start adding the timber roof. The next meeting promised to be very tricky.

We were up by 6.00 a.m., cups of tea in hand, ready to take Lynne to the airport.

Because of the early departure from Alombada, we didn't hit much traffic until Porto but then ground to a halt a few kilometres before the airport. We crawled along, dropped Lynne off and returned to similar traffic jams on the other side of the road heading south. Reaching Sernada we had time for a coffee before moving on to Arrancada for our meeting with Aldina and Adrio.

First, the telephone was discussed and Aldina made contact with PT to ask why our phone line was still dead. Apparently there were no problems – it just hadn't been connected at the exchange and would be done that very same morning. We pretended we hadn't heard that one before.

Next, we were given assurances the apartments would be finished by the end of October, which would be perfect timing for our move out in November. We both emphasised that we would be moving over with all our furniture and belongings during the third week in November and the apartments had to be ready for us to live in whilst the house was being built. This was imperative; otherwise we would be arriving in Portugal with nowhere to live – not a good start for our new life. Adrio gave us every assurance that we would be able to move in and we needn't worry.

The third topic was more of a poser. We asked for a temporary letter box to be fitted so we could run a trial for our own mail before coming out. This caused great consternation because, although we were going to be living in the apartments, we did not as yet have our 'Licence to Live.' The post office is equally bureaucratic and would not deliver mail to any address, even if they did happen to be living there. Used to Portuguese officialdom, we weren't greatly shocked, but the next stipulation did stagger us. They insisted that the correct size and shape of the opening to the letterbox was to their specifications – you couldn't just have any old hole in the wall or door – so Adrio agreed to put a proper letterbox in the outside wall of our land.

Fourthly, we asked for small windows to be put in both the downstairs bathrooms in the house instead of extraction units, and a window on the inside wall of our office to light the passageway with natural light. These modifications were all agreed.

The next stage payment was then discussed (up to roof level) and agreed – Aldina and Adrio were no doubt already congratulating themselves that the meeting had gone so well when I dropped the bombshell.

Our house upstairs had always been intended as a cathedral style, with exposed beams to the roof in the kitchen and living room area. This would give us height, space and a distinctive individual feature. It was something we had discussed and impressed on everybody all the way through the planning stage. I had had a nagging feeling that something was wrong but hadn't been able to put my finger on it until I had my revelation in the early hours of the morning.

Adrio gesticulated: "It's in the plans, Mister Ken."

"We agree it probably is, but we're not architects," I replied, "and you must have seen all along our schematic drawings of the interior showing quite clearly exposed beams."

"I don't recall them," he muttered.

We were quite surprised when Aldina interjected: "I was also involved in that conversation and remember the request quite clearly."

This would cause Adrio a huge problem, not least of all the extra time it would take. Once again out came the standard excuse: "The Camara Municipal won't like it and it'll take an extra three months to pass it." He shuffled nervously, hoping this would forestall us.

Sue blew this out of the water. "We compromised in your favour over the position of the apartments – we will not give way on this." We had both set our hearts on it and were not prepared to be thwarted.

Adrio offered us a wooden veranda awning, which he would build at no extra cost. "It would allow you to sit out on the veranda in the height of the sun."

"That's fine," we said, "thank you very much – but we still want the exposed beams."

Aldina appeared to be wavering. I asked her a simple question: "What if your builder had put a low ceiling right across your entrance hall, would you be happy?"

At once she understood the full implications – her entrance foyer to her newly built home is floor to roof, all marble and wooden beams. She was suitably horrified at the thought and made further and more earnest representations to Adrio in Portuguese.

"If the plans can be changed, I'll make the application to Camara Municipal whilst the building continues so as not to hold things up."

Adrio appeared resigned. It was decided, with reasonably good grace on his part, that he would discuss it with Leonardo and if he had no objections to the planning or structural work, his men would remove the concrete from over the kitchen and the lounge area, leaving it – obviously – over the master bedroom, and he would then wooden clad the inside of the roof, making it the feature we wanted.

Before leaving, we also discussed briefly with Aldina the chance of arranging an appointment with her accountant in Aveiro, as well as the name of her landscape gardener, and we gave her more details for the Portuguese wills we had to make.

"I'll phone you later on today – any preference about time?" Aldina's hand was poised over her organiser.

"Any time at all, even two or three in the morning," said Sue, glancing at me, somewhat resentfully, I thought.

Earlier, Adrio had offered to treat us to lunch after the meeting with Aldina, before going to look at new tiles for the other apartment. I had gone into total decline and was really not feeling well again; no matter how many paracetamol or ibuprofen I took, the symptoms still came in waves and by the time we reached the restaurant all I could manage was a bowl of house soup and a large bottle of water. It probably did me more good than Sue's meal, however – a cheese and bread starter, pasta and huge chunks of pork in a red wine sauce, swamped down by half a bottle of wine with a whisky chaser...

After lunch, Adrio took us to Agualinda, a local specialist in swimming pools and left us there to see what deal we could make with them. It was essential for us to have one for our tourist business. We would rather have had a hot tub on the veranda but, being practical, we thought for 12 or so visitors a swimming pool was best.

We discussed every aspect of the pool and by the time we left some two hours later we had ordered an oval swimming pool, liner, ladders, pump, the complete installation. They agreed to start around January, but it would definitely have to be completed by the end of March, so as not to interfere with the landscape gardener's schedule.

Here, too, bureaucracy took over and by the time they had taken the usual photocopies, produced a five page contract in triplicate for both parties to sign, with further receipts for our deposit cheque, most of the afternoon had passed. We left their offices in an ebullient mood but reality soon hit home.

"In England would we have just walked into a swimming pool centre and spent that amount?" Sue was quizzical.

"No matter how much money we had, you're probably right."

"It's not so much as if we bought a pool, it's more as though we've acquired another vital asset." She was adept at justifying our move.

"Right. That's the next part of the jigsaw put in place."

Reassured, I drove us back, took two more paracetamol and within two minutes I was in bed and asleep. Sue went to check for e-mails but, ominously, Lynne's telephone was dead. It so happened, just at that moment, the lady from PT phoned our mobile to say our phone was now connected and the engineer had been and made sure it was working. Sue told her, half in trepidation and half exasperation, that Lynne's phone wasn't functioning now and asked what the fault could be. The spokeswoman assured her that it wasn't our doing, but it was possible that in putting our line on, the engineer had accidentally disconnected Lynne's.

She asked Sue if somebody would be there from next Wednesday onwards because that was the first time they could attend. Unfortunately, as we were due to fly off on Tuesday we would have to leave a note for Lynne on her return.

"Somehow I don't think God meant us to work this weekend," said Sue.

Adrio arrived with the welcome news that Leonardo had no problems with changing the plans for the roof. I was still asleep, serenely unaware of this until later.

When I eventually surfaced, we went down to the apartments and thankfully had the foresight to ensure the laptop worked off the main line telephone (as the bluetooth still didn't work). Amongst all the rubble and dust, amid the noise of men fitting doors and cutting tiles with grinders, we finally made a connection onto the internet.

We marvelled at all the windows and doors that had been installed so quickly and neatly, especially the side windows which opened by the main doors.

"Do you remember our bet?" said Sue.

"Dead right I do."

The bet was due to our lack of understanding Portuguese, since Sue said that the windows would open inwards whereas I was sure the window people had said outwards.

Sue triumphantly opened the windows inwards. "You owe me another pound."

"Come off it, it was obviously euros not pounds."

Buoyed by the news about the house, I had a brief period of feeling better so we capitalised on it and drove down to Sernada for a bite to eat. We went to the delightful local station café where I had steak, chips and salad to get my strength back. Sue (still full after her lunchtime feast) contented herself with a cheese omelette and salad. We swilled it down with a garafe of house red, delivered in a litre bottle with an obscure label, although the owner explained that the wine we were given was not the same as the label. Later we saw them decanting more out of a large 5ltr garafão – it was a very good local wine but we never did find out what it was. We discovered it to be a common practice in all the local cafés, especially with the 'prato do dia' (dish of the day).

The omelette and steak were superb. Our entertainment for the evening was more variable as it was 'The Price is Right' with a Portuguese host and contestants on the television in the café. We found that every café and restaurant had a television switched on, usually with the volume turned up, making conversation at best difficult and in some cases impossible. This was also mandatory for every public place including doctors' surgeries, dentists' waiting rooms and even some cinema foyers.

We returned to catch up with the 10.00 news, but fell asleep during it, woke up and shuffled off to bed.

"This was definitely the day for non-working of computers, telephones or electrics," I yawned.

"Oh yes, guess what?" Sue reminded me. "We've had no call from Aldina with any of those appointments or phone numbers."

"Some things never change." But I was too tired to worry overmuch.

I had another relapse, and failed to get up Saturday morning, feeling absolutely wretched. Sue went off alone to the market to find something for our dinner later on, then on to the hypermarket to buy ingredients for a couple of nights' suppers, but failed miserably to obtain a simple product like Lemsip or an equivalent. This was a pointer to bring a reasonable medicine chest over with us next month (we found out later that only chemists were registered to sell pharmaceuticals of any kind at that time).

On her return I had just surfaced and finished having a shower. My scalp was very itchy, sore and felt almost on fire. Sue said there was a noticeable swelling around my forehead and on both sides of my face. The nape of my neck felt tender to the touch – all this along with my flu symptoms. We had a sandwich and met up with Adrio in the early afternoon. We thought we were going to choose worktops and bathroom units so left the house in the rain fully equipped for a trip down the mountain with him, but not a chance.

He indicated we should follow him to the apartments where he went over the earlier decisions of floor tiles, bathroom tiles, and then on to the house where we got a further concession from him that we would have exposed beams from our bedroom right the way along, and not just after the staircase. Quite something considering this probably meant him removing a further half ton of concrete slabs from the present roof area. He also agreed to place a water header tank in the loft space above our bedroom and put double access doors so we could use the considerable area for storage – this though never materialised.

We had a fairly leisurely afternoon trying again to get the bluetooth working (still no dice), so Sue typed up our diary whilst I watched Rugby – a fair division of labour I reckoned.

When the match was over, I thought I'd better check our e-mails so went down to the phone line in the apartments (which is the only one that seemed to work in our corner of the village). Unfortunately, the tilers in their wisdom had locked up the apartments when they finished work and taken the keys for security – we were now unable to take interior photos or exteriors with the doors open until Monday, and certainly couldn't access the internet. It would all have been very frustrating, except that Sue's ears had started playing her up so, allied to my ailments, between the two of us we really couldn't care less.

The weather had been very mild but with several downpours of heavy rain we kept getting soaked to the skin, adding to our despair.

"Now I know what they mean by stair rods," I shivered.

We retired for the day, having failed miserably to achieve most of what we wanted to accomplish.

After supper, we collapsed into bed. But I was even more restless than before. The pain developed in my neck and the lack of sleep finally got to me so I rang my homeopathic practitioner in the UK in desperation. She was sympathetic but was obviously unable to do much about the treatment from a distance. However, she assured me that, homoeopathically, it was exactly what she had been hoping for. Naturally. Although the reaction was severe, she told me it was a good sign and meant that she could now treat the cause directly. Could I possibly persevere while the symptoms subsided over the next 24 hours or so? I reluctantly agreed it seemed a shame to quit with the end in sight. At least I knew why I'd been suffering such exaggerated distress.

"A local lady told me a good night time remedy," said Sue, who needed sleep as much as I did. "You mix fresh lemon juice with three teaspoons of local honey, hot water and whisky." Alombada honey is used by the villagers for all ailments from colds and broken legs through to heart attacks.

"Well, someone has to be the guinea pig, I suppose."

"I'll heat up the water and make it for you then." Sue turned the gas on – nothing.

"Easy, just change the bottle." But I couldn't find the right connection.

We tried them all, but the one for the hob eluded us. Nor could we find any more gas bottles so we decided there must be one outside. Unbelievably the batteries were flat in the house torch. I gave up and had a lukewarm toddy with water from the tap, followed by yet another fitful and painful night.

Sunday, I was still in depressingly dire straits, and hunt the gas bottle was not what I considered my favourite pastime. It was as elusive in daylight as it had been by night. However we persevered and Sue eventually discovered the little devil loitering under the patio, miles away from the cooker. Having discovered its hiding place we replaced the empty bottle with a new one and, with another hot toddy, I downed some toast and a couple of boiled eggs and flopped back into bed. Meanwhile Sue went for a long walk half way back down the mountain and up again.

"An hour or two of that each day and I'll definitely be as fit as I was in my teens," she declared cheerfully.

"That's good. It's cheaper than the gym," I said, pulling up the covers. "Alombada isn't likely to have one for quite a time yet, anyway."

By now, I was at my wits' end with frustration and the pain so I phoned the practitioner again.

"You'd best take the homeopathic antidote," she said.

"What's that?"

"Three mugs of strong, black coffee and loads of peppermints."

We fortunately had a couple of packets of peppermints in the car and the coffee was easy enough to produce so I took them with great relief. I tried to sleep again, going back to bed around 9.00. Sue followed two hours later, and brought another hot toddy in for me to get a better night's sleep. It seemed to do the trick.

In the morning the fever broke – I had finally sweated it out and felt better than I had for days. Still taking it gently, we had a late breakfast after a much needed lie in.

Adrio was due at 11 a.m. for a meeting so we pottered around until he arrived, and went over all the minor snaggings which until then hadn't been discussed; for instance, the outside tap and where the gas bottles for the cookers would be stored (much on my mind).

"We also want propane not butane with automatic change-over when empty," I added.

"Yes, Mister Ken."

"Don't forget we'd like a hydro-bath in the downstairs bathroom and a steam room shower in the master bedroom, with larger shower trays throughout," put in Sue.

Adrio agreed, scrawling notes with his pencil, no doubt grateful we hadn't dropped another bombshell, and off he went: "Bom viagem tomorrow and see you safe in November." His car vanished.

At that point it really sunk in with both of us that this would be our last visit to Portugal. We would be residents here next time. Was our gamble going to work?

Fortunately, I no longer felt like a rag doll half an hour after leaving bed, so we took all the photos we could and had a small outing with the camcorder around our site. Feeling adventurous after our illnesses, we took the car into town and had a walk in the hot afternoon sun. As we passed the English language school, I had a thought.

"Let's go in and see what we can discover about teaching EFL." It was an idea Sue had for boosting our income if necessary once we had moved out here.

In we went. "Fala Inglês?" Sue asked politely.

"Não," said the lady behind the desk.

We both burst into laughter. Imagine going into a French language school in the UK and asking if they spoke French. But this was Portugal and anything could happen – and usually did.

"Do you speak French?" Sue followed up in French.

"Indeed – I am French. Please take a seat."

This was more like it. Another bizarre experience was in store. We were in her office for a good half hour, as she chatted away about her parents, her grandfather who originally came from Ireland, how she was twenty when she left France and came to Portugal and now had three children all over twenty three (they were good children but the youngsters didn't seem to want to get married these days). At last the flow ceased.

"And what are you doing out here?" she enquired.

"We are going to be letting holiday apartments in Alombada," explained Sue.

Incredibly, she'd heard of it.

"I will let my sister know about them because she always rents a place for one holiday a year near here," she said enthusiastically.

Leaving there, we agreed it had been a remarkable impromptu meeting. She had opened up instantly, probably because she was really pleased that her mundane afternoon was changing for the better with some interesting conversation in her mother tongue. She was also genuinely interested in us and not only liked the idea of our apartments but told us that a lot of people would use them – especially where we were, up in the mountains – as a long weekend retreat.

We drove back to Alombada through the back roads, the traffic dying away, savouring the beautiful countryside as tourists for one last time. We settled in for a quiet evening, watching the News.

It was the day of our departure. Breakfast was a light affair again but with the packing to do and clearing up, washing and all the other chores associated with leaving, we took our time.

Beatriz came over and we showed her around the building site. She was amazed at the waste – finding about 15 used nails on the floor she promptly bent over and picked them all up for future use. Pointing to the land, she explained how we had to clear all the bindweed, brambles and undergrowth before we could replant there. She indicated that she and Augusto would assist us – we had to confess that, at 75 and 84 respectively, they were a darn sight fitter than ourselves.

As we were showering there was a call from the living room. It was Beatriz with a telephone engineer. This was lucky, particularly as it would save Lynne and Jeremy a lot of trouble, but there was an obvious question. I asked it.

"Why couldn't you have come here on Tuesday when we reported it?"

"The system is one of rotation. We answer in strict order."

"Since Alombada is off the beaten track, so to speak, why didn't your office call our mobile to see if anybody would be in?"

He shrugged.

"If nobody had been here would we have gone to the back of the queue whilst people waited for us to enquire again?"

He nodded slowly. It was sheer good luck that we were around.

At least, there was nothing wrong with the phone line

inside so he went off to check the junction box. An hour later we received a welcome phone call saying all was now working.

There was just time to visit Agualinda to change the pool we had ordered to a slightly larger one, which we did after they had assured us that planning permission would not be required for its installation. Having agreed to the change in principle (hardly surprising as there was more in it for them), they told us to come back in November, sign new contracts in triplicate and pay the extra deposit. However we were assured they wouldn't require more proof of identity. We returned for a final check on the house and I loaded the car whilst Sue sifted through our e-mails.

"Ohhhhhhhhhhhhhh, Yes!" came an ecstatic cry from the other room. I hurried to her side, wondering what on earth was going on.

There on the screen was our first official booking for the apartments next year. From June 12th 2004, two couples wanted one apartment for two weeks – they had already booked a car and flights and just required accommodation.

We were officially in business. There could be no turning back now.

To celebrate, we had a beer with the builders and told them we would be back for good with all our furniture in November – they reassured us everything would be finished. They had made great progress in removing the concrete ceiling in the house and by the time we left they had taken away three quarters of the required stuff and gone for lunch! We said our goodbyes to Beatriz and Augusto before driving through the village and setting off for Porto.

It wasn't that easy. The airport was still having major surgery. Every time we went there were huge differences, not just in terms of roads, access points, and car parking, but also in shopping, duty free and refreshments. We chomped on an old style, British Rail type sliced bread sarnie each and drank a small beer – which came to the same price as our main meal in the station café the other night.

"All airports are the same," mused Sue.

"It does seem a bit of a rip-off," I agreed.

We flew back to England for the last time as tourists, glad we could now concentrate on our move to Portugal.

It was only a month away and nothing was perhaps as important as our own transportation there. We searched the web to book our passage and personal belongings on the ferry from Portsmouth to Bilbao. After the usual questions and answers and credit card details, we were asked if we wanted to confirm our booking. We looked at each other searchingly. This was the point of no return. We held hands and both pressed the button:

"Yes."

Chapter 8

D-Day minus 3: our flat in Newbury had still not been let so we were forced to find alternative agents and new tenants at the last minute (not easy with 72 hours to go). That was merely the biggest of our problems, because the sale of Sue's car was at an extremely delicate stage, the printing of the brochure for our holiday apartments had to be collected, the Newbury flat cleared, and the office closed. Not forgetting the most important missions, visiting Cathy, as well as my mother, for the last time before our departure. Fortunately they were both still happy with our move to Portugal and wished us all the luck in the world. A bit melodramatic since we would be returning in less than six weeks but we were thankful they were both relaxed about it.

It amazed us how many last minute tasks cropped up which couldn't have been done earlier. We must have eaten at some time but I don't quite remember when, if at all. If moving is always hard work, then moving countries is a damn sight harder.

D-Day minus 1: the removal guys, Barry and Dave, arrived about 9 a.m. and worked solidly putting the contents of both our homes, plus all the office equipment into 2,500 cu.ft. of lorry. Needless to say the weather obliged us with a steady downpour all day. Eventually, everything was loaded and we contemplated the sum of our belongings.

Barry turned to us. "How much do you think that weighs?"
"No idea."
"Five and a half tons."

Sue whistled. It was the best response, really.

"Makes you think," I said. Barry thought a bit.

"Well, we're off to Croydon now." They turned to get back in the lorry.

"See you Saturday evening on the ferry," Sue called out.

"You hope," he said. We laughed nervously. Dave grunted, his customary mode of expression.

We cleared as much of the office paperwork as we could, transferred all the new data to the laptop and prepared ourselves for the trip. We went back over to Newbury to say goodbye to a few friends, had a pint in our local, The Nags Head, collected a take-away curry, returned to my flat one last time and opened a bottle of wine while discussing our past and future lives.

D-Day: we were up bright and early, not just because of the anticipated move but something equally important. We were both determined to watch the Rugby World Cup Final, England versus Australia. I spent the second half pacing up and down, I couldn't keep still with frustration as decision after decision went inexplicably in favour of Australia, while Sue shouted at the television, but the last second drop goal by Jonny Wilkinson ensured the correct result in spite of the referee. We hugged each other in delirious triumph.

"I'm hoarse," admitted Sue afterwards.

"What a day to leave when England has just won the World Cup!"

"We ought to put Jonny Wilkinson on our brochure."

"And David Beckham," I said, more in hope than conviction. The European Championships were barely six months away.

It was raining even harder. We finished loading the car and the roof pod – nearly everything had gone in the lorry so we only needed to take the few remaining personal items. It was amazing to discover how many there were, as the car sagged on its suspension.

However, we said our farewells to Hampshire and headed down to the South Coast in the still pouring rain to meet up with Sue's daughters for a late-afternoon meal before catching the 8.00 p.m. ferry from Portsmouth to Bilbao. We had a great time with them and were delighted to receive, as a farewell to England gift, something which became very precious to us as time went on – a leather bound Visitors' Book for all our future guests at Casa Sulo. Having said our emotional goodbyes, we very nervously took our place in the queue ready for departure. How come the ship's crew had placed us in the wrong line? It seemed that everybody who arrived after us was getting on the ferry first but an hour and a quarter later we were on board at last, collecting the key to our cabin. It was rather fun – spacious, with good bathroom facilities, a large double bed, a window (sorry, porthole), bowl of fruit, plenty of coffee, tea and chocolate – this was a good place to call home for the next 36 hours – equal to any four star hotel.

As the Pride of Bilbao slipped her moorings we stood on the upper deck in driving rain and saw Sue's daughters waving to us from the quayside, lit up by the car's headlights. For a brief moment I wondered whether I was doing the right thing but then, with my arm around Sue, we walked back inside to enjoy our mini-cruise.

Barry and Dave were in one of the bars when we finally met up with them so we were then able to relax. A swift drink later, we left them there watching the on-board cabaret and crashed out in our remarkably level cabin.

We entered the Bay of Biscay early next morning with a force seven gale blowing, gusting to force eight, but the Pride of Bilbao was one of the largest P&O ferries and an ex ice-breaker. Thankfully, we didn't notice any swell or movement, our fears about seasickness were groundless – neither of us suffered any adverse effects.

In the afternoon we watched the dolphins jumping and flirting with the bow wave and obviously enjoying themselves. We went up to the top observation deck for the last hour before darkness fell and scanned the horizon for whales. Unfortunately, though, they were all hiding. Not realising it wasn't yet six o'clock, we were the first in the restaurant for our evening meal and lingered for a most enjoyable couple of hours. It was such a change to have nothing to do. After dinner we went off in search of Barry and Dave and discovered them in the same bar as the previous evening.

"Have you been here the whole time?" Sue asked, not unreasonably.

"Naah," replied Barry, much to his disgust. "They kicked us out at three in the morning."

Dave grunted in agreement.

Whilst the ship docked, we enjoyed a good breakfast having asked for an early call, to ready ourselves for the 800km journey across Spain to Portugal and ultimately Alombada. We were luckily one of the first off the ferry – perhaps those quartermasters at Portsmouth had known what they were doing after all – and took advantage of it even though it was rush hour and, of course, still raining cats and dogs. Freeing ourselves from the Bilbao area in less than three quarters of an hour, the skies cleared, as did the roads, so we had a great journey through. To help us along the way we received many text messages of support from family and friends. It was heartening to see so many people sharing our adventure.

As we crossed the border into Portugal, much to our surprise there were no customs sheds or passport control – welcome to the EU on the continent – and we drove over the mountains cheered by Vilar Formoso and headed straight for Guarda, the forbidding city looming on its hill above the motorway, skirted the northern edge of the Serra da Estrela, the highest mountain range and plateau in Portugal, marvelling at its arid grandeur, before making our way westward towards Viseu. Its lofty cathedral was visible from a great distance, seducing us closer to our goal. This was no day for seeing the sights, however, so we kept to the motorway over the hills until we started dropping down towards the intersection where our roads became narrower, more familiar, and we were finally climbing that last tortuous but already beloved hill into the village.

We were home and it felt good.

Along with Barry and Dave, we were due to be staying at Lynne and Jeremy's and, having arrived in Alombada, there was little else for us to do but visit the apartments and await the arrival of our furniture.

This gave us the first shock of the day. The apartments were unfinished – all our praise for Adrio went temporarily out of the window – the interior had been painted in the wrong colours, although they were bearable, the central heating hadn't been installed, the lights were hanging by loose cables – even the outside and wall lights – none of it had been cleaned and prepared for our arrival and there had been no work done on it recently. Apart from that, fine.

We reckoned Barry and Dave should be 2-3 hours behind us. Mindful of the five and a half tons of furniture approaching, we called in to see Natálio.

"Could we take up your offer and use your barn to store some of our excess belongings?" asked Sue.

"No!"

I was horrified: "Why not?"

"The barn is far too damp over winter," he explained.

"Oh," our faces fell.

"But I have a better idea."

He had just bought a house in the village which had been owned by an elderly lady who had recently died – it was still empty and he thought this would be an ideal place to store our furniture.

So, walking down the village high street like a bunch of vigilantes, Natálio with a huge key in his hand (all we lacked was the Morricone music), we investigated this possibility. It was everything he had said, dry, warm and secure.

"This is great," enthused Sue. "Thank you very much."

"How much do you want for it?" I asked, trying not to embarrass him.

"Nothing," he replied, "since you're friends, you can keep it as long as you need it."

It wasn't the fact that no payment was being sought, it was that we had found people in our village would always help a friend in need, without looking for anything in return. Frankly, this was the reason we had moved here, not just for the sunshine and scenery, although that helped.

About 6.30 we had our second shock. There was a call from the removal men and at first we were really surprised they had arrived so soon. But it was good news followed by bad. Barry said he didn't think he could cross the bridge. He had stopped before it but reckoned it was too narrow and flimsy to get the lorry across.

"I've researched it very, very carefully and I know your lorry will definitely fit and the bridge will take the weight," I was adamant.

"Okay," said Barry, "I'll give it a try."

Five minutes later the phone went again. It was Barry.

"Naah, no can do, both tyres are sitting on the edge of the bridge. There's no way it'll go, I'll have to park up for the night and think about an alternative for the morning."

"All right," I agreed. "Park up and Sue and I will come and collect you – stay with the vehicle, whatever you do." I had visions of all our possessions disappearing into the night as they caroused in a nearby bar.

We knew the roads and, having gone over the bridge we thought would be the problem and not finding the lorry there, we carried on back up the next mountain towards Chãs. Passing under the only other bridge which we reckoned he could possibly have been at, there was still no sign of Barry, so we pulled over and I phoned him.

"What exactly does this bridge look like?"

"Er, it's a sort of temporary metal thing, you know, very narrow construction."

"I know exactly where you are and it's the wrong road – thank God. Reverse back the way you came if you can and we'll see you at the bottom of that hill."

We crossed the bridge at Sernada, which even he couldn't have got stuck on (it doubles as a road and railway line), turned right and saw an amazing sight. There was this huge great lorry negotiating a very narrow 'S' bend, having managed to turn round in Christ knows how many metres of spare road. It was truly time for thanksgiving.

They followed us back up the mountain and parked for the evening ready for the main event the next day. We dined with them and hit the sack. Barry and Dave were still happily playing darts and having a few beers. However, before we took our leave we asked them a question which completely baffled us:

"How on earth, having followed our very detailed directions all the way from Spain, could you possibly have missed the most fantastically well illuminated railway and road bridge across the river at Sernada?"

"We don't know," was all Barry could say. "We just didn't see it."

It remains to this day one of the great mysteries of the universe and we remark every time we cross it, "how could they miss THAT bridge?"

A good hearty breakfast saw us ready for action but we immediately hit our first snag. When we looked at the dirt track that should by now have been a driveway down to our apartments, we knew the lorry definitely couldn't reverse down to offload. It was like Passchendaele down there. So, again we had to call on the villagers' generosity.

Once more, they came up trumps. Unquestioningly, they gave up their day's work, hitched their largest trailer to the tractor, and everybody helped load and offload whilst Paulo drove. Naturally, a certain amount of curiosity helped: there was much interest in our belongings and a lot of merriment at some. Sue's exercise bike excited particular admiration.

Fortunately, the weather changed, the sun shone and the whole exhausting job was finally finished by mid afternoon. As we thanked everyone for their help, we felt exhausted – the thought of unpacking and sifting through boxes in both the apartments and the new storage area, which now needed six new tiles on the roof as they had been knocked off by the removal lorry, filled us with abject horror.

We had some business to attend to, so we dropped Barry and Dave off at the café in Sernada and went into town. We sorted out the bank in record time, bought a load of continental plugs, and dashed into the local computer shop to arrange for our internet to be installed on a semi-permanent basis in the apartments. They agreed that Carlos would come up and put us online when we had unpacked, plugged in the computers and had them up and running.

On our return, the builders were working on our roof and Augusto was explaining to them how he produced wine in his cellar.

"Would they like to try some?" he asked innocently. Do bears defecate in the woods?

"A sample of the local wine might be in order," said Barry, who had barely finished a beer. Dave burped noncommitally.

"After all it is getting on in the evening," agreed one of Adrio's men.

"And it looks like it might rain some time in the next couple of days," I added with more sarcasm than I meant. So we, the removal guys, the builders, dogs and cats, all went with Augusto to his cellar, a small room filled with five 250ltr ancient wine barrels on their stillages, a concrete foot press for treading the grapes, a wine press and an old table with tumblers for tasting. An hour and a half of conviviality saw us ready for a meal.

Because of the chaos in the apartments, we decided to make full use of Lynne and Jeremy's for a few more nights.

Barry and Dave left early in the morning for their return trip to the UK and we set to work. Suddenly it was like Act One of a comic opera, with simultaneous entrances stage left and right: the plumbers to put in the central heating, the painter to re-paint, the electricians to put things where they should be and Adrio to explain why other things hadn't happened, leaving us utterly bewildered. It was a constant nightmare moving one box from A to B to create a space, knowing full well that it had to be put back 10 minutes later in exactly the same spot to make way for another box to be put elsewhere. Mind you, at least the cast were turning up as advertised.

Amidst all this chaos, we struggled to find the correct boxes with the computers; finally we located and connected them – but they refused point blank to work, no matter what we did and, of course, it had to be Carlos's day off.

We had the further handicap of not being able to put anything outside to create space because of the rain –

welcome to the real Portugal, now the weather had changed again. We soon discovered that the roof was leaking because of several broken tiles and water was dripping down on the inside doorways, the window ledges were damp and moist, making the apartments humid. We carried on like this until eight in the evening, before returning to Lynne's.

Another day, another problem. The plumbers said they had not been asked to put in any radiators/towel rails in the bathrooms and they had also been told that the central heating was going to be gas. Ummm, this was not the case. So they downed tools – and we had to stop work on setting up the office to resolve the problem with Adrio. After much cajoling, he agreed that for a further consideration a 1.3m towel rail would be installed in each of the four bathrooms and the central heating would have a 1,000ltr diesel tank for the boilers. The reason for diesel instead of gas was the cost of running it, since diesel would be cheaper – how prices leapfrog over the years!

In the afternoon, we gave Carlos directions to Alombada – it's only about 7km as the crow flies though hardly anyone has been there or knows of its existence (which is music to our ears). With the plumbers now installing the radiators, the painters deciding there were too many people around to paint, the computer boffin getting us online, a welter of UK business telephone calls, not to mention unpacking more boxes and moving others to and from storage, the rest of the day passed in a bit of a blur.

More rain the next day, so no plumbers or electricians. Instead a 40 ton lorry made three deliveries and blocked the whole of our entrance drive with hardcore, ready for the bulldozer to create our patio area. However, because it was pelting down they decided that no work could be done, so we reverted to sorting the apartments and made substantial progress. It seemed typical for our project that we enjoyed days, if not weeks, of glorious sunny weather but every time an outside job was planned, the heavens opened to delay, if not stop, work.

At the end of the day, we both agreed that it was

beginning to feel like home. We were extremely happy and more than a little proud of our achievements. Not just ours, however. No words could do justice to the hard work that had been put in by so many people. So we decided we'd get them some liquid refreshment instead. We were grateful for the goodwill and generosity of all concerned. It had been a genuine eye-opener for us.

Over a meal of trout we received our first mail – a Good Luck card from one of our friends, a bill from Vodafone for 49 cents and notification that the redirection of my mail from the UK to Portugal needed several signatures from leading Directors in my organisation before they could act on my instructions. After a lengthy telephone call the Royal Mail agreed I was a sole trader and not a PLC, and re-agreed to redirect the mail to Portugal. This was a great relief. There was also confirmation from our bank that the deposit for our first bookings had been received – we were definitely now in the tourist business.

God gave us a message this morning, in a roundabout sort of way. As usual we were up early and Sue was in 'full soap and shampoo' in the shower when all the electrics blew. After much investigation of various fuse boxes, all very Heath Robinson-ish, which terrified me, Lynne made a snap decision.

"I must close this side of the house down and wait for Jeremy to return," she announced.

"When does he get back?"

"In three weeks – he'll sort it out."

"What?" I almost exploded.

"We've got no electricity at all in our room," Sue hissed at me.

"Sod it, this is obviously an omen," I said.

This forced us into taking the decision to move into our apartments and making do. We settled our account, said our thanks to Lynne for putting up with us and explained it was probably fate. I went down to the apartments and had my first shower there – it felt great. There was no shower curtain, the floor was dirty, but the water was warm and although not very powerful, bliss.

We then made ourselves some scrambled egg on toast, tea and more toast with jam, our first meal in our temporary new home. Hardly likely to appeal to the Egon Ronay Guide, but there you go.

The apartments were drying out slightly now because we had had the foresight to bring out several electric radiators which had been the object of great mirth when the villagers had been helping us. There was a power cut. In the middle of this mayhem, Adrio arrived with a Russian labourer who moved all the hard core from the driveway to our patio area.

By late morning, the electricity was back on when the satellite man turned up to enquire where we wanted our dish placed. We gave him various options but he shook his head – none would be suitable for the signal. He then made several suggestions, which we rejected as they were either close to our home and apartments or in the middle of our field – the last thing we wanted was to have our beautiful views spoiled by a 3m satellite dish. Like everything else, a compromise was reached and he agreed to put it on the roof where we could not see it. Pragmatism is a wonderful thing when people choose to apply it.

Finally, as we finished for the day, I realised we should have collected the laptop. It had blown a gasket earlier on one of the frequent electrical power cuts. We decided to see if the shop was still open – to our surprise it was and although the laptop wasn't ready, we were able to rescue all our disks to load on to the main computer. We returned for our first night in our new home.

"Wouldn't it be great to open my works leaving present?" Sue suggested.

I agreed it certainly would – especially as it was a single malt Providence whisky and a rare specimen indeed. What better way to celebrate our new, although temporary, home. After the first glass we phoned Paul, Sue's ex-boss and a close friend, thanked him and gave him all our news, only to be told:

"I was thinking of you guys and was going to call you

tomorrow. I'm so pleased that you appear to be settling in well."

"See, our timing has always been good," Sue said – we celebrated with another couple of glasses.

The bedroom was warm, dry and ours. We slept like logs: in my dreams I could hear the sound of distant drumming.

It wasn't hard to work out the reason behind my dreams. In the morning, I woke refreshed, heard the constant battering on the roof, looked out of the window, "Oh no, more rain."

And how it did rain. The river in the valley below was in flood (it had been the merest trickle in the summer), as were many of the fields. Acting on the maxim that when the going gets tough, the tough go shopping, we spent the day at the shops. Well, not what Sue's daughters would call shopping, but we bought essentials for the apartments, like shower curtains and rails, loo roll holders, cutlery trays, sink tidies – the list seemed to go on for ever. We also needed food for the cupboards and freezer and a five litre garafão of red wine for the decanter. Laden with household goods and goodies, we returned home, settled down for the evening, updated the diary and chatted long into the night.

It was the end of a great first week. Fair enough, we still had lots of problems to solve with the apartments but all the wrinkles had for the most part been small and not insurmountable.

And we had that first payment nestling in the bank already. Not much could go wrong now. Could it?

Chapter 9

Things were starting to lag behind schedule – we called another three-sided meeting. Our solicitor was half-hidden behind her usual teetering piles of papers when we arrived, a few of which fluttered to the floor when Adrio hurried in shortly after us, looking justifiably nervous.

"Couldn't we have a single diesel boiler to replace the two gas combies?" I began.

Adrio tapped distractedly at a notepad with his pencil.

"We told you the gas boilers for the showers and hot water were not man enough for the job," Sue carried on.

"They only stay hot for a short time," I persevered.

"And even then they're only strong enough for one shower at a time," finished Sue.

"You promised they would be adjusted," I twisted the metaphorical knife. Adrio looked wildly to Aldina for help, but she refused to catch his eye.

"Er..." he started.

"You don't understand our regulations," he protested feebly.

Unexpectedly Aldina decided to come to his aid. "It would cause great problems," she pronounced.

"Also, we need the paintwork cleaned, the doors made to fit, our electric light fittings and sweep fans installed, the fly zappers hung, and our ovens purchased and connected," Sue checked the items off our list.

"Not forgetting buying a spare gas bottle with automatic change-over, plus the patio requires a quote before being paved," I added.

"Can you do all these things for Sue and Ken?" quizzed Aldina.

Adrio was still wavering under our combined onslaught.

"Providing it doesn't rain too much, everything will be ready in a week," he said quietly.

"Great. And can we have a meeting on site with the plumber/electrician tomorrow?"

"I'll see if Ricardo can make it. I know he'll be free by six."

"That's fine," we chorused.

Ricardo duly arrived on Friday evening and we started to go through our list of over 30 items which all required urgent attention or installation; leaking radiators, rusting plugs in the sinks and so it went on. We insisted he wrote every point down as we said it, having found through bitter experience it paid to be precise with all the sub-contractors.

Ricardo was extremely small, about 5ft, and was distinguished by a permanent 10 o'clock shadow. He had watery big baby blue eyes with long eyelashes, and a thinning hairline. It was clear that he was extremely competent and really knew his stuff but, on the other hand, he was unpunctual, unreliable and it soon became obvious he wasn't especially interested. His workmen, on the whole, were equally adept with some notable exceptions – including a pair of plumbers whom we nicknamed Mick and Montmorency, who were in a class of their own for incompetence.

Since this first meeting was taking place well into the evening, it soon became evident Ricardo was mumbling, "Yes" to everything and not really taking much notice.

"He's obviously thinking about his supper," whispered Sue to me.

Nevertheless, he did write everything down as requested. "Is that it?"

"When can you come out and take us to choose our light fittings and bathroom fitments?"

"On Monday, if that's okay," he replied. It was.

"And how soon can you do all this?" I enquired, gesturing at his piece of paper.

"They will all be installed and the apartments finished whilst you are away in the UK next week." Folding up his list, Ricardo was full of breezy confidence.

At least we thought that's what he said.

Our Saturday started as usual – very early – and we had a go at clearing and cleaning another of the bathrooms. We also managed to clear one of the bedrooms at the same time and put another load into storage. After completing all these tasks, we decided to shower before going into Aveiro and look at furniture for the apartments. Half a shower later and with soap – isn't it always the way? – all over her, Sue called out:

"There's no bloody water. What's happened?"

"Don't know."

I went outside and soon found out – half the villagers were standing around looking at two ends of our main water pipe and discussing it.

Now, as it happened, a few days earlier we had mentioned to Beatriz that the silvas (brambles) were looking rather an eyesore and when we had a chance and a break from everything else we would have a go at cutting them back. She had obviously told the other villagers and, without a word to us, they had very kindly decided to clear them all for us from behind our apartments. This was a godsend, because when we eventually had visitors, they would have a much better view of the apple orchard and sheep from their bedroom windows. But as luck would have it, Paulo, wielding the heavy duty strimmer with more enthusiasm than finesse, had sliced clean through our water pipe. A repair was required urgently.

I watched as Augusto demonstrated a potentially effective way of repairing plastic piping. First, he lit a newspaper underneath one end of the pipe, and when it was sufficiently soft, he inserted a cooler pipe into the heated end. The idea was that it should shrink on to it and form a perfect seal. So much for a good theory. Unfortunately, the pipe caught fire and with no water handy, there was much jumping up and down on it, greatly to the amusement of all concerned.

By this time Sue had dried herself whilst the rest of the village had arrived to offer advice and enjoy the entertainment we were unwittingly providing. Messengers were sent off in all directions to obtain connectors, bolts, spare pipe, more newspapers and matches, and various other useful items. It might have seemed arbitrary but it clearly wasn't. We were amazed at the speed with which everything was achieved. One elderly gentleman produced the correct pipe connector complete with screw-in fitments and within half an hour we had water again.

Yet again we were impressed with the ingenuity and stoicism of our village friends; nothing ever seemed to be a problem for them for very long. Nor were things often plain sailing, as we were to find out.

The setback had not dampened their enthusiasm to get the brambles cleared and a couple of dead trees cut down so off they went to the music of chain saws and strimmers. Soon the task of cutting down the brambles was over, and they turned their attention to the offending dead wood. A much larger chain saw was produced. Now, bearing in mind that the main protagonists in this saga were loggers by trade and manage all the eucalyptus forests for miles around, this should have been an uneventful task. We watched as they prepared to fell this 3m ivy covered stump. As the first cuts were made, I noticed the lie of the land with a sinking feeling and pointed rather dramatically to the telephone wire.

"If you cut it that way, you'll take our telephone line down with it," I shouted out.

"No problem, we know what we're doing," was Paulo's smiling reply and he continued to buzz away.

As predicted, the stump began to lean heavily on the telephone wire so they produced a binding wire and looped it round the stump, pulling in the opposite direction. This was asking for trouble, and it soon arrived. The binding snapped, everyone fell backwards and tumbled on the ground, whilst the stump broke at the base, and tottered for a second before falling towards the telephone wire. It bounced off the line a couple of times and landed within centimetres of our apartments.

We dashed inside to see if our telephone was still working. Much to our relief it was, and so we acted on the principle of least said, soonest mended. They were trying to be helpful, and disaster had been narrowly averted. The telephone wire to the house was now very loose and stretched, though.

Glossing over any misgivings, we opened some rather special red wine for the villagers to celebrate the hard work they had put in. As with every impromptu get-together, it was much appreciated and we had a great party for an hour or so. Our neighbours produced more wine, we brought out cheese and bread rolls, and all stood around in the blazing sun conversing happily.

Surprise, surprise, Monday came and went and no Ricardo arrived to show us fittings or continue the work.

Sue called Aldina in the afternoon.

"Can we come in to see you tomorrow?"

"Sure. Do you want me to notify Adrio?"

"No thank you. That's why we want to see you."

"Oh, all right. In my office at 3.30."

Our patience with the sub-contractors was starting to run out.

We woke on Tuesday to absolutely torrential rain again so obviously we would not see any workmen. To our great surprise, at 9.00 a.m. Ricardo arrived with a big smile on his face and off we went in his car.

"Where were you yesterday?" I asked.

"Problems," he grinned.

He seemed to take forever to get to the bathroom fitment warehouse but the selection was minimal with only three types of mirror, all too large, and about four different types of loo brush holders. To say it was a small selection was a misnomer – our local corner shop in the UK would have had a wider choice. Grudgingly, we chose a couple of items. He then spent a further three quarters of an hour making detours to other building sites of his before finally arriving at a lamp fitment warehouse.

This warehouse sold light shades and light fittings exclusively but they were still hard pressed to understand the concept of a small vanity light over the top of a mirror in a bathroom. The salesmen came out with 300 watt spotlights, strip lights, flood lights and wildly ornate lights until the proprietor's wife intervened and explained in simple terms what was required. As is often the case, female practical logic cut through the waffle and got to the point. She went off into the back room and returned with four perfect single vanity lights for the apartment bathrooms. Her male colleagues were glumly unimpressed.

After a particularly long wait in the car while Ricardo conducted other business we told him we had a meeting with Aldina at 1.30 p.m., and therefore had to be back in Alombada sooner rather than later to collect all our paperwork. Of course this was a little white lie, we knew full well that the meeting wasn't until later but the gap meant that we could check we had all we needed beforehand.

As he left, Ricardo reiterated that everything would be completed by the time we got back from the UK on the 18th December.

We went for our meeting with Aldina. She greeted us, looking somewhat perplexed.

"Did you tell Adrio about our meeting?"

"No, why?"

"He phoned two hours ago to say he was in the area and would be only too pleased to join us for the 1.30 meeting."

"What did you say to him?"

"I said you were my clients and if we wanted him along there I would phone him. I also said the meeting had been planned for 3.30 not 1.30."

"I can guess what has happened," put in Sue. "Ricardo obviously phoned Adrio with the time of our meeting. He must have sensed a problem was looming and didn't want us discussing it with you without Adrio being there."

"There's a reason we wanted to see you on your own rather than with Adrio, as you probably guessed," I said. "There are a lot of issues with the building programme – the timing and quality of work is not progressing as promised. Left to his own devices, Adrio is very capable, an excellent builder and he's doing a first class job. But he's the main contractor and, as such, we feel the plumbers and electricians – who he uses as sub-contractors – are a law unto themselves."

"Pretty much the same as everywhere else in the world," added Sue.

"They're clearly making promises to him and not keeping them. In our opinion that's his problem, not ours."

"Also, Ricardo and others are presenting us with separate invoices for work they've carried out. We haven't paid them because they should come directly through the main contractor. If we start paying everybody individually, we will soon have an administrative nightmare. The budget will get out of hand and nobody will know who's paid what and to whom," explained Sue. I thanked our lucky stars that she was so good with accounts.

"I see," said Aldina, trying to look composed.

After we'd been outlining our problems for about 10 minutes the telephone rang. Aldina answered it. Sure enough, it was Adrio – she switched to speakerphone.

"Would it be all right if I join you in five minutes, because I just happen to be in the area?"

Aldina left the answer to me. I was polite but firm.

"We're having a meeting with Aldina because we're off to the UK in the morning. If she has any questions from us for you, she'll contact you tomorrow."

There was the sound of a deep intake of breath, before the line went suddenly very dead. Adrio was not a happy bunny.

We concluded our meeting with Aldina and agreed that she would contact Adrio to ensure that all the outstanding works would be completed within the timescale and that our return to Portugal would not be as unsatisfactory as our arrival less than three weeks earlier. We dashed back to start packing. It definitely felt very strange to be going back so soon after our arrival here, but we needed to do the Christmas run.

First thing next morning we set off for the three hour trek to Lisbon where, on this occasion, we were catching our flight – we normally fly from Porto airport, only about an hour's drive away. We arrived in extremely good time only to find that fog in London had created havoc with flights across Europe and that ours had already been delayed by four hours.

However, my paranoia for arriving early at airports came into its own. We were told that because we were in such good time they would transfer us to the earlier flight, which should have already departed. We were greatly relieved because the delay in the later flight would have meant us getting back to the UK late at night, if at all, and having to alter all our plans. We congratulated ourselves on our good fortune – rather too soon, as it turned out.

The flight should have taken off at 11.30 a.m. and at 12 noon, a merely respectable delay, we were called into the departure lounge where we proceeded to board. Apart from the usual scattering of passengers there was a large contingency of Japanese tourists, clearly all part of the same package holiday, who seemed unable to sit in their seats for any length of time. The tour guide – Japanese but minus the obligatory umbrella – paraded up and down the aisle explaining in great detail what was, or rather wasn't, happening on the plane. They still looked as baffled as we did. We all had good reason.

We were left sitting in the plane on the tarmac with the doors to open for three hours. The stewardesses explained to us at various times that because the doors were open, they couldn't serve us with any refreshments and they were waiting for London Heathrow control tower to give them a clearance for landing in the UK before taking off. Finally, we taxied out and took our place in the queue ready for departure.

After an uneventful flight we were on our descent, when the pilot informed us that due to the earlier problems at Heathrow we would be circling over the M25 for a further 35 minutes. Upon landing at last, he announced that we hadn't been allocated a landing bay. So there we sat, stewing in the plane on the tarmac by the perimeter fence for another 25 minutes until a parking bay became available. What should have taken two hours 20 minutes had kept us on the plane from 12.15 to 6.30. Goodness knows when our scheduled flight might have arrived.

Even so, we made good time out of the airport and called in on the way through to see Cathy. She was still enjoying herself which eased away some of the tensions of the day, and it was good to hear, having moved close to Sue's sister, Judy, she was receiving regular visitors from the rest of the family and Judy was even able to take her out and about a bit. Finally we arrived at our Hampshire flat, unpacked, sorted out e-mails and appointments for the next day, and wrapped up all our Christmas presents for family, friends and customers.

Friday – a routine day, but a vital one – we visited our banks and cancelled all the unnecessary direct debits and standing orders with companies whose services were no longer required.

In the evening, we wandered over to Newbury and spent a very pleasant couple of hours in good company in The Nag's Head.

"Back so soon?" boomed the landlord. "I told you, it wouldn't last."

"Just doing our holidays in reverse these days," I countered. "Though we don't think much of your weather. Only 3° - it's 22° at home!"

We returned with a take-away ready to meet my son Chris who was due to arrive around 10.30, having been on an army battalion exercise.

As we were pulling into our street, we received a text message from him informing us that he had already arrived, turned on the television and for us not to worry what time we returned. We hurried in and cooked him two huge steak sandwiches, but refused to share our meal with him – we were in withdrawal mode and nobody and nothing was going to prevent us from having our Madras curry and tandoori chicken!

Saturday, we were out of the house really early, heading up to Manchester with Chris to see my mother and brother.
The car we had rented had been upgraded by the hire company and proved very comfortable on the 680km round trip. We wondered how Bozo would have coped. Probably broken down on the motorway. Both my mother and brother were delighted to see us and we filled them in on all the newsy bits, swapped presents and arrived back in Hampshire in the early evening. Chris, no doubt still brooding about the curry, made a rapid departure back to Kent.

A pleasant drive took us to Romsey on the Sunday to meet up with Lucy and Mary (Sue's daughters) for lunch. They were driving from Bournemouth and Portsmouth respectively. Having booked a table and met up with Mary, we wandered around the town before returning to the restaurant for coffee, waiting for Lucy to arrive. After an hour and still no Lucy we moved into the dining area just to make it look as if we were going to dine. Shortly afterwards Sue's mobile rang.
Lucy sounded rather breathless. "I'll be there shortly – just to let you know I've brought my friend, Helen," she gasped.
"Oh God," exclaimed Mary, "this'll be the blonde leading the blonde! Goodness knows when they'll arrive."
"Good," said Sue into her mobile, glaring at Mary to keep silent. "We were wondering when you might show up,."
There was a brief pause. "Where exactly is the restaurant anyway?"
Sue told her and she and Helen walked in shortly afterwards. We all had a fine meal; gifts and presents were swapped again, two bags each for the girls, of course (one for Christmas, one for

birthdays) before we made a rapid departure for a meeting in Winchester.

The following two days were spent in a flurry of activity visiting family friends and clients as well as a final 'sorting out' time before going home.

With a final meal in the evening we celebrated the conclusion of our week in the UK and the sale of Sue's car. He had a bargain but at least we were shot of it – one Bozo was quite enough.

We headed back to Portugal – no problems with flights this time, fortunately, and we reached Alombada around midnight after driving from Lisbon in heavy rain.

On arrival, we had a quick check on progress and found, to our horror, a distinct lack of it. The builders and contractors had promised faithfully to finish everything during the week we were away. After all that time little had been achieved, although the marble thresholds to the apartments, which we had complained about being raised above the tile level, had been ground down and smoothed off, so there was now no lip between the floor and outside, making it easier to sweep dust straight out of the apartments. This was just as well.

Unfortunately for us the workmen had failed to put dustsheets over anything and hadn't even bothered to close inside doors, so we returned to a 5mm layer of marble dust over beds, furniture and kitchen area, the lot. Guess what we were doing for most of the next day? It was amazing how recalcitrant marble dust could be. We spoke to Adrio in the morning and gave him a blasting on the phone.

Early Friday morning we were sitting debating what to tackle first during the day, me in the buff, and Sue in a dressing gown – not a pretty sight (well, I'm not) – when Adrio turned up promptly to sort the problems we had returned to. Within half an hour we had workmen coming out of our ears – plumbers, electricians, the satellite dish people, and others to re-do the gutter (in our absence they had put up a white one and it should have been green, the same as the rest of the exterior fittings).

It reminded us of an Ealing comedy, or the Keystone Cops, with everyone falling over each other and trying to get into the same area at once. We felt redundant, and found we couldn't even shut ourselves up in our office without interruptions, so we went and did a bit of Christmas shopping and left them to it.

Brenda had advised us to join the ACP (the Portuguese equivalent of the AA/RAC) because they were 'ever so helpful' and reminded people when their cars needed taxing, spoke English, sorted out the bureaucracy and were generally invaluable. They had an office in Aveiro, and when we'd finished shopping, we decided to check them out. We eventually found the office and queued to see the official.

At last our moment arrived. The man examined us from under hooded lids.

"Do you speak English?" I asked brightly.

"No." So much for that. I explained in my limited Portuguese that we wanted to join.

"Because we live at the same address, can we join under one membership?" Sue asked.

"No! You must have two memberships because you have two surnames. Fill out these forms," was the essence of his brusque and rather officious reply.

We had found out they would re-register our UK Peugeot and obtain Portuguese licence plates for us. If successful, there would be no tax to pay because we had owned the vehicle in the UK longer than six months and were now resident in Portugal. It all seemed a great idea – on paper.

As we started to fill in the forms, it became apparent that a simple thing like joining the ACP was going to be a nightmare. People were queuing up behind us, chattering away about these English people joining their organisation – not unkindly, just observing – whilst the functionary pointed out various sections, all of which had to be correct before we could become members.

There was one number about which he was particularly agitated and demanded that unless we supplied it he could do no more. He asked for our número de contribuinte which we proudly presented to him.

"There – certified, embossed, signed, sealed and it's authentic," I said.

"It is," he said, "still only a temporary piece of paper."

"Every other organisation including banks, solicitors, notaries and Camara Municipal has accepted the number," Sue pointed out.

"Even when our plastic card comes through it will still have the same number," I pleaded. He shrugged. We were definitely dealing with a jobsworth and getting nowhere. It was time to beat a retreat.

"Not to worry, we'll come back when we've got our permanent cards."

He smiled sourly as we departed.

This had been our introduction to the 'friendly' bureaucratic ACP organisation in Aveiro. It may be different in Lisbon, Porto or on the Algarve, for all we know, but here in this part of Portugal everything is done by their interpretation of the book.

At least we were now the proud owners of a very smart, comfortable and welcoming pair of apartments. We made them ready for Christmas with a tree, lights and loads and loads of cards, both wishing us good luck in our new home and for Christmas, which were greatly appreciated. Armed with invitations to various parties and family gatherings we were really looking forward to our first Christmas in our new home.

Chapter 10

Christmas Eve

We woke up to a wonderful bright, clear and sunny morning and checked our mail. Along with our usual business mail and plenty of Christmas cards, we received a wonderful surprise in the form of our official número de contribuinte cards – we had been waiting for these for nearly three years.

Flushed with triumph, we celebrated with two cups of tea and decided that we were ready to take on ACP's bastion of officialdom. We would return to its hitherto impregnable stronghold on Boxing Day and finish all the paperwork – we had discovered that in Portugal Christmas Day was the only official holiday and everybody returned to work on 26th. They certainly don't overindulge themselves – if a bank holiday falls over a weekend then that day is observed with was no alternative holiday given on the Monday or Tuesday.

The Portuguese therefore treated Christmas Eve as the main celebration for family and close friends, and held a huge festa in their homes during the evening. This would be a sumptuous banquet, consisting of starters, usually a main course of bacalhau, followed by various other courses, volumes of wine and the obligatory desserts.

For ourselves, we had less elaborate plans, involving a Christmas Eve dinner just for us. As we plotted our festivities, Natálio strolled over with a seasonal invitation.

"You must join our family and friends this evening because you are now part of the village. And in Alombada, that means you have become part of the family."

"It is very good of you to say so, Natálio." I was struggling to think of a way of refusing gently.

"What's more, it is an excellent way of introducing you to other people in the area who will become your friends."

There was no way round it – I had to bite the bullet. "Natálio, please don't be offended. Because this is our first Christmas in our new home, we've really set our hearts on celebrating Christmas Eve in a more traditionally English way on our own."

He took this philosophically and, in the Portuguese manner, suggested a workable compromise.

"Of course you must do that, but after you've finished your main meal we would be very pleased if you would join us all for desserts."

Visions of those tempting sweets swam in front of our eyes. I glanced at Sue, who was similarly powerless to resist.

"That would be perfect, thank you."

Having finished our meal at home, we were getting ready when there was a knock at the door and Sandra arrived to summon us. We arrived and found two empty places at one of the long trestle tables with at least 25 fellow diners, ranging from young children to great grandparents, in a companionable fug. They were just starting the desserts. Apart from all the other sweetmeats, the pièce de résistance was the 'Bolo Rei' (King cake). This is a traditional Portuguese cake usually produced for the 6th January – Epiphany – to commemorate the arrival of the Three Kings. It is a heavy doughnut shaped fruit cake with candied crystallised fruit garnishing the top, and tastes delicious with a glass or two of chilled white port.

The lively chatter and good-humoured banter between the guests did much to enhance the atmosphere; even though there was no music, radio or other artificial means of entertainment, the sound of conversation and laughter fully enriched the evening. Our knowledge of Portuguese was still limited, although improving daily, but we understood only too well what a good time was in any language.

During the evening we were introduced to a lovely 10 year old girl, Carolina, who was learning English at school and took great delight in correcting our obvious and glaring errors in Portuguese. She also had a younger sister, Mariana, who proudly counted from one to ten in English – and she was only five! It rather put us to shame.

Eventually, Natálio raised his hands. It appeared the end of the meal was the time for giving presents. We had put some thought into what our hosts and other villagers would have liked whilst we were in England. We sat back and waited for the cries of joy as we distributed our presents. They did not materialise – it seemed to be incidental that we had actually given them gifts because it transpired the villagers were great givers but poor receivers. So, when it came to our turn, we were given chocolates, a bottle of port and an empty aguardente decanter. This was soon taken back from me by Natálio who ushered me down to the cellars where, with exaggerated and slightly drunken care, he filled the decanter with his local firewater; whereupon we returned to the table and it was promptly shared by all. By this time everyone, apart from the children (and we weren't too sure about some of those), was extremely merry and the mince pies we had brought back went down well.

There was a sudden hush.

"What's happening?" Sue asked as I shook the empty decanter over her glass.

"Everyone is going to drink a toast to my birthday," slurred Natálio.

"It's your birthday as well," I exclaimed.

"Didn't you wonder why I was called Natálio?" he laughed.

So, as the bells rang midnight, everyone sang Happy Birthday in Portuguese (a two verse version with every line apparently different), then English and French, accompanied by yet more alcohol. This time, Natálio produced whisky, and it wasn't long before that bottle was fast diminishing.

About 2.00 a.m, we staggered back down the little hill to the apartments. Sue went to bed whilst I just floated around. It had been one of the best starts to a Christmas I could remember.

Christmas Day

Surprisingly, neither of us had a hangover (or only a hint of one), so after a reviving cup of tea, we opened all our gifts from family and friends and phoned them in the UK with our thanks, before swapping presents with each other. Most were unsurprisingly related to our new home, which couldn't have suited us better. We wandered outside, where our neighbours were excitedly discussing the previous night's party whilst feeding the livestock.

This was the day the whole village – or so it seemed – descended the loggers' track on trucks, tractors and trailers, spiralling down through the woods to the base of the mountain to Tony and Lydia's. It was a tradition that they fed all their family and friends on Christmas Day and, as they had lived in England for a long time, it was always roast turkey with all the trimmings including fresh sprouts, a rare commodity in Portugal, which Lydia had bought at great expense from a contact in Lisbon. The kick-off was at exactly one o'clock – no excuses could be made for late arrivals because of the timing of the food.

So, just after 12.30, we all set off and took the very bumpy, twisty and narrow track down. Although there was no snow on the ground, there was something of the spirit of Christmas about our descent. Perhaps it was because every villager was crammed into one of the vehicles, with dogs yapping around us as outriders, as we made our slow way down the rocky mountainside, the tractors grinding in low gear. The eucalyptus trees were swaying ever so slightly in the breeze, as if they were dancing a stately minuet around us. And there, at the end of our journey, was the fairytale castle waiting in the woods.

The welcome from Lydia and Tony, as usual, was enthusiastic and friendly and there were many people present whom we had met at various times over the preceding three years. Without any of our own family around, the sheer conviviality of this family orientated meal was very special to us. Needless to say, the turkey was beautifully cooked, moist and tender, and there was also a huge leg of pork which we were all 'forced' to have seconds of!

As on Christmas Eve, there then followed the usual desserts before we men took ourselves off for a game of boules. There was a difference to the French method of play. The Portuguese pitched a 9cm x 10cm thick heavy metal disc instead of balls. I rolled up my sleeves and joined in with enthusiasm until I got the hang of it.

Sue watched us all from a distance before coming over.

"Can I have a go?" she asked.

"I'm sure you can," I agreed, even though I was unsure of the etiquette.

And she did, proving herself adept at the accuracy required, and inspiring much applause from all competitors.

Once again, Tony took it upon himself to show us his various orchards, a cornucopia spread over about three acres of land. Among all the citrus fruits there were also six kiwi vines dripping with fruit.

"You see those?" Tony pointed to them. "They've produced over 600 kiwis in the last year alone."

"Would it be possible to let us have a couple of oranges?" I asked. "We're going to roast a duck for Boxing Day and we've forgotten to buy any."

"No problem," he replied. In traditionally generous fashion, four plastic carrier bags were produced and these were quickly filled with oranges for juice, oranges for eating, tangerines, lemons and a whole bag on its own of kiwis.

"This is amazing. Thank you very much indeed," said Sue, as our arms became laden with fruit upon fruit.

"Now I know the kiwis are still unripe and hard, but to ripen them, all you have to do is put one or two in a bowl with a couple of apples for a few days," explained Tony. "There is a chemistry between the two which soon ripens them."

We tried this and it worked.

But we still had to sing for our supper, as it were. After the dinner, drink and festivities, it emerged that there was another tradition, though no trophies or medals were to be awarded afterwards, for first-timers at the feast to cross the latest of Tony's bridges above the river raging about 10m below. The bridge was approximately 1.5m wide with a steel hawser as the main support, steel pillars at both ends and wooden slats as the walkway, spanning this roughly 90m wide river. We watched a dog trot across it, and quivered as the bridge shook slightly. I'd have felt better if I hadn't known how often he'd rebuilt it.

Of course, it turned out that we were the only ones who'd never crossed the bridge. Sue and I both took deep breaths and began our ordeal.

We tried to imagine that we were two intrepid explorers crossing that jungle bridge in the Indiana Jones film, hand in hand and eyes closed. Was it the alcohol or the bridge swaying – they certainly weren't swaying in the same direction, were they? Meanwhile, the two large dogs took great delight in running backwards and forwards and jumping up at us, making the bridge sway even more alarmingly. We were certain they'd been trained to do this. The crowd on the bank cheered our every step wildly.

Anyway, we were (we considered) very brave, made it to the far bank and back without any mishaps and were relieved to have our feet firmly back on terra firma.

"Now that we have made the journey by bridge both ways, we can revisit them by parking on the main road, and crossing the river," I wheezed.

"Maybe, but we would have to telephone first to ask them to unlock the security gates," replied Sue, ever practical.

Only too soon the flotilla of tractors and trailers was preparing to climb back up the mountain. Arriving back early evening, we quietly drifted through the rest of Christmas Day.

Boxing Day

In theory, this is a normal working day in Portugal. Adrio

had told us that a machine, along with two or three workmen, would come up early to flatten the hardcore on our patio. By 10 a.m. they still hadn't arrived so we gave up waiting and took ourselves off to Aveiro to complete the paperwork at ACP.

As our footsteps echoed through their building it was clear we were the only customers – so much for the full working day... Satisfyingly, the same unfortunate official we had met before was presiding in lonely splendour and he could only watch in horror as we approached his desk. We produced the envelopes containing our shiny new número de contribuinte cards with a flourish. His harsh look softened and he almost smiled as he accepted them and produced the forms we had half filled in a few days earlier. We had definitely cracked the code.

However, after he had taken our money for a year's subscription to the organisation x 2, plus €12.50 for administration, we moved on to a new subject, which proved we still had much to learn.

"Is it possible to re-register our car in Portugal?"

His frown returned.

"I require the make, type, cc and year of your vehicle first."

We supplied the relevant information.

Out came new forms, folders, dossiers and various other pieces of paper from assorted filing cabinets. It appeared we were about to use up another forest. He set to work with a calculator and spreadsheet and, after some frenzied key punching, informed us with no hint of an apology:

"The tax you will have to pay to have your own car re-registered here is €5,103.84."

I was flabbergasted. "I know for certain that if we have owned the vehicle more than six months, which we have, have left the UK, which is part of the EU, and are now permanently resident in Portugal, which we are, and that it is our only vehicle, which it is, we don't have to pay any import tax at all."

He, in his turn, produced a string of reasons why we

would have to pay the tax – not least because we hadn't actually applied for, or been given our proof of residence by our local Junta de Freguesia (local council office) or Camara Municipal. This, it turned out, was not the número de contribuinte which we had obtained, but yet another set of documents. We might have guessed it. He took great delight in explaining this to us. What a great Boxing Day celebration this was turning out to be for him.

"There is nothing I can do," he shrugged, examining his fingernails carefully. "If you care to return to this office on 7th January when more people are on duty, one of them will be able to escort you round to the Customs and Excise office (the Alfândega)."

"Will that help us?" I had my doubts.

"In a way. They, too, will explain why you have to pay the tax."

This was quite typical of Portuguese bureaucracy and Catch 22 for us, because the ACP man knew it was doubtful that we would obtain our proof of residence until we had lived here long enough for it to be issued – this could take anything upwards of eight to nine months. Meanwhile, our vehicle, with UK registration plates, could only be driven here for a maximum of six months before the tax was liable.

"Better call Aldina to obtain yet another piece of gratuitous official documentation as urgently as possible," advised Sue. "Otherwise, if nothing happens within the next couple of months we'll be driving the Peugeot back to the UK on a one-way ticket to be sold."

Undaunted by events at ACP, we returned home via our local watering hole in Angeja. This put us in a much better mood because the Patron came out after our second drink and insisted that because he hadn't seen us for all of Christmas, he would pick up our bar tab. We argued with him, of course, but to no avail.

Returning home there was still no sign of the builders so we gave up hope. Judging by experience, we knew that if nobody had arrived by 2.30 (after their lunch break) we wouldn't see anyone. This being the case and it still being

Boxing Day and a beautiful warm sunny one too, we set about assembling the large gas barbecue, washed and prepared the duck, potatoes and all the trimmings to go with our meal, lit the barbecue, and went indoors whilst it heated up.

Suddenly there was a crunch of gravel and a cacophony of voices. The workmen had arrived, complete with their tampa tampa machine, to level the patio. Cursing our luck, we turned off the barbecue, moved it, the gas bottle, the table, and all the chairs out of the way whilst they hammered away. This took the rest of the afternoon, so we settled down and watched something stupid on our satellite TV. Well, at least that now worked – we had hardly had a moment to view it previously.

We enjoyed the duck when we eventually ate it – late in the evening. However, whether it was because we ate rather later than we intended, we both had disturbed nights, and had a nasty shock when we woke up next morning. As we dyspeptically looked out of the window, there was a row of sheep's backsides looking at us looking at them.

"Sheep's bum in morning, shepherd's warning," declared Sue.

We knew that two of our neighbours owned sheep; Beatriz and Isabela kept theirs cooped up in their pen most all the time and brought the fodder to them; whereas João had an equally small flock but would lead them each day to a different field for grazing, which helped to keep the weeds and grass cropped. These? Anyone's guess.

A couple of days later we met Aldina to enquire about the papers we would require to set up a Portuguese company for the holiday letting apartments and re-register the Peugeot. At the same time, we asked her about the certificate from the Junta de Freguesia stating that we were now resident in Alombada. Aldina said she would sort the latter certificate out for us but that we would have to apply for our residencia in person, telling us it would take at least three to four weeks before we would even be considered for an appointment prior to getting the correct forms filled out.

However the telephone is a wonderful tool. Within 10 minutes of the phone call commencing at some office somewhere a few kilometres away, Aldina told us that if we were to go down to an office in Aveiro and speak to a man called Miguel; he would be able to sort out the necessary forms.

"Miguel! That's just like John in the UK!" I fulminated.

"Michael, actually," corrected Sue. "Anyway, we'd better try and find it. You know we desperately need our residencia."

"I suppose so – and if we don't get it soon we'll have to pay thousands of euros as import duty to re-register the car."

Putting aside such grim thoughts, we set off happily enough to discover where exactly in Aveiro this magical Miguel was to be found. We guessed it must be near the Loja do Cidadão from Aldina's somewhat vague directions, but didn't realise that the offices we were being sent to were in the very same building.

When we pulled up and parked outside we both looked at each other, remembering past vigils here and our faces said it all.

Sue sighed and voiced what I was thinking: "Do we eat first, or perhaps take a flask of coffee, a jug of wine, a bottle of spirits and a picnic in with us or do we just brave it and hope that we get out before midnight?"

Oh, we of little faith. The experience was a joy and most unlike our previous visits. First, the security guard looked at our handwritten note from Aldina and said in perfect English:

"Certainly Sir, Madam, come this way, it's not far."

He took us along to a small booth, pressed a button for our numbered ticket, placed it on the counter and informed us:

"Please sit down, you're next in the queue."

Almost immediately a courteous young lady attended to us: "How can I help you?"

"Er, Dr Aldina Rainhas, our solicitor, telephoned a 'Miguel' here about some papers, and if possible can we see him?"

To Sue's delight this rather dishy young man appeared and took control of things. He spoke some English – rather well – and produced a form for us to fill in.

I wasn't used to such efficiency. It was all moving too fast for me. I glanced at the form, baffled: "What do I put on this line? I just don't understand it."

Sue didn't want to look like an idiot in front of Miguel and curtly responded: "Read the question, it's in Portuguese, German and English."

This surprised me because this was the first form I had seen in any language other than Portuguese.

Whereupon the form filling was child's play and after the obligatory photocopying session, it was only a matter of minutes before we were told that within three to four weeks we would receive a letter from his Department asking us to return to sign on the dotted line, give a fingerprint, pay €2.50 and we should then receive our residencia identity cards. Miguel gave us a 'cover note' to tide us over until the official ones came through. These were blue pieces of pre-printed paper with a couple of official stamps, dates, names, and squiggles, no actual numbers, but they did show we had applied and covered all the official requirements.

"Thank you, Miguel. And how do we go about re-registering our UK car to Portuguese licence plates?"

"Simple. Go round the corner to the next booth, produce this cover note and there will be no problem re-registering it. A very good day to you both."

"He was fantastic, wasn't he?" remarked Sue. I harrumphed.

Ah well, all good things come to an end. We had it explained to us at this next counter that it wasn't quite as simple as that and first we had to go to the Alfândega, one of the few offices not located in the building, no doubt for historical reasons. And, of course, we'd have to make an appointment.

The next few days we spent re-cleaning all the bedrooms, windows, and floors and tidying the land at the back of the apartments. The weather had turned beautiful without any hint of the rain that had prevented the workmen from finishing the roof on the house. This was becoming a worry because until that was done there could be no further progress.

Because they were partly the reason we had moved here, we invited Lynne and Jeremy for a meal one evening as our first guests and had a great time. Unfortunately for Jeremy, who had always dismissed fly zappers as an expensive gimmick, we had just installed ours.

"I was told a long time ago that they were no good," he announced with an air of authority.

"What? Even though every shop, restaurant and bar in the world has them?" I replied.

"Quite so, a ridiculous waste of money and electricity."

Naturally, ours were zapping insects all evening.

Lynne became highly excited by this and squealed each time: "There's another one zapped!"

Jeremy flinched at each buzzing death rattle: "Beginner's luck," he intoned.

But Lynne's bloodlust was aroused. "I'm going outside to catch some more just to zap them," she said malevolently.

"That's another good purchase which we bought over here that's proved its worth ten times over," I said, gleefully rubbing salt into his wounds. "You'll have to buy her one now, Jeremy."

He had an almost pathological hatred of paying for electricity and took it all with rather bad grace.

Whilst in Sernada the following afternoon, we were sitting enjoying a glass of wine, when we were approached by two elderly gentlemen – locals – who had seen our UK registered car with GB sticker. They examined the bottle from which we were drinking.

"Do you really enjoy this Portuguese wine?" asked the older one with interest.

"We certainly do," I replied, draining my glass.

He cocked his head on one side as if to determine whether we were telling the truth. Evidently satisfied by our honesty, he cordially invited us to his home overlooking the river and valley. It was only a ten minute walk at none too fast a pace, and the views were spectacular.

It was a bachelor home, long johns on the washing line, a few empty glasses on the table and a hotch-potch of crockery in the lean-to. The owner vanished and returned with a litre jug of wine proudly proclaiming it to be from his own vines, adding:

"I don't like it as red but I mix it with my white wine to make rosé."

I thought this sounded rather unscientific, but nodded and said nothing. It was certainly dry but after two or three glasses we both agreed that it was palatable. He gave us a conducted tour of his winery, a stone built room with wine press, barrels and a few hundred bottles laid down.

This sort of thing kept happening with amazing regularity – it seemed that whenever we spoke English to each other in public, a Portuguese person would hear us and feel impelled to engage us in conversation or, as in this case, invite us to his home and shower us with hospitality. It has to be said that most of these excursions and talks occurred because the people concerned, or a member of their family, however distant, had either worked or lived in some English speaking area of the world. But even if there were an element of nostalgia on their part, it still indicated remarkable friendliness.

Thanking the elderly bachelors, we returned home.

We had an amusing incident in the computer shop whilst attempting to pay an invoice for the massive sum of €14.39. It caused absolute consternation for over 20 minutes while we waited patiently wondering what on earth was going on. We knew the people, they knew us, we even had an account there; it was only a small local business and not part of a national chain, but all the staff kept going to their computers and attempting to correct something.

The proprietor finally came over and apologised most profusely for the delay: "We have just installed a new accounts package on our computer and your invoice said €14.39 and not €14,39," he explained.

Neither of us were any the wiser. "And...?" I said.

"This has confused the system and it has actually credited your account with €14,390!" He looked mournful at such a projected loss.

"Of course," Sue interjected. "They use commas instead of full stops here."

"Don't worry – for the fourteen thousand euros credit we'll be more than happy to have that computer, that computer and that one!" I pointed at the most expensive I could see.

He smiled rather thinly. We paid him cash to cheer him up.

"I'll post you a receipt when we've sorted the computer out," he promised.

Next door was our mobile phone shop. Another interesting anomaly here – we had just taken out a rather good contract with them – €59 per month any time, anywhere in Europe, any network and 240 minutes call time. When we asked the salesman for a mobile phone upgrade because of the new contract, we were told we couldn't have one unless we could prove we ran a business. This was unlike the UK where businesses received nothing and usually the private customer gained. We were happy to oblige him.

The following night was New Year's Eve, and it saw us out on the tiles again. Some friends in the village invited us for an evening meal. We were looking forward to spending a couple of hours of pleasant company, returning back home soon after midnight and breaking open a bottle of bubbly to celebrate in low key fashion. Arriving to a warm welcome and a well prepared meal, followed by the mince pies we had brought and some delicious wine, we were having coffees and chatting when Natálio burst in and invited us all over to celebrate the New Year with them.

"It can't be your birthday again," exclaimed Sue.

"This will be as good," he smiled wickedly.

"Oh God," I groaned. "Not another Natálio'ing!"

Natálio'd – description of a person who has been in the company of Natálio in his wine cellar or home for a few hours 'sampling,' the after-effects always being rather blurred.

Again, and in traditional Portuguese style, there were about 15 family members there. Natálio had already begun to enjoy the festivities with a vengeance and it wasn't long before we were all involved in the party. As well as bread, cheese, cold meats, olives, cake, nuts, and plenty of drink he had contrived to get a really good party spirit going, with music and dancing.

Whilst Sue was questioned eagerly by some of the women of the village, I was invited to participate in a strange game of cards. Once I had sorted out the basics as the evening progressed and realised they only played this game with a pack of 40 cards, I began to win a few hands. At this point Natálio – for some obscure reason, whether or not connected with my prowess at the card table – decided to show me round their home. We toured the bedrooms, kitchen, bathrooms, winery, even the piggery (there were three porkers, all destined for the pot) and pigeon loft. This was most unusual, a great honour and demonstrated the considerable respect of one man showing another his wealth, but at the same time demonstrating openness and friendship. When I returned to Sue, she was looking somewhat dazed.

"What's the matter?" I asked, "aren't you enjoying yourself?"

"Well I am, but I can't understand what any of the women are talking about. "

"Why ever not? Your linguistic skills are better than mine and we both make ourselves understood and hold reasonable conversations with the builders."

"Yes, I think that's the problem – I don't know any Portuguese words which relate to babies, cooking or knitting, which is all they seemed to be talking about. Now, if they had asked me how deep our cesspit was going to be or what colour and style we were going to have in the bathroom, the conversation would have flowed!"

"Point taken."

At midnight more drinks were poured and everybody celebrated even more raucously than in the UK. Shortly after this six young lads appeared, obviously friends of Sandra and Paulo, one of whom entertained us painfully on the accordion with the only tune he knew.

"He's suffered for his music, and now it's our turn."

Then it was fireworks time. Now, believing them to be a danger if handled improperly, we were quite amazed and horrified to see these enormous fire rockets and fire crackers being hand held, the blue touch paper lit and pointed skywards, only to be released when the rocket was really fired up. No such thing as health and safety or a metal tube to hold the rockets – just a hand and a dash of bravado. Natálio led the way, laughing devilishly as yet another whooshed into the sky.

As for the fire cracker boxes, these were lit and held in both hands whilst the thunderbolts blew skywards with enormous explosions and a myriad of sparks and coloured lights. After five or six of these, we vanished inside where it was obviously safer.

The rest of the evening became a total blur but somehow we woke up the next morning at our own home and in bed, wondering which part of the celebrations overtook us – was it the firecrackers or the champagne?

"Never again," vowed Sue.

New Year's Day

With hangovers we rose rather gingerly and planned the day. Although we had been told that nothing would open here on New Year's Day, we had understood that to mean that some filling stations and grocery stores would be open, along with restaurants and cafés, similar to the UK.

So, having had breakfast we decided to drive up into the mountains and have lunch out. It soon became pretty obvious that we had miscalculated as we drove for kilometre after kilometre without seeing any cafés or shops open nor indeed did we see another car. It didn't look as if our original plan of having a meal out was going to happen. However, we decided to try Águeda because, apart from anything else, we were beginning to run low on fuel and every petrol station we passed was closed. In our part of the world 'Nothing open' evidently meant just that. It appeared to be the most sacrosanct of public holidays.

"Let's give it another five kilometres or so along the main road and if we don't find a petrol station open, we'll head back and eat at home," I suggested.

"I've got a funny feeling we'll be OK," said Sue.

Three kilometres further on to our delight we saw an open garage, filled the tank and decided to follow our plan and drive on up into the mountains. We breezed through an empty town and took the road alongside the River Águeda towards the heart of the Serra do Caramulo. It was as though we were the only survivors of a post nuclear apocalypse. Occasionally a chained dog twitched moodily at the roadside, and there was a flock of sheep on a hillside pasture from time to time, but gradually we left even these last vestiges of civilisation behind as we cruised through the mountain range, vast vistas of the rocky landscape falling away from us on either side.

All day the roads were deserted, the views grew ever more spectacular and we had a wonderful time exploring and getting lost again along the mountain tracks, returning home via Talhadas. This small town is reasonably close to us, high in the mountains, surrounded by a lunar landscape of ancient granite boulders. One huge rock had even split in two hundreds of years earlier and now loomed up towards the sky, naturally smooth and polished by the weather, straddling the road as though it were a gateway to the parish.

Needless to say, no cafés were open, and, ravenous when we got home, we raided the freezer for our evening meal.

A couple of days into the New Year, we had a site meeting, not a particularly friendly one at first because there was still a big problem over the boilers. Adrio and Ricardo were digging their heels in and Aldina tried heroically to keep the peace.

I spelled out our case: "There is no reason to have separate gas boilers for hot water in each apartment and another diesel boiler just for the central heating. It's uneconomical."

"It's the only way," asserted Ricardo.

There followed a long and convoluted discussion with Aldina interpreting for both parties. Ricardo and Adrio slowly backed down and eventually we reached agreement.

"Can I summarise by saying that Ricardo will come up with a price for taking out the existing diesel boiler which isn't large enough to cope, removing the two gas boilers and replacing the whole system with a larger diesel boiler?"

With some rather reluctant nodding of heads after Aldina's translation, we all shook hands. Sue and I watched them drive off.

"We'll just have to wait for the price he comes up with," I sighed.

"I've worked out the figures," Sue said. "If it costs us another €1,000 it will take us over four years to start breaking even and it's not worth the aggro or extra money."

"Irrespective of whether it costs us more or not, we will have to change the system," I argued: "Because at the moment the gas combi boilers are not good enough to have more than one shower at a time. They keep cutting out and producing cold water. Disastrous."

It wasn't the best way to start the year. Our first guests were barely five months away.

Chapter 11

Twelfth Night – with any luck some more Bolo Rei would be on the cards later. We had already had our first cup of tea of the day and it was still only 6.30 when we heard shouts and calls, cars and lorries squealing to a halt and the clanging of tools and iron scaffolding. It could only mean one thing: the rain had stopped and the roofers had arrived to insulate and tile the roof. This was their first day back after Christmas because of the awful weather we'd been suffering.

It seemed they were determined to make up the lost days – in no time at all half the roof timbers had been added and the batons were being placed on the sides and front ready to tile. But there was still no chimney – nobody knew how to read plans all of a sudden. Sue and I kept asking the roofers:

"Where's the chimney?"

The response was always a blank stare, a smile, a shrug of the shoulders and a 'mais tarde' (later), whether we used Portuguese, French or English.

"So will we be having a fireplace in the lounge?" I queried in exasperation. This met with still greater incomprehension.

Sue soothed me: "Let's discuss the situation with Adrio when we see him."

And there I had to leave it.

João arrived that morning while we were working in our temporary office. When I glanced outside an hour later, he had once again cleared the field behind us of all shrubs and brambles. He had though replaced them with a dazzling but totally naff plastic orange fence – so much for the aesthetic look!

In the afternoon we went to see Hernani, the landscape gardener who had been recommended by Aldina. He had promised to get the top part of our land around the apartments and swimming pool ready for spring and our first visitors.

"Don't let anybody tell you that Portugal is cheap," Sue exclaimed as she examined the costings en route.

"Landscape gardeners certainly aren't," I replied, "but it's essential to have the lawn laid as turf instead of grass seed because of the time factor. In other words we haven't got much of it."

Hernani, a tall and wiry man with a permanent air of nervous tension combined with raw energy, most untypical of the Portuguese, listened thoughtfully to our plans.

"We also want to plant some mature trees with fruit to give our first year guests a real taste of Portugal."

"When are your visitors due to arrive?" Hernani's gaze was fixed on the middle distance, as if in anticipation.

"In time for the European Football Championships in June."

"Leave it to me," he said. And with a nod, our meeting was at an end.

"I reckon he's a real professional and knows exactly what to produce and how to get the best out of the land for the money," I said as we drove away, mentally crossing my fingers – I was only half right.

"Only time will tell. We'll see when he starts work how good he is," Sue replied, filling in the cheque stub.

At least we had already seen some of his projects and were impressed with both the look and the speed they had been transformed from bare soil to living gardens. Our design though was in two parts: the first, especially for the tourists, was mainly lawn, shrubs and some fruit trees. The second stage covered the remaining two and a half acres which we intended to maintain as naturally as possible with existing wild plants and flowers, merely cutting a winding path through the undergrowth and planting different fruit trees on either side.

"It'll look great once we've cleared the brambles down there," I enthused.

Wild foxgloves, heather, gorse, mint and fennel already grew in abundance on our land. There were also many established but young sweet chestnuts.

"It really will attract all the birds and wildlife and give us another interest," agreed Sue. "They'll certainly be thanking us."

An absolute downpour of rain stopped work on the roof. However, as the roofers disappeared, the advance party from Agualinda arrived – one man and a digger. In part, we rather wished he hadn't.

With a tape measure Jorge, whose drooping moustache drooped still further in the rain, slowly proceeded to mark out the area of the swimming pool, ensuring meticulously that he was in the right position and that we were quite happy. The rain, if anything, increased in intensity. When we finally agreed on the precise position of the pool, we vanished inside the apartments absolutely soaked and watched through the windows, drying ourselves frantically, while he staked out the corners, created an arc for the oval shape, chalked the outline, climbed into his digger and scooped out a hole for the pool to be sunk into.

After about an hour and a half, it appeared we'd soon have a natural pool. I shouted at Jorge from the porch:

"We have to go out, but we'll be back in an hour or so."

"No problem," Jorge said, "I'll be gone by then. The rest of the team will come tomorrow or maybe later, depending on what they are doing."

There was nothing more to add. It was in the lap of the gods.

We drove through the storm into Aveiro to find out if our residencia cards had arrived. The receptionist had a quick look in her in-tray and said she had nothing for us. We asked how long they would take. She phoned another department and enquired. It didn't sound good.

Replacing the handset, she asked when we had made the application. We told her, off she went into the back room and returned, started looking in drawers and various other cupboards until eventually she appeared with our original applications, complete with photos and still unbanked cheque.

"I'm sorry for the delay," she said, "but they have obviously not been sent off."

It was abundantly plain they had sat in the cupboard since our last visit.

"So much for the beautiful Miguel," I voiced to no-one in particular, Sue scowled.

However, receptionist assured us this time they would be forwarded and would only take a couple of weeks to come through. But we'd heard that before.

Leaving there we went in search of furniture for the apartments. It wasn't like buying a bed for the spare room – we needed four twin beds as well as two bed-settees for the lounge areas, tables and chairs. Although we'd bought many things with us, we felt it would be a false economy to mix-match some of our existing furniture.

"I want things to look just right," said Sue, and I wasn't going to disagree.

When we got home, we found there'd been seven electricity cuts throughout the village in two hours. This had confused the hell out of the computers, one of which refused point blank to reboot. The other one got into a right pickle and went through all its rebooting several times on its own accord before finally settling down to having no screen.

We used to think that the anti-power surge plugs would protect them from most things but, living up here at the top of a mountain with only one power cable to serve the whole village, we were seriously considering buying a UPS. This is a kind of battery which smoothes out the peaks and troughs, thus allowing the power to continue for some minutes to a few hours after a power cut, depending of course on the amount of money one wished to spend.

"For a modest €2,000 you can protect your whole house and apartments for approximately 30 minutes," the salesman had advised us.

"Good value," I dripped sarcasm. "However, if we had a constant power supply it wouldn't cost us anything."

Sue drew me to one side: "It's a small price to pay for living up here in the peace and quiet."

"Surrounded only by drills, hammers, spades, builders' shouts and calls, bulldozers and stone cutters, which not only cut through the stone but seem to pervade the very soul of the mountain," I carried on, warming to my theme.

"The residents of Alombada have been requesting a substation or transformer from the electricity company for the past ten years and now we've been promised an enquiry," she reminded me.

"Sure, and with only 20 residents maximum I reckon the pigs will actually be landing after a very long flight before that happens!"

We decided to reserve judgement on the UPS until after further investigation because it appeared that the majority of the problems with the electricity – apart from the obvious – were our computers and it might be a lot cheaper to protect just those.

We returned to the ACP offices in Aveiro with our temporary residencia certificates, but, because it was only 1.40 when we arrived, we had to wait until the doors re-opened at 2.05 – we had forgotten the Portuguese never failed to take their two hours for lunch.

The offices finally opened and we saw a new man behind the counter who very suavely explained that because he hadn't enrolled us, we would have to wait for his colleague who would be back shortly.

"He will be able to assist you," he said, almost visibly congratulating himself on his own legerdemain. In so doing, he had neatly sidestepped a potential involvement, leaving the rest of his day free.

Shortly afterwards, our very own ACP man arrived and momentarily paled, but put a brave face on his ill fortune.

"I think he actually managed a smile," I whispered.

"Looked more like a grimace," muttered Sue.

We had the distinct feeling that he thought we would never pursue the matter any further. He was, though, courteously polite and told us in Portuguese: "Go and collect your car, park up outside, and I will show you the way in my car to the Alfândega where we can arrange the transfer."

After obeying his instructions and following him for a few kilometres we entered the dockland area of Aveiro, parked in the compound and entered a long, low and very unattractive, typical concrete Government building. This was to be our home for the next few hours – in fact weeks.

"Boa tarde, como estão," boomed our ACP man. Much bonhomie flowed between him and the two customs men in the office. I heard many times the words 'Inglês,' 'carro,' 'matricula' and 'número de placa' mentioned.

"What are they saying?" I hissed at Sue.

"Rough translation is 'bloody English, wanting a registration change, hah, no chance. Got their own car without buying one in Portugal and paying our extortionate taxes – they must be joking. Let's see what bureaucratic rules we can change in our favour'."

"Thought as much."

Eventually we were included in the discussion: "Let's see what papers you have," said one of the customs men.

In turn our passports, driving licences, número de contribuinte cards, car documents including MOT, log book, proof of purchase with date, price and tax paid, certificate of conformity for the engine and vehicle, certificate of insurance and road fund tax were all produced. The two young customs officers were looking crestfallen. Up to now every piece of paper was perfect. Next, they requested our residencia and looked even more downcast when we proudly produced our newly acquired blue piece of paper to show we had applied for it and it was official.

It seemed as though we were making progress until

another official arrived who seemed to have a better way of playing the game. He was an older man and had obviously had more experience in thwarting anyone stupid enough to want to achieve something within their office in a day.

He asked: "Do you have an official piece of paper which says that you have left the UK?"

Sue smiled and produced our change of address officially stamped by Her Majesty's Royal Mail.

"That should do it," she announced, and it probably would have done, but for the intervention of a very officious woman who had just walked in. There then followed a heated debate by everybody including our ACP man, the new woman, the two original administrators, the third older official, and from nowhere another four. After about 15 minutes, a syrupy, smiling spokesperson proclaimed it had been decided that anybody could ask for mail to be redirected without actually moving. We showed him our receipt for our removals proving that everything from cutlery to cookers had arrived here in Portugal.

"No, we're sorry, but we have an official form here which quite clearly states that you must also have these three documents."

This was out of a list of twelve, and we had already produced nine of them. The remainder consisted of a letter from Her Majesty's Government stating the date we had left the UK, a form from our Junta de Freguesia confirming that we lived in that area and a further document from Águeda Finances showing we had not lived, earned or paid any taxes in Portugal for the preceding three years.

As far as the letter from Her Majesty's Government was concerned, I replied: "When a person leaves England the only thing our Government says is 'bye-bye, would you like to take some others with you to reduce the burden on our National Health Service'."

They laughed: all the officials were more relaxed because they now had a bureaucratic line which would certainly preclude us from re-registering our vehicle that day, thus putting off the inevitable work for them with quadruple forms to fill in and generally much paper pushing. At this point, yet another member of staff, who had been listening to the discussion for the last hour and a half, helpfully produced a photocopy of a letter from the British Consulate in Porto, similar to the one they required.

"Do you know the British Consulate's telephone number and, if so, can we phone them from your office to enquire about the form?" asked Sue.

This didn't seem to faze them at all and appeared to be the most natural of requests. They even dialled the number for us, then handed the phone to me. I spoke to one of the Consulate's administrative staff and explained.

"No problem. This is quite a normal application here – if you'd like to come to our offices in Porto, on any weekday between the hours of 9.30 and 3.30, we'll provide one. There will however be a small fee for this."

"How much?"

"Ahem, er, €52.50."

"What, for a single piece of paper? That's a disgrace. I just can't believe that the British Government is charging over €50 for something saying we've left England when by doing so we're saving them a fortune."

My wrath had a beneficial side effect, besides giving vent to my frustration. It really pleased the Customs officials because those who spoke English understood what I had said, and all of a sudden they relaxed even further and their attitude changed – when I put the phone down, they were all smiling and chattering.

"What's going on?" I asked Sue.

"They're saying things like, 'typical Government, getting their ounce of flesh and tax, all Governments are the same' as far as I can gather," she explained.

However, sympathetic or not, we could not pursue the matter any further until we had acquired these three documents so we looked around for the ACP man.

"He has gone to the café for his afternoon refreshments, but will probably return if you want to wait," said the older official.

We said we wouldn't, asked them to thank him and say goodbye for us and took our leave. Ten arms waved us their farewells as we departed. At least it might now be the beginning of the end of the red tape for re-registering the car.

A friend of ours, Peter, who has a holiday home in the Algarve, phoned as we were on our way home. Sue told him of our latest trials.

"How familiar it all sounds. My wife and I have this theory that all officials are actually on a career programme, moving on only when they have perfected skills of delaying, ignoring, repeating the obvious without a facial expression and appearing to be busy. The ones on the 'Fast Track Career Path' move from the electricity company via the Avis desk to TAP check in where they can nod to you when you request leg room and a seat near the exit."

"Whilst they book you into the smallest seat on the plane," said Sue.

"Exactly. But, all in all, it's a wonderful place and the people are great."

As soon as we arrived back, Natálio called in to see us and said he would take us to a friend of his who sold agricultural products, including strimmers, which we would need if we were going to successfully clear the embankment and the rest of our land of brambles, gorse and other thickets.

"Otherwise," he hinted darkly, "you will be constantly asking other people to do the job for you."

We took the hint that this was not a good way of living in a small community and climbed aboard his truck. The rain had finished a couple of days earlier but the mountain pass roads which he took at speed in his usual cavalier way could have been really scary if either of us had kept our eyes open. We screeched to a halt outside a large house in the middle of nowhere and walked down the driveway to find a massive garage containing strimmers, chain saws, tractors and other agricultural implements, gleaming brightly amid rows and rows of dead and dying scooters.

Natálio's friend was most co-operative and they sorted out between them exactly what we required – we had no say in the matter. Considering Natálio had farmed our field for years, he was best placed to know. Still, we weren't entirely redundant. There was a debate some 15 minutes into their deliberations as to whether we required the full professional model of strimmer that was slightly heavier, or the 'advanced' amateur one. We lifted them both up without a harness and decided that the full professional would last longer and do a far better job in the long run.

So, we left there, a few hundred euros lighter, but armed with a brand spanking new Husqvarna top of the range strimmer, harness, helmet, visor, three different blades, tools for maintenance, two-stroke oil to mix with the petrol and an instruction book, in Portuguese.

"Very helpful," I scoffed.

Sue flicked through the book: "Well, it's mainly in pictorial format."

"I bet there are still quite a few technical bits which we need to know."

She closed the book and her eyes as Natálio prepared to screech round a particularly muddy and dangerous bend.

"If we get home," she prayed, "let's have a go tomorrow morning on some of the land."

Her prayers were answered, so early next morning we took the strimmer and attachments down to our starting point. If you've ever experienced trying to put up a deck chair for the first time you'll realise how difficult and confusing it was trying on a new shoulder harness complete with brackets and adjustment straps. Firstly we put it on the wrong way – then upside down. A small, appreciative crowd began to gather. We were in for a sociable weekend. Sue tugged and pulled at the straps, which only made me blue in the face and left big weal marks round my midriff. Changing course we decided to look at the instructions and discovered the correct procedure, fortunately explained in pictures.

After that it was a piece of cake. I started the motor and

the strimmer strummed. With visor down and ear protectors on, I soon entered a world of my own, sensing that Dustin Hoffman must have felt a similar isolation walking across the grass with his frogman's outfit on. I worked methodically for the first 20 minutes, blissfully unaware that I was creating great entertainment for the villagers who were standing behind me and watching my progress.

Eventually, Isabela threw a stone in front of me to attract my attention. It appeared that I had the throttle on full and was probably doing 1km per litre. Natálio, not wishing to miss out on a new toy in the village, asked if he could have a go. That was the last either Sue or I had a chance of using the strimmer for about an hour, in which time he had cleared about 100sq.m of the 2m high brambles.

While all this was going on, Sue put her culinary skills to the test by deciding what to make with the ingredients we had in store for Beatriz's Sunday lunch to which we had been invited. Discovering we had some oats, sugar, ginger and butter – with her ingenious girl-guide attitude – she set to and made flapjacks. After cooking them and prising the crispy offerings off the baking tray, she broke them up a bit and tried to make them look respectable on a plate. She then covered them tightly with cling film in the hope they would survive scrutiny and the villagers would accept that they should be pieces rather than round cakes.

Meanwhile, Natálio handed me back the strimmer and I finished off where he had started for another half hour or so. Then I came in and we relaxed before going over to Natálio's for fresh rabbit stew. One of his friends had been out shooting and these rabbits had been marinated in wine, cooked as a stew with rice added about 20 minutes before everybody sat down to eat. This was, we discovered, predominantly a male gathering but we settled down and enjoyed it.

We did find that when the huge stew bowl is put in front of you, whatever you end up with on your plate is what you get. The Portuguese are not fussy about what goes into the pot – if it has meat on it will not be discarded, including the heads. I discovered one on my plate and it surreptitiously found its way back into the pot without, I hoped, anybody noticing.

As it was a male gathering, Sue retired early and left me with the men of the village. With great self-restraint, I stumbled home only a couple of hours later having had a rather good time! Need I say more?

On Sunday we woke to find another beautiful clear sky, encouraging Sue to have a go at the strimming. I had to start the motor with the string pull for her, but it was soon an extension of her arm and although she found it hard going, achieved great things. Together we cleared about half an acre over the two days.

This was celebrated with our invitation from Beatriz for their family Sunday lunch. The meal was fantastic: they had slaughtered and butchered a pig a few days earlier. A huge plate of fresh cabbage, boiled potatoes and broccoli was topped by pork steaks, which had been broiled. These melted in the mouth and we ate our fill, leaving just enough room for our desserts. After five minutes or so of chat over another bottle of wine, Beatriz vanished into the house and reappeared with what can only be described as the same again, only this time the pork was roasted. Surely not?

We weren't the only ones who'd miscalculated. Lynne, who had been to many of these functions over the years, had not only failed to inform us this was the norm but had fallen into the same trap. We couldn't believe it, so to save face, we cut down on the vegetables on the second course but had some of the meat. After that came desserts, including the flapjacks which were a huge success – with some fine tuning Sue will have to produce these at nearly every occasion and, laced with ginger, they really appealed. Usually, the Portuguese decline anything with ginger exclaiming it to be too hot and spicy, even though they drip tongue-shrivelling hot piri-piri on most meats.

"Even the women praised them, which was a great compliment," Sue said happily.

After this grand meal, we walked it off through part of

the eucalyptus forest, meandering along the many tracks and feeling cosily surrounded. There was a fresh wind blowing from the west and the trees appeared to be putting greater energy into their dance, approximating to that of a waltz. Yet again we were delighted by how secluded we felt from the hurly-burly of life, that our environment was genuinely rural. Arriving back at the village, we were pleasantly tired, and ready for a rest.

The morning saw everybody back at work on the house, our workmen for the patio, others for the swimming pool, and Hernani to check the lie of the land. All went well until one of the guys from Agualinda asked us where we wanted the housing for the electrics and the pump. We showed him the rough position.

"So what type of housing do you want?"

"What types are there?"

"There's the fibreglass box completely submerged in the land or one which is half in and half out of the ground but which looks like an artificial rock. For the artificial rock, you would have to pay an extra €200 on top of the €500 for the one sunk into the ground."

I was getting quite wise to these tricks: "Look, it's your electrics and your pump so what do you propose to do if we don't have a box – leave it on top of the soil as a garden ornament?"

That confused him – I don't think anybody had ever said they wouldn't pay extra for the pump box.

We pointed out that we had paid enough already and increased our costs by having the larger swimming pool, so an extra 500 or 700 euros which we considered part of the equipment was out of the question.

This debate had all taken place in Portuguese so to get his message across (and some moral support), he telephoned his head office where there was an employee who spoke good English.

All she did was reiterate: "You have to pay extra for the pump housing."

My reply was simple: "No. We'll have the subterranean one at no extra charge."

She conceded: "Up to last year we used to put the boxes in free of charge but some people already had outhouses, so we decided not to include them in the price."

"If I had an outhouse, would you be knocking €700 off the price of the pool?" My argument, although very logical, seemed to be beyond her comprehension.

"I'll have to refer the matter to my boss."

She made several more phone calls saying that we would definitely have to pay and I continued to stand my ground. Eventually, it was decided that the box would be put into the ground at no extra cost. Sue and I cheered silently.

It proved to be a pyrrhic victory. The next day we went down to pay our second instalment to Agualinda. Before we could write the cheque we were told there was a problem.

"There's an increase in the cost of the pool because the pool liner you have chosen is thicker and more expensive than the standard one. Unfortunately the girl in the office hadn't been working here long enough when you ordered it to tell you the difference in price."

"Surely you must stick to your quoted price," I said.

"Yes, but if you care to look at your contract (we did – it was there, all in very, very small Portuguese print), you will see that the quote only applies for standard liners. You will have to pay another €700 if you want the stronger liner."

I conferred rapidly with Sue. Since we did want the stronger liner and better pattern, I entered into negotiations about how much extra we should be paying and, once more, the poor unfortunate girl who spoke English was phoned. I agreed, as calmly as I could in the face of her mounting hysteria, that the liner was indeed more substantial and would be of benefit to us in the long run but that €700 was far too much to pay for the extra when it wasn't our fault.

"Besides," I concluded, "we hadn't calculated for the extra money. However, we think €200 will be acceptable."

The horse trading began. "€600," she suggested.

"300," I countered.

"€400," she said.

"Done."

"So, we can either look at it that we've got a better quality liner for €400 extra and be positive," summarised Sue on the way home.

"Or admit it cost us an extra 400 for nothing."

We preferred the former view.

A bang and a slight whiff of smoke that evening changed our lives for the next few days. A lack of electricity had, once again, succeeded in plunging the mountain into darkness. I contacted the power supplier to find out what the problem was and they advised me that a major fault a few kilometres away had affected the whole area and they were desperately trying to restore power. There was nothing for us to do but wait. We were used to the vagaries of our electricity, there is only one cable serving the village and this causes regular surges, tripping the switches and blowing the fuses.

Usually, the loss only lasts for a matter of hours so it was rarely anything more than a minor inconvenience. However, on this occasion, it lasted from Thursday through to Monday and, because an enormous surge had taken place, not only had we lost power, but it had damaged over 20 appliances, including the fridge and freezer, computer equipment and television along with various other ancillary smaller appliances on standby or recharge. The other consequence was a lack of fresh water from our bore hole because it all had to be pumped – there was no mains water.

This was obviously going to cost us a fortune. Discussing it a couple of days later before power was restored, Isabela laughed and explained that because the damage had been caused by the electrical company they were insured and all we had to do was submit a detailed list including the date of the incident; we would then receive compensation in full. Living with candles and bottles of water suddenly seemed less of a hardship and was quite romantic in a rustic sort of way. Fortunately, we cooked by gas so the early morning cuppa wasn't a problem.

Armed with this information we confidently entered EDP's reception area and enquired about a claim form.

"Certainly," we were told, "we understand the problem. There are a number of people like yourselves who have already submitted claims for this rather unfortunate incident."

We filled in the forms. The official was then able to access all our details on his monitor and, with a syrupy, smug smile, he explained to us that, although he sympathised with our predicament and confirmed it had been caused by them, our €1,400 compensation claim would not be processed because we weren't on a permanent contract.

"What the hell do you mean? Do we have a contract and does EDP supply the power?"

"Yes, but if you look at your contract it is only for obras (works)."

"Is it the same electricity?"

"Yes."

"And what will happen when we have a permanent contract as opposed to a works contract? Will the line and cable be the same?"

"Yes."

"So why aren't you paying out compensation to us?"

"Because it's a temporary works contract."

I gave up. We certainly wouldn't receive compensation and it was all in a word and the stroke of a pen.

Isabela hadn't told us this one.

Because of time constraints, we were forced to landscape expensively around the swimming pool and not a half-finished mishmash. We had also decided we wouldn't appreciate planks to and from the pool over a hard soil base because if we were on holiday it would be rather too reminiscent of resorts from hell programmes.

So we went back to see Hernani, who had created a plan of what he would like to do with our land. It all looked fine but rather ornate, so, having discussed with him what we wanted again, he agreed that our ideas for a simple lawn with some 'scrubs' (he couldn't say 'shrubs') and an area of flowers immediately in front of the patio would also look very effective.

All was agreed so, as we were in Aveiro we contacted Rui, and invited him for lunch. For a tiny sum we had a superb three course meal including wine and coffee, all served by a most friendly waitress. We were about to tip as normal, when Rui stopped us and explained in great detail where you tip and where you don't.

"Here," he said, "because a lot of people are out shopping or on their lunch break, the waitresses would consider a tip an insult."

So we obliged and didn't tip. It didn't appear to count against us. When we left, we received a lovely smile and a "Goodbye, and thank you" from the waitress.

"Did you feel guilty about not tipping?" I asked Sue.

"Of course, but tradition is tradition and we'll just have to get used to it."

After taking our leave, we visited Aldina's new home to see how her 'in the wall' automatic vacuum cleaner worked. The amusing part was that Aldina hadn't a clue about housework, or how to use the vacuum. She didn't even know where the hose was stored, and ruefully admitted that her daily housekeeper was the only one to use it. Even her children didn't know. So we had to ask her housekeeper a few questions about the advantages of the vacuum. She explained it and gave us a practical demonstration concluding with what we thought was probably the best feature. In the kitchen even the hose was unnecessary – all the crumbs, dust and food scraps were just brushed on to the floor and, at the flick of a switch, the offending matter was sucked into the machine through a letter box style slit below the kitchen units – we were sold on it.

Aldina then showed us round her home, beautifully designed with every conceivable mod-con, including speakers and televisions in every room, a cinema style foyer entrance hall and glass panelled corridors overlooking her land. It really was quite magnificent and exactly as she had described it to us when she first moved in. However, just like those cobblers whose children have the worst shoes, there was a catch.

"Our home took five years to build," she admitted.

"Why? It's great, but that long?"

"I forgot to tie up the paperwork with a finishing date. I thought the builder would have been quicker because he is an old friend."

We both made mental notes to check her paperwork more carefully in future.

Day's work over, we headed back to our village but I decided on the way home to go a different route and found a new bar. On entering we saw the garage proprietor where our ill-fated Bozo had spent much time. He welcomed us with open arms. At the bar were eight men ranging in ages from about 50-odd to late 70's and each of them, it appeared, had bought a bottle of wine, which they shared amongst themselves. This was a new experience for us. We were soon integrated into this session and several bottles later we were cordially invited to reciprocate, which we did willingly. After another hour or so we settled our account only to discover the whole session had cost us an amazing €3. We realised it was high living but what the hell, it had been a night to remember.

Unfortunately, arriving home in the dark we discovered there was no running water in the apartments. We knew the Agualinda people had been in so, with torch in hand, we followed the pipe back up to the bore hole, checked the connections, checked the bore hole was connected to the pipe and that the valves were open. Still no water. So reluctantly we had to telephone Adrio who we thought would send one of the lads out. He arrived himself some 35 minutes later and after much pressing of pipes and valves, had a brainwave. He promptly ran back up the hill, torch in hand.

There was a shout of triumph and seconds later there was a flood gushing out of all the taps which we'd left open on full, instantly soaking all the floors. But at least we had water. It appeared that in their haste to depart before dark the workmen had failed to turn the electrics back on to the bore hole. This sobered us up after our bar session so we had a restorative scotch with Adrio.

A very smart looking man arrived on site in the morning. We watched him walking around tapping the walls and wondered what on earth he was doing. It turned out he was the vacuum man who proceeded to explain what the machine could do and, after pointing out where we would require all the outlets and pipe work, gave us a price for the installation.

On earlier advice from Aldina, we rejected his offer because this was only a 1,200 watt motor and she had advised a larger one.

"But the smaller motor is adequate."

"We don't want adequate, we want perfect," I stated.

"We want the one which sucks up dust, bits of stone – and water if necessary," said Sue, mindful we were still mopping up from last night.

He then came up with a much improved specification with a cost to match. We negotiated the price down a little and everybody was happy.

Nobody was coming today, or so we thought. We had just enjoyed a leisurely breakfast before showering and getting dressed. There I was, once again in the buff, Sue in a dressing gown (just in case, and how right she was), when there was a knock at the door. It was Mr. Vacuum man – he wanted to start work and needed to know where we wanted the pipes. I almost told him (from the other room) exactly where he could shove his pipes, but Sue explained that we would come over to the house shortly. We dressed quickly and sorted out the logistics of the pipe work.

He asked for his deposit cheque but we explained that we had ordered a new cheque book from the bank and would payment next week be in order. He understood the situation and agreed with us that the banking system here in Portugal was archaic – he had worked and lived in France and Germany where the system was totally different. Getting a new chequebook is not as simple as in the UK, where one automatically arrives. Here, you have to go into the bank and order them and they usually arrive within the week. You also have to pay for the privilege of having them. Our last request, we had been told by the bank, would be posted to us that same week. Nothing arrived for ten days. So we went to the bank and enquired where they were.

It transpired they hadn't been ordered and would take yet another week to ten days to arrive.

"It's very embarrassing because we have certain bills to pay and we've told people the cheques are on the way."

"That's no problem at all," said the cashier. "Just tell us the amount and who you want the cheques made out to and we will willingly write one of our cheques for them out of your account."

"How much will these cost?" I was wary, from bitter experience.

He replied casually: "Oh, not much at all, we charge a percentage of the amount of the cheque – a mere 2%."

"Look, it's your fault we don't have our cheques." I was indignant.

He just smiled happily at us: "I agree, but there's nothing I can do. Head office sets the rates and that's how much it would cost us."

Just then the English-speaking cashier came over and took charge. "I will personally request an express delivery of your cheques – they should arrive by Tuesday morning so you can pay all your debts before leaving for the UK on Wednesday."

There was nothing further to be said. When we returned to Alombada, our equally friendly postman had posted a card in the letterbox to say we had four registered letters to collect from the main post office on Monday after 2 p.m. This was a real pain because the time of the card was less than 15 minutes earlier. Have you ever had knowledge of post and not been able to recover it for three days, especially registered mail (these were from the Camara Municipal)?

Life can be extremely frustrating.

We continued to strim the bottom part of the land, cleared out all the young eucalyptus and thinned out the pine trees. On Saturday morning we began work again on the land, making sure that we took it a step at a time and cleared as we went. It was hard work but eminently worthwhile. The felling of the sapling trees was especially tiring using the small crosscut saw we had bought specifically for the job. On advice, we bought a couple of attachment blades for the strimmer to remove them. This would make life a lot easier.

It was clouding over as we returned home so we put off completing the job for another day.

Sunday morning I got the pressure hose out and hosed down the new patio area and cleaned all the outside garden furniture. It certainly looked better afterwards. Late morning, out came the strimmer again, and after changing the cutting disk we both cleared a further 60sq.m or so before strimming suddenly ceased. We checked for fuel – there was plenty. We just couldn't pull the cord. The whole thing had seized up. It was a dead strimmer.

Nothing else could be done on a Sunday so we packed it all away and the iron came out for the first time since we arrived, the only reason being Sue had a very creased shirt which no amount of pulling and jumping on, putting under the mattress or anything else would un-crease. Out came the instruction booklet, Mrs. Beaton's book on household chores and, being in the frame of mind she was, if it didn't move fast enough it was slammed onto the ironing board and flattened. Everybody, including the local dogs and cats, ran for cover.

"Why on earth did I start this," she shouted. "I'm not going back to the UK ever again if I have to do ironing."

There were many other similar but less decorous phrases that rang out before the job was complete. Whilst all this was going on, I took refuge in a careful study of Augusto and Natálio's wine cellar, coming back only to barbecue a chicken.

After the weekend our electricians turned up to install cables in the house, the Agualinda people to do the pool, Mick and Montmorency to plumb and Hernani's landscape gardeners to survey. Many exhausting questions later, it seemed everybody knew what they had to do so we left them to it and returned the strimmer to the shop for repair under the guarantee.

This was easier said than done. It was quite a tough task to remember the exact roads that Natálio had taken to this most reclusive of retailers. Besides which, one mountain road looked much like another and the rugged landscape, imposing though it was, was generally devoid of helpful man-made features that would show us we were on the right path. I was just about to give it up as a bad job and slink back to Natálio for directions, when Sue pointed and I saw the owner tinkering away with some machinery outside his establishment. We parked up and showed him the stricken strimmer.

As we approached the mountain store, Natálio's friend's face was a picture of abject horror. Nobody had ever brought a new machine back to him so soon – broken. Without waiting for an explanation as to what had happened he took it into his workshop, put it on the bench and attempted to pull the starter cord. Nothing.

He looked up and said accusingly, "This is a two-stroke petrol engine and you haven't added any oil."

"I assure you we did."

He didn't look as though he believed us and proceeded to strip the engine down without saying a further word. Then he took it out into the yard where the light was better and had a look at the innards. Thankfully for us, he could see a glimmering of oil on the surface of the piston, after which he stripped the rest of the engine down and discovered the piston rings had broken inside the housing.

"Okay, it will be repaired under guarantee."

I felt completely vindicated.

It was now after 2 p.m. so we collected our registered mail. We had to show our passports before being given the four letters. We couldn't wait to open them but when we did we wished we hadn't. There were four identical bills, two addressed to Sue and two addressed to me, all demanding payment of €8,000 to the Government Finance Ministry.

This was a bolt from the blue – it was, we thought, a new tax which the Government had introduced in November decreeing that all land which had been purchased and was in the process of having building work done on it, was liable to a tax of so much per square metre. We had a few thousand square metres of land, of course – it reminded us of that horrible hotels' and houses' tax in Monopoly. Because the land was in joint names we had each received a bill for the respective amounts for the same land twice. To make matters worse, it had to be paid in nine days, we didn't have that kind of money in the bank and we were off to England the following day.

We just had time to catch Aldina's assistant, Paula, in her office before she left and asked her if she would give Aldina a photocopy of the invoices and letters as soon as she came in the next morning. Furthermore, could she find out what it was all about and explain to the Finance people we would not be available for the next ten days. Paula said she'd do this and at the same time she told us that our other forms for the car were being processed and would be with us on our return. At least one thing was going right.

Life wasn't getting any easier as the days went on but we were still enjoying every moment out here. It was becoming increasingly obvious to both of us that Alombada was our home and we talked about how we'd miss it as we packed. The main reason for our trip was to deal with the dreaded quarterly VAT return. Some treat.

We flew back from Porto, brooding on the difficulties we were leaving behind us.

Chapter 12

The quarterly VAT returns were already proving to be a logistical nightmare because, although HM Customs & Excise would readily bank our cheque for the VAT on the UK business and accepted our postal address was now in Portugal, they could not legally mail the VAT form out of the country (which the important part of the VAT, not the cheque). By the time we left for the airport we still hadn't received the form even though all our mail was being redirected.

As I drove, Sue made a frantic call to the VAT office to ask if they could send a duplicate form urgently to our accountant and use his address for future correspondence. They were very friendly and helpful and agreed, but said they would need it in writing first, and not via e-mail. Sue promised to fax them a letter on arrival in the UK.

"Bureaucracy being bureaucracy, I bet we don't get the form through before having to return here," she sighed.

I didn't give her odds.

There was a deal for the car in the long stay car park, working out at €45 for seven days, which seemed reasonable. We checked in our baggage and I called Aldina about the problem of our four invoices from the Camara Municipal Finance Department.

"Don't worry, I'll take care of it all whilst you're away," she breezed.

"Have you managed to read the them yet?" I asked.

"Er, no, I haven't had time."

"So are we safe, or what?"

"I'm pretty sure you wouldn't have to pay them in nine days and, anyway…"

"Yes?"

"Even if you did, we can argue the point later by sending them your airline tickets to show you were out of the country and thus unable to pay."

The tannoy announced our flight and I rang off, passing on the news.

"That really fills me with confidence," said Sue.

The temperature when we left was a comfortable 22º but we were anticipating a very wet and cold south of England, so on our arrival at Heathrow we were pleasantly surprised with a clear sky and 16º. We collected our hire car – they gave us an upgrade again. It was obviously our lucky day with weather and transport.

"Let's enjoy it whilst it lasts," I said, thanking the rental people and jumping in the car before they changed their minds. Singing tunelessly along with the radio, we drove back to Hampshire.

The next week raced by with 2,400km on the clock – amazingly we received the VAT form so spent a day preparing the accounts. Sue had a call from the letting agent to say the washing machine in the Newbury flat had broken and they were also calling in someone to clear the drains.

Wherever we were, our lives seemed to revolve around water problems.

Britain's unseasonably warm weather couldn't last. We woke to the aftermath of blizzards – there was snow everywhere and we were catching the early flight back home. However, Sue had missed out on her skiing and we were now living in sunny Portugal so we had half an hour of fun with a snowball fight. We then inched our way through the queues on the M3 and the M25, but the snowfall predictably proved to be a problem at Heathrow with a two hour delay.

This had an unforeseen consequence when we tried to

leave the car park at Porto airport. I handed a €50 note to the attendant.

"Not enough: the bill is €62," he demanded.

"What? Why it isn't €45 as displayed last week?"

"Ah, hah," he explained patiently. "You left the car at 11.45 according to the ticket, but it is now 12.30 so therefore you have an extra day's parking charge."

"But the flight was delayed because of snow."

He shrugged. The barrier remained down.

"And why is it a full day, not just an hour's extra charge?"

"These are the rules."

Evidently we were going nowhere unless I paid up so I found the remaining coins from our motorway toll fund.

"I can't believe three quarters of an hour makes that much difference," said Sue.

"Another reason for suing the Met Office," I chuntered.

"And the car parking authority."

That wasn't the only shock. On our return home we discovered to our horror that in his enthusiasm to please, Hernani had demolished the bottom half of our land and left it a naked, barren waste. Not only had he stripped away all our natural wild flowers but he had also felled the 15 sweet chestnut trees which Natálio had planted two years previously. We were heartbroken – all our plans for a natural pathway through the foxgloves, primroses and wild fennel were back at square one. The area would now need careful cultivation and re-sowing in the vain hope that it might be green by the time our first visitors arrived.

In the mailbox was our original VAT return form.

The next day Hernani came out to see us, smiling in anticipation of our thanks.

I pointed to the barren land. "What on earth have you done?"

Taken aback, the smile left his face and he became very defensive.

"I thought you would want to clear everything and start afresh."

"Don't you remember our last conversation? We liked your ideas but we didn't want you destroying our natural wild field. Why didn't you listen?"

Hernani was crestfallen. "What do you want me to do?"

"For a start, you can sow a range of new wild flower seeds along the bottom of the land and plant nine or ten sweet chestnuts. We must have it looking at least halfway decent by early summer."

Whilst I was extracting firm promises from Hernani to make good the carnage, Sue phoned Aldina who gave her some welcome news.

"Your letters are not invoices but estimates of the value of the land which will be the basis for your rates when the house is completed."

"Maybe so," replied Sue, "but we still have the problem of the property being in joint names and us receiving separate invoices for the same amounts. Clearly there is only one plot of land and one home, so there should only be one joint invoice for rates."

Aldina explained. "In Portugal once you have a número de contribuinte they have to assign the rates to each person, unless you are married. Then you must go through the rigmarole of explaining exactly what the situation is between the two parties."

"Such as?"

"Whether you're both intending to keep the property separate if it was owned by you prior to marriage, whether all the property is owned solely by your husband, or whether it is jointly owned."

"And what if we have no intention of getting married?" Although we were very much in love, that wasn't part of our plans.

"Single people unfortunately do not come into any category," stated Aldina.

Sue relayed the news to me. "So we'll now begin another round of bureaucracy which will probably take years in and out of Camara Municipal, financial houses, solicitors and so on."

"It's all part of life's rich pageantry and the joy of living together out here," I reassured her. Her sigh seemed endless.

There had been no work on the house whilst we were away (not greatly to our surprise) and the rain absolutely pelted down all day Saturday. It was still pouring on Sunday so we caught up with the office work.

Just as well, really, because on Monday morning there was a deluge of workmen. The electricians and plumbers arrived and continued laying the electrics, telephone wires, satellite cables, and even the gas pipes. Unlike builders in the UK who would cut a channel through the bricks, insert the conduit and plaster over it, here they took out a hammer, similar to an ice pick and, because the bricks are honeycombed, broke the outer skin and pushed the tubes inside, adding a blob of cement every few metres to keep them in place.

After a few hours of activity, with cables reaching the full height of the walls, I enquired mildly:

"Are you sure there'll be enough strength left in the walls to take the weight of the upstairs of the house?"

Maybe my Portuguese was at fault, or maybe they considered it a daft question. Either way, they didn't seem at all concerned.

"I suppose we shouldn't worry," Sue consoled me, "they've been doing it this way for years."

"Do you think they repair the brickwork?"

"I think I heard someone say they'll smooth it out with cement afterwards."

However, when they had finished the day's work there were hundreds of cables, water pipes, and telephone wires – all in their respective tubes, running the length of the house along the floor, up the walls, through the concrete ceilings and into a monstrosity of a grey metal fuse box which was placed in the entrance hall, a wonderful welcoming view.

Sue asked: "Can't you put that underneath the stairs?"

"It is a bit of an eyesore," I agreed.

Apparently not, according to the foreman. "It is the law that the fuse box has to be placed immediately inside the doorway of any building for safety reasons. If there's a fire or any other emergency, there must be easy access to turn off the electricity."

"But it would be highly unlikely that we would be standing in the hallway if there was a big problem."

"Now we know that and you know that, but the Camara Municipal doesn't recognise it, so everybody has to have it in the same place."

We looked at each other in resignation.

"Okay," I said, and capitulated as gracefully as I could in the face of yet more intransigence.

"Look, if you don't like the appearance of it, and I can't really blame you, the simple answer is to hang an even bigger picture over the top," he suggested.

This really seemed to defeat the object of the exercise. But I nodded in agreement. It was the way of things around here.

Just before noon, I glanced out of the window. Natálio was walking past pushing a wheelbarrow with four legs sticking up in the air.

"I've just seen Tuesday's lunch going by," I called out.

Sue came over to the window and watched as Natálio, assisted by Paulo, took the freshly slaughtered hog along to their outhouse to be butchered and marinated.

"That's what I call back to basics," she said.

It was the anniversary of the birth of our village, a very big day in the calendar – 3rd February – S. Braz. Again, a festival was being prepared around mountains of food. However, there was a difference. For once, Alombada's tiny chapel was opened, and the priest arrived in a very old chauffeur-driven Volvo to conduct a service before the feast.

"He doesn't drive because he enjoys his wine," Natálio whispered to me.

Alombada was rewarded with sunshine. Our builders were highly amused at the locals' antics. After the sheep had been gently herded back into their pens, all the local landed gentry arrived in their finest. Many had come from miles away and had family connections with the village from way back. There were about 40 people crammed into the chapel, which would normally only take 16 comfortably.

As the village newcomers and in deference to the villagers, we stood in the church doorway listening to the proceedings; these, Natálio had assured us, would be timed to perfection. It began with a surprise. The priest regarded us earnestly and in perfect English said:

"I'm sorry, I don't speak English so I shall conduct the service in Portuguese." Then, with a smile, he continued.

The bells continued to sound the quarter hour as usual. The priest had just begun his sermon when the clock struck midday. It was the full works – ding dong ding dong several times followed by twelve echoing chimes – with the amplified speakers sounding from the pole above the chapel, his voice was utterly drowned out.

"It has happened every year since he has been conducting the service and the sermon always starts at the same time," muttered João, happy that tradition was being upheld.

Meanwhile the priest ignored the bells and, even though nobody could hear a word of what he was saying, continued his sermon. There was much tittering and many sideways glances at Augusto, who was the keeper of the bells, from certain quarters in reproach. These glances, evidently time-honoured, seemed to say: 'have you been tweaking the volume up again for the service? You could have turned the speakers off for it.' Augusto, in his equally traditional and wordless reply said it all with his eyes – a gentle shrug and 'he only comes once a year, the bells go on for ever.' Although the villagers obviously respected God, they had even more reverence for the land and tradition.

No-one really minded: the priest carried on unflustered and the congregation had evidently heard it all before.

After the service most people milled around the square, gossiping, while we said our farewells and strolled back to the apartments ready to restart work in the office after lunch. I was opening a bottle whilst Sue broke off some bread when there was a knock on the door. It was Isabela.

"What are you doing?"

"We're just having a snack."

"Don't you know you never need an invitation to our home when there is a feast? And certainly not on festival days."

"We thought it was only for family and long-established villagers."

"Pah!" she signified disgust at such exclusive thinking. "You are just as much a part of local life as anybody."

There was no escape. Our stomachs groaned – we knew we were in for a five hour blow-out.

The hog had been bred specifically for this party and fed on sweet chestnuts to make the meat even more tender and moist, and it worked. We would have to go a long way to have pork as tasty and sweet as this one. Sure enough, it was 6.00 p.m. before we departed, with the tacit agreement that we would both return at 8.00 to continue the festivities. The meal so far had consisted of six main courses, each being a full one, with no shilly-shallying such as counting cheese and biscuits. These were big – and pacing yourself was very difficult when people either side and opposite kept on insisting on piling your plate higher.

The desserts were varied, all home produced and as delicious as ever. Throughout the day the village wine had flowed, and most people were getting merrier by the hour. Beatriz's twin sister had arrived from afar and the pair of them sat opposite us giggling away like two schoolgirls, apparently discussing us at great length. Eventually we just had to ask Beatriz.

"What are you two whispering about?" enquired Sue, summoning her best Portuguese.

"We were guessing how old you must be," she replied.

Sue told them.

It appeared from their exclamations and Beatriz's answer that they couldn't believe we really were in our mid-fifties. Naturally, Sue found it very flattering.

After a rest for a couple of hours, we slowly walked back up to Natálio's to carry on what we thought was talking and relaxing. No chance. We were met with an identical meal but some newcomers had replaced those who had departed.

"I don't know if I can eat it all again," groaned Sue.

However, it didn't take us too long to discover the whole point of the evening was to mix and enjoy each other's company. We also worked out that, if we didn't really want to eat anything, we could sit there with a bowl of soup and chat away quite happily. Provided there was something in front of us, everybody was content. We slept extremely well that night and fasted the next day.

It all started with the builders arriving to continue their work, followed shortly by the Agualinda people. The pool saga was developing: Jorge had dug the hole, two men had covered the base of the hole with concrete, and now another two arrived, discovered the concrete base wasn't big enough but still proceeded to fit the aluminium frame over the undersized concrete base.

Even I could see the error: "It's not going to work," I told them.

"No, no, it will all be smooth in a day or two, there is no problem at all."

"But it doesn't fit," cried Sue, exasperated.

"I looked at the plans, and the size is correct," was the obdurate reply. Next, another team arrived to fit the liner.

We were starting to learn from bitter experience that the Portuguese never confront a problem as it happens – they just build on it until it becomes gargantuan, instead of stopping and correcting the mistake immediately.

"Look, the sides aren't level or upright," I pointed out.

"It's okay. After we go, someone will come and do the final fitting and they use a big machine to straighten it all out."

There was no telling them, and we had errands to run. We arrived back in the dark and there was our pool filled with water but without the flagstones around the top.

The next morning a different pair arrived as advertised, although there was no sign of the aforementioned big machine. We had meetings with Aldina and Adrio, which took up most of the day, and on our return the latest pool people had vanished.

With no-one on site and the job obviously completed we had grave misgivings, which were soon corroborated. The guys had laid all the flagstones but to compensate for the wavy sides of the pool had cut and laid curved corner flagstones along the supposedly straight edges. This was not the only flaw.

Soon, we discovered another. We were sitting on our patio with the light on looking across at the pool when Sue suddenly jumped up and said:

"That pool dips down in the middle!"

On closer inspection not only did it dip down in the middle but the lining was also bulging away, full of wrinkles and wasn't even in contact with the aluminium sides. We were furious that all our warnings had been brushed aside. Not to put too fine a point on it, it was a complete dog's dinner.

The next morning we were on the phone complaining bitterly about the shoddy workmanship. We achieved nothing on the phone so went down to see Catarina, the salesgirl in their local showroom.

"Can I help you?" she enquired brightly, but soon wished she hadn't.

"Your men have done the most shoddy and unprofessional job I've ever seen, and we want it put right at once," I said, flicking the contract across to her.

Her face fell. She rang their head office and gave me the telephone to speak to her German counterpart, Greta, the one who was fluent in English. The poor woman didn't get much of a chance to show off her linguistic skills, because the conversation was rather one sided. At its conclusion, she promised to send out their chief surveyor within the next 48 hours to see what the problems were at first hand.

In the meantime, Hernani, who was on rather a tight schedule himself, had arrived and started to lay the lawn turfs up to the swimming pool. Within two days he had almost completed the work, built the rock garden boxes in front of the patio and installed the automatic sprinkler. It really did look a picture.

Two days later the swimming pool surveyor arrived on site, took a look at the pool and agreed tentatively that it probably wasn't up to the standard they would normally expect from their workmen.

"Unfortunately," he droned on, "now the job has been completed there is nothing we can do about the liner but as compensation we will give you one of our automatic swimming pool vacuum cleaners. We'll also refit the top flagstones around the pool so they look aesthetically better."

"Compensation! We're not interested in compensation at this point – we just want it right. Compensation can come later after the pool has been installed properly and to our satisfaction."

I distinctly saw him flinch, but he said nothing. After a beer he left, assuring us that he would explain the problems to the boss but he reiterated nothing could be done about the liner and the unevenness of the sides.

The following day I complained again to Greta, and explained how bad the pool was looking.

"There is no problem," she asserted, a trifle nervously, "because the surveyor has told my boss about the situation. There is not much more we can do at this stage."

About an hour later another two workmen arrived, complete with hammer and chisels and masses of cement. They proceeded to remove the tiles from around the pool. We were quite happy at last because we thought they were finally going to do something about the sides.

Not a hope. They had ignored our pleas – if indeed they had been informed – and the only thing they had been told was to level the middle of the swimming pool by putting extra cement underneath the tiles and straightening the flagstones. Sue went out and gave it to them:

"It's a waste of time doing that before the pool has been completed satisfactorily."

One of the two replied. "I'm afraid we have only been told to take the flagstones off and straighten them up, nothing else. We're paid to do our job and that's all we can do."

I joined Sue by the whole sorry mess of a pool and said, as politely as I could:

"In that case it's best if you pack up your tools and leave. Why not have a beer with us before you go, but at the moment you're wasting energy, cement and time because we'll never accept the pool looking like this."

Sue nodded and headed for the fridge. We felt it wasn't their fault so there was no point in taking it out on them. They downed a beer, packed their bags and left.

Meanwhile, I once again contacted head office, explained what we had done and that the job was totally unacceptable. Greta flannelled miserably – we were getting nowhere. Then I had a bright idea:

"Why don't I take some close up digital photos of the state of the pool? I can then e-mail them direct and you can show your boss on the screen how bad it is."

She accepted this proposal with some relief. It only took a brief time before photos were taken, downloaded, and winging their way through the ether. Now, bearing in mind this was a quarter to 12 and lunch takes place from 12ish to 2ish, we were greatly impressed when at 12.40 the phone went and Greta told us that her boss had seen the pictures of the swimming pool.

"He says up till now he had not appreciated how bad it was, but will drive over to see you tomorrow, assess the problem and discuss how best to resolve it." Perhaps we'd see some action at last.

That afternoon we had a strange visitation. It was ostensibly another representative from the pool people: he was Swiss so conversed with us in French.

"I have been a swimming pool specialist for many years and this is the worst constructed pool I have ever seen," he declared.

"That's what we've been saying."

"As a favour, I consider you need a cold water shower by the pool for your guests. I can install this at a greatly reduced price as a special concession: what colour tiles would you like for the base?"

At this point, even though the temperature was around 26º with a beautiful blue sky, our temperatures had risen to way above 45º. Sue's French became very eloquent as she explained exactly where his showers should be placed. He almost ran for the car. We weren't sure whether he was a salesman from another company who sold swimming pool extras or whether he worked for Agualinda. But it felt good to vent our spleen on someone.

The following day, a mere hour and a half late – he had lost his way – the grand patron arrived from the big head office in his 7 series BMW. He reluctantly shook our hands, examined the pool, shrugged his shoulders, smiled genially, and explained quite carefully without admitting liability:

"I'm sure my people could not possibly be responsible for this job. Nevertheless, we are obviously faced with a predicament. As I see it, we have two options. We can either remove the flagstones around the pool, straighten them up extremely neatly and push them forwards in towards the pool itself so that, looking down from the top, one wouldn't be able to see the wavy sides. This is obviously the quickest, and in my opinion the best option."

"And the other one?"

"Well, yes, there is an alternative but in view of the time it would take and the damage it would cause to the newly laid turf, I don't think you'll want us to do it. In short, that is to remove the existing swimming pool in its entirety and replace it with another one, giving it a concrete surround first before the liner."

Guess what we told him to do. He blanched and gulped. "Are you sure?"

"Quite sure, thanks."

Stammering, he agreed that, starting the following Monday, the A-team – personally supervised by himself – would arrive at 9.00 a.m. promptly, remove the existing pool and replace it with a correctly laid one.

Of course, it was never going to be that easy. Monday

morning came – and went. No sign of any workmen or the Big Boss. Finally at 2.30 two workmen arrived on site, one of them being the original 'balls up' merchant, and, to the great delight and amusement of all the villagers and our builders, proceeded to remove the flagstones. The patron had told us that the work would take five days maximum and that within the week our landscape gardener could restart and finish his project. Three days later the swimming pool still hadn't been completely removed.

I asked the two workmen on site: "How much longer will it take?"

"Oh, at least another week."

"But your boss said five days."

"If that's the case, maybe he should have been here to help."

"You've got a point there."

There was nothing more for us to do but hope the work would be finished sooner rather than later and that this time they'd get it right.

Friday came. At 3.00 we were informed that Agualinda had bad news for us – one of the workmen had called in sick and nobody would be there that day. We had already assumed that by 10.00 a.m.

"You see," explained Sue sardonically, "Yesterday was a bank holiday and today, well it's almost the weekend so that will be lost too." She was right.

Adrio came up during this hiatus and spent over an hour with Ricardo and us, marking the electrical power points in the house. For some reason, they found it extremely funny that we wanted more than two sockets in the kitchen. God only knows what they had in theirs. As it was, every socket we were having was a double and we'd earmarked lots of them. We had to decide the style and type of lighting we required, and confirm that the underfloor heating system had been ordered. Finally, we reiterated we definitely wanted only one diesel boiler for all hot water and central heating. Sue also informed Ricardo that the position where he planned to put the boiler would be immediately underneath our veranda so unless he piped the exhaust fumes and muffled the sound it would be unacceptable.

"Where else can we put it?"

"Round the side," Sue suggested, "with a flue going straight up."

Isn't it strange how things go full circle? Our original design had a fireplace in the lounge on the left hand side but Adrio had assured us it was impractical and out of the question because of the newly redesigned timber roof. Now it seemed Adrio had decided the most practical thing to do was to have a fireplace in the left hand corner of our lounge with a chimney which would not only take the smoke but would also be shared with the diesel boiler flue and the cooker extractor fan from the kitchen. Ain't life quirky?

The following morning we woke very early, roused by some knocking, and there were two electricians at the door. They had come at long last to fit the sweep fans throughout the apartments.

"Okay," Sue said, "great, there they are in that corner. They've been here awaiting your tender loving care and attention for five weeks."

Fortunately she said this in English and the workmen merely looked blank. Shaking their heads in bewilderment, off they went for their tools, returning a few minutes later to unpack one of the fans, the type being the same found in any DIY shop in the UK and around the world with the same fitting instructions. We left them and drove off for one of our labyrinthine negotiations with the bank, returning $3\ ^{1}/_{2}$ hours later expecting to find all six, or certainly some of the fans in place.

Um, not quite! Only one had been installed but they had used the extension pole from the ceiling and had thoughtfully inserted the metal ring screws in full view. Furthermore, although we had specified energy saving light bulbs, the one fitted was 250 watt.

"The glass dome was too shallow to take the energy saving ones," was the rather feeble excuse.

I pointed out another error: "Half the fan blades have

been put light side down and the other half dark side. They're also only about 20cm above our heads – rather dangerous, don't you think?"

So, not a very successful job. However, they said they would remove the pole but they didn't know how to. They packed up their tools, took one of the sweep fans away with them to consult with their boss, explaining they would return the next day and install them all, including this one, correctly.

"I bet those sweep fans remain in their boxes in the kitchen for at least another three weeks," said Sue. She was right again.

We had some good news from Adrio at a meeting with Aldina. He reckoned he would be able to finish our house sufficiently for us to move out of the apartments by the end of April. This would give us six desperately needed weeks to fit the apartments out with beds, wardrobes, chests of drawers, blinds, curtains, cutlery, crockery and all the other thousand and one items which would be required by mid-June. These were still languishing in the departmental store's warehouse waiting for our instructions for delivery.

Not to mention fitting the sweep fans.

After our meeting, we went to the Post Office to buy more stamps for the UK. We knew exactly how much they were – 54 cents each. So, we ordered 30 x 54 cent stamps in perfectly rehearsed Portuguese. But we had not factored in that in Portugal everything, like the motorway tolls, increases in price in January. The stamps now cost 56 cents – so much for our well-prepared Portuguese. Of course they didn't have any 56 cent stamps and sold us 54 cent stamps plus two 1 cent stamps per letter. We have this problem every year in January and it is quite normal to have to continue buying the old rate of stamps plus one, two or three cent extra stamps well into August when they finally start selling one stamp of the correct value.

But we were getting slowly closer to our dream.

Chapter 13

"I bet you," said Sue over the weekend, "the pool workmen don't come on Monday because Thursday happened to be a religious festival." Foolishly, I took her on.

I handed over a crisp yet scarcely imposing €5 note at supper.

"What do you think the excuse will be?"

"Stomach upset, without a doubt. Care for double or quits?"

"No chance." It was just as well.

On Tuesday morning the same two workmen reappeared, one of them rubbing his stomach melodramatically to explain how violently ill he had been for the last three days. His colleague, though, was grinning from ear to ear, which rather gave the game away. However, at least work recommenced, still minus the Big Boss's supervision, of course, and by Thursday evening they had removed all the old concrete base – well, put it by the side of the pool – along with the lining, aluminium sides and uprights. They had also started to lay blocks to form a new outer wall to prevent the sides collapsing.

"Why wasn't this done in the first place?" I asked Sue, exasperated.

"That we will never know," she replied. "But, having experienced the company's ability to charge for extras, it would probably have been one!"

We left them to it and went into Aveiro partly on errands and partly to protect my blood pressure. It merely delayed the inevitable. On our return, we discovered they had re-used the old aluminium side, complete with creases and holes already cut out for the old filters, pumps and lights.

"These obviously won't fit the new ones," I explained, "because we can already see where the skimmers and the connecting pipe work are being placed."

Our man of the violent stomach pains shrugged dismissively.

Sue was firm. "I'm sorry, but this is not acceptable. You must use new aluminium."

A gesture indicated there wasn't one. Work stopped while I phoned their head office again and told Greta about this latest folly. She promised to speak to her boss. Sure enough, three hours later (he must have had a good lunch break), she phoned us back.

"I am happy to tell you a new aluminium side will be provided. Please put on one of our men so I can let him know."

Tummy ache nodded to me as he put down the phone. He had his revenge, however. The following morning, we found they had taken off the old aluminium side, rolled it up and thrown it in the bushes at the bottom of our land, rather than dispose of it properly. We also discovered half way down the mountain they had, like many other Portuguese, taken the easy option of tipping the rubble and waste rock from the pool over the edge. It could be seen and identified for miles around.

Later that day, they returned and completed the task with the new aluminium side. Reinforcements then arrived – we were quite surprised to see the paving around the swimming pool being put on by a different group of workmen prior to the plastic liner being fitted. It was a pleasant surprise: the job looked entirely different to the first cock up and the new team leader, obviously a liner specialist, informed us that a new liner would be put on. Meanwhile, the old one was stretched out on the lawn, dried and taken away.

The next part of the operation went well and remarkably, a good job was now in danger of being completed. The pool was filled and the water allowed to settle before a technician arrived, poured a settling chemical in, cleaned the bottom of the pool and attempted to connect the lights. The length of cable that had been installed was, unfortunately, too short and said he would have to return next day to extend it.

"I might have known it was too good to last," groaned Sue.

He returned a week later and once again cleaned the pool, moved the electrical connection box but still didn't extend the cable.

"We will have to wait for a committee to arrange a proper installation for our lights, I suppose," I said wearily.

"Two months to go – we should just about manage it," she replied with all the cynicism of accumulated knowledge.

The swimming pool itself was now absolutely crystal clear and looked wonderful in the afternoon sun. It was the spring equinox. The temperature outside was a glorious 28º with clear blue skies. We had been working on the land planting vegetables, clearing more brambles and rough vegetation before finally stopping for a spot of late lunch. I decided to have a swim because it looked so inviting. Unfortunately, I forgot that the water hadn't been in 28º quite long enough to warm up so it really did become a very quick dip. Lightning, in fact.

"Aren't you going to christen the pool as well?" Shivering, I upbraided Sue.

"My big toe's having a swim but the rest of me's staying on dry land!"

We had another phone call that evening from Greta asking if everything was okay. It was by now getting dark and, although we did point out that we hadn't checked the electrics for the pump and the pool lights still weren't working, we confirmed that as far as we could see things seemed to be all right.

"Apart from the water being a bit cold, but we can't blame your men for that."

"I'll raise the invoice for the final payment," she added tentatively, "which will include the extra cost for the thicker liner."

I almost choked when I heard this.

"What about the compensation? How's it going to be paid?"

It was her turn for a discreet cough at the other end of the phone. I decided to elaborate for her benefit (and ultimately, that of her boss).

"Are we going to receive an automatic pool cleaner or should we knock the cost of this off our bill?"

"I don't know," she mumbled miserably, "but I'll phone back tomorrow."

She was as good as her word. At 10.00 the next morning, Sue took her call.

"My boss considers the pool being finished is compensation enough."

Sue maintained a stony silence.

"There's another thing…"

"Yes?"

"Did you order two lights for the swimming pool originally, because it has now been fitted with two and only one is included as standard?"

"You're joking," snorted Sue.

"I'm sorry. He asked me to pass this on."

On hearing the news I almost fell about laughing and grabbed the phone from Sue.

"I can't believe this cheapskate attitude from a company like Agualinda. Doesn't your boss understand customer relations?"

"I know what you mean but unfortunately I can only tell you what my boss said. Even if I agree with you, he's still my boss."

I couldn't get riled with Greta. She was doing her best in very trying circumstance.

Sue agreed: "It's his fault, and he doesn't even realise what a gem he has working for him."

Hernani and his team of landscape gardeners came in as

soon as the pool was finished and within three days, they had transformed what resembled a building site into a lush green lawn with camellias, lime, lemon and orange trees. So, whatever issues were outstanding, we were now the proud owners of a wonderful looking pool and surrounds. That was the good bit.

On the other hand, we were still in dispute with Agualinda and, to a lesser extent, Hernani, over several things which had not been completed to our satisfaction. These were mainly mistakes we did not notice at the time because of the lack of daylight. But the worst slight of all was that the pool people had had the gall to insert one of their paving slabs with their own company logo in the most prominent position around the pool. I rang to ask for this to be removed at once.

"I don't know if we can do that now," said our long-suffering Greta.

"Fair enough," I replied, "but if you can't, then tell your boss our fee to advertise his company around our pool will be the exact same sum as our final payment for the pool."

She sighed, but we noticed it didn't take them long to have one of their workmen return, remove the offending tile and replace it with an ordinary one. It was a success of sorts. We knew we would have no further input from Agualinda from now on and that the so-called guarantee would barely be honoured. However, Greta had been so helpful we felt it only right to show her our appreciation even if her boss didn't. We went down to the local florist and organised a bouquet of flowers to be sent direct to her at her office.

After our last trip to the UK, we had brought back our very own Lancashire speciality, Bury black puddings. We had seen similar looking products over here and tried many of them but, good as they undoubtedly were, as far as we were concerned there was nothing to equal the taste or texture. We thought it would be a good idea and a way of breaking the ice, culinary wise, for Augusto and Beatriz to sample these. So, we took them across and described in great detail the two methods normally used to cook them, either sliced and fried or whole and boiled.

With great solemnity, Beatriz and Augusto took the proffered black puddings and promised they would follow our instructions carefully and eat them either that night or the next day. We thought no more about it until we met up with them a few days later.

"Did you enjoy those Bury black puddings?" asked Sue.

Beatriz had the grace to look a little shamefaced.

"We didn't understand the cooking instructions so we gave them to the dogs."

On cue, four dogs bounded in, licking our hands eagerly, with every sign of having enjoyed the feast. We were aghast because we both love black puddings and, with great reluctance, had only brought enough for them, but we forced tolerant smiles.

"Next time, we'll cook them for you," declared Sue.

Amazingly, we now had all the relevant documentation for re-registering our car. The crowning glory was the residencia cards we had finally collected after five wearying trips down to the Loja do Cidadão. At each visit an official repeated the mantra: "It has been sent for signature and will be here in the next day or two."

We returned to the Alfândega with our sheaf of documents where their officers recognised and greeted us, not exactly as long lost friends, but certainly with a slightly warmer welcome than on previous visits. The Customs Officer in charge of our vehicle sifted through the sheets of documents, asked for our passports, which thankfully we had included, even though they had photocopied them on a previous visit. Now, we thought, we were home and dry.

Not so fast. Every page of our passports – including all the blank ones – had to be document photocopied again, and every document re-photocopied and put in a separate file. Now that she had all these various files she gave us the photocopies, signed a new top copy certificate and explained:

"You must return in three days when I will give you back your original documents. Meanwhile, you can still drive your car over here."

"What about us not having our passports or residencias with us?" asked Sue.

"There is no problem because the top copy I have signed is proof of their existence and that the Alfândega is responsible for them." She pointed helpfully to the statement.

Sue turned to me as we walked out of the building. "I feel very naked leaving with just a pile of photocopies."

"What do you mean?"

"I just hope nothing happens in the next few days, that's all."

Fortunately it didn't – but we weren't out of the woods yet.

Judy, Sue's sister, came out to stay with us, our first family visitor from England. In the midst of her holiday, we thought we'd show her some real Portuguese life. We returned with her to the Alfândega at the designated time.

"You'll be amazed. The old Turkish Grand Vizier had nothing on the bureaucracy here," whispered Sue to Judy.

Nobody was in the office, of course, but we soon discovered the reason why. 10.30 was a vitally important time because all the staff had just had their coffee break. We spotted 'our' official and called her over. When she mentioned that we had to have an IPO (MOT) on the car, we produced our UK certificate, which was valid for six months, as proof of its roadworthiness. However, with a mirthless smile, a shrug of the shoulders and a cursory wave of the hand, this was ignored.

"No good. You have to go through a Portuguese inspection. When the car passes, you must return to us with the certificate."

I sighed. "Where do we have to go?"

"There is one nearby." She pointed out of the window to a small group of buildings about a kilometre away in the distance.

We immediately drove along to the testing station, and asked for the required inspection, producing the paperwork we had been given by the Alfândega, and were duly charged €25.50. The car was then driven into the testing station and had a similar test to that in the UK with one or two additions on a rolling road – the test was extremely thorough and the mechanics very efficient. This was by no means to our advantage.

Because we were asking for Portuguese licence plates, all the car's stamped numbers on the chassis and engine had to be seen and certified. But ours was a five year old vehicle and, sure enough, the mechanic could only read seven or eight of the twelve digit engine number because of dirt and oil. So we were refused a certificate until it had been cleaned off properly and he could read the number clearly. The car also failed because the UK lights had not been adjusted for driving on the continent.

The lights I could understand, but the numbers…?

"I thought you'd asked our local garage to adapt them," said Sue.

"Dead right I did," I replied. "Guess where we're heading now."

We stopped in at our local garage on our way home. The proprietor affected to be pleased to see us. Given our outlay so far, he probably was.

"Why didn't you adjust those lights as I asked?" I demanded.

"Because you did not approve the expense in advance. New lights alone are €120 each plus VAT because there are no adjustment screws on the UK light fittings. So you must have new ones."

"Can't you go to a scrap car dealer and get some second hand ones to fit?"

"I suppose so." The proprietor whistled doubtfully through his teeth.

"And at the same time, try and clean up the engine number. We'll need to have it visible soon. It appears that we only have 30 days to complete the work, otherwise, from what we can gather, the whole process has to be re-started."

Leaving Judy relaxing and sunning herself, we returned to the garage to find out if they had been successful in obtaining second hand headlights. Not entirely to our surprise, the price for 'factored' headlights was only €30 more than second hand ones at €80 each. So we went with those and the mechanic assured us that the other requests from the IPO would be fulfilled within a couple of days.

"Clean engine?"

"Sim, senhor."

He nodded, before summoning a mechanic to drive us home.

We collected the car a few days later, managed to read all twelve digits on the engine number, paid the outstanding balance, and returned to the IPO centre in the sure knowledge that everything this time would be all right. With quiet confidence we presented the receptionist with our failed certificate along with the appropriate paperwork and paid the required €7 for the re-test.

Our confidence was misplaced.

You would have thought we had violated the Pope and abused their President. Apparently, we were a piece of paper missing and her demands became more and more agitated with much hand waving, finger pointing, examining the pile of papers and finally an outright refusal:

"We cannot do the inspection without this document."

"But we've given you everything. We don't have any other pieces of paper apart from those in the folder."

It was a mystery. We knew we'd been meticulous in ensuring every relevant piece of paper, past and present, was in that damned folder. One helpful officer, on entering the reception area, listened for a couple of minutes and, with an inspired piece of deduction, telephoned the Alfândega office to enquire about the missing document.

"All is clear. The Alfândega officials have retained the missing piece of paper until you returned for the inspection, but now I have explained they will personally bring it round straight away."

"What did I tell you?" chuckled Sue. I was too relieved to do more than agree.

The sun shone once more, the smiles were back (no apology of course) and we concluded the office work once the piece of paper was brought round. The inspection was completed and with one minor fault, that of the lights still not being adjusted exactly right ("but I suppose it's just okay" grimaced our mechanic), we returned with our 'pass' certificate to the Alfândega. They processed the documentation and gave us another certificate for six weeks, which would allow us to insure the car here on a temporary certificate until we had our Portuguese registration plates. Until the matriculation change, our UK insurance was still valid but was now nearing its renewal date.

Armed with this certificate, we had the bright idea of asking our garage if they could advise us on the best insurance company. Instantly they knew somebody.

"He is local and will do you the best deal in the whole of Portugal," enthused the proprietor.

It appeared that their networking skills would put most proficient businessmen to shame in the UK. We followed him in our car round to the house where this local insurance man operated. I explained what we required.

He was polite but full of regret: "Much as I would love to help you, unfortunately I can't. My company is the best in Portugal, probably the cheapest, but it can do nothing unless you have Portuguese licence plates."

"Back to the drawing board," I said in the car.

"Didn't the Alfândega give us the name of an insurance company?" Sue reminded me.

"Where's it based?"

She shuffled through our mound of papers. "In Lisbon, with no local offices apparently."

"That's that, then."

We took our leave and headed into town in search of the business sector. Finding another insurance company's office, we tried again. The lack of plates was clearly a hurdle. After much discussion between several obviously junior clerks they approached a more senior official who waved us over with a grand gesture and invited us to sit down.

He told us: "There is no problem – I will sort the paperwork out for you here and now."

"Thank you," said Sue. "You'll need this, I expect."

She produced our bulging folder, crammed with our documents. He looked warily at this mountain of paperwork, gingerly poked through it with a pencil, and extracted the IPO certificate, log book and Alfândega certificate.

"You can put the rest back. I'm not interested in wasted paperwork."

It sounded too good to be true – and it was. He immediately proceeded to produce what seemed like seven or eight copies of each document.

"Thank God he's being frugal," chuckled Judy, who was becoming ever more baffled by the never-ending saga.

We finally came to the financial part.

"Your insurance cover will be €200."

"How long is that for?" It sounded suspiciously low.

"It is only valid for the six week period of your stamped Alfândega certificate."

"What?"

He was almost apologetic: "I'm afraid there is nothing else I can do until you return with either the registration number or an updated certificate from the Alfândega."

"And if we don't?"

"If you don't have the registration number by then it will be another €200 for a further six weeks."

I conferred with Sue: "This could go on ad infinitum."

"Let's get out of here."

We went back to the Alfândega and asked if there was any way they could process our metrification sooner and explained the financial implications. There was some sympathy but precious little practical advice.

Luckily, a Portuguese gentleman overheard us.

"There is a good insurance company in Águeda which can help you," he called out, and gave us its name.

"Whereabouts are their offices?"

"I can't recall the address for the moment, even though I'm insured with them." But he did explain what they could do.

It seemed to be a different type of policy and we were now pretty hopeful that within a few more weeks we would have our registration numbers to change on our car. He soon disabused us of this notion, laughed and showed us his Alfândega certificate. It had been updated bi-monthly for 18 months.

"But there is a problem with my car," he admitted.

"Join the club," Sue and I chorused.

Our Alfândega girl hastened to assure us: "Don't worry. Your case is more straightforward than his and it will not be such a long process."

On the way home, we sought out this elusive insurance office. With hindsight, we should have taken the time to look up the address of the company in the telephone directory before setting out on so dubious an adventure. We kerb crawled around Águeda, asking various people who had absolutely no idea either what we were saying or where the company's offices were, until at last we spotted a gang of street gardeners.

"If anybody knows, they should!" said Sue, and asked them.

"Yes, she does," they said, and called over their foreman, a young lady, who gave us very detailed directions. After she had finished and we thought we had understood everything she said, we thanked her and drove off.

"The poor girl's deranged. She hasn't got a clue where the place is."

"How far away did she say it was?" Sue asked.

"About 10km in a little suburb which I've never heard of."

"Oh."

"It's the equivalent of standing in the middle of Westminster and asking someone directions to a very small company in Holborn. It's obvious they would know."

"Anything better to suggest?"

After following her directions we found, greatly to our surprise, the small offices exactly where we had been told.

"I take it all back. I'm eternally sorry for ever doubting her," I confessed.

We enquired about insurance for our car. The receptionist was all smiles.

"Yes, we can insure it straight away."

"What about when the registration plates change to Portuguese?"

"We just amend the records at no extra cost to you."

She quoted us what we considered a very reasonable rate but when she produced the final documentation there was an extra €32 to pay.

"It seems there's already an extra cost."

"Well it does include roadside assistance, household insurance and various other bits and pieces."

"We don't drive our house, you know, so what does that mean?"

"Er, no, I'm aware of that," she said, "but this is in case your home gets broken into, covers structural damage by fire or whatever, it's inclusive."

What a great system! We duly signed on the dotted line, paid the money and were fully insured for another year.

During Judy's all too brief visit, we had taken a few days off and visited some of the beautiful and traditional towns and areas of inland Portugal, such as Viseu and Buçaco. It was great to get the chance to see Viseu properly for the first time. We were able to park quite close to the main shopping district, stroll through the mainly pedestrianised alleyways, keeping a wary eye open for the occasional car or scooter that chugged along them obliviously, and climb through ever narrower passageways up to the cathedral, whose gaunt exterior belied the beauties within.

Buçaco could never be accused of being sombre from the outside. A fantastic former royal hunting lodge in the middle of one of Portugal's most sacred forests, it is now a romantic hotel surrounded by a warren of walkways, lakes and a huge variety of trees, brought back by missionaries from all parts of the world. We saw where the Duke of Wellington had stayed when he plotted the defeat of the French in the battle there during the Peninsular Wars and took many photos against the backdrop of the wedding cake building, before enjoying a picnic and relaxing for an hour or so in the grounds. Then off to visit the nearby prosperous spa town of Luso.

Judy was eager to undertake these trips, and naturally experienced plenty of the local food and hospitality. We were delighted that she enjoyed the area, food and culture as much as we did, because it backed up our hunch. We dined out regularly but inexpensively in the small local restaurants and cafés.

There was one notable exception. Judy had wanted to visit Coimbra, the oldest university city in Europe, similar to Oxford and likewise usually full of tourists. It was just over 40 minutes to the south. We had an easy journey, parked and wandered around the semi-deserted streets, soaking up the atmosphere and gradually working up a thirst. After ambling through a myriad of narrow, cobbled streets winding steeply from the river to the university, passing through a Moorish gateway and climbing more lung-bursting steps, our need for refreshment became imperative. Being out of season and a Sunday, most of the places were closed but we found a small café in the town centre and asked for what we would consider a normal round of drinks – three coffees, one brandy and two ports. These would usually cost us under €5 locally.

When the waiter produced the bill, I got a shock.

"What do you mean? This says €14.75."

"That is the price," confirmed the waiter, yawning.

I argued with him briefly but to no avail.

"Look at the receipt," said Sue. "You can tell we're being overcharged because it clearly shows two ports totalling €6.75."

"You know 6.75 does not divide equally by two," I pointed out.

"Must be a special offer," hazarded the waiter. "Anyway, it's what the boss is charging."

We left with a bitter taste, unhappy that for the first time we had fallen to a tourist rip-off. It was a great shame because it's a beautiful city, unworthy of such rapacity, made even worse because Judy had insisted on paying as her treat to us. This was, though, the only downside in a very pleasant trip and she returned to the UK next day delighted to have seen parts of inland Portugal as well as the Atlantic coastline – in fact, much of the Beiras region. She also had a bit of a hangover because she had been Augusto'd in his wine cellar that evening after returning from our day trip out.

Augusto'd – much the same process as being Natálio'd. Even tougher, if that were possible.

We had ordered new stationery when we were last in the UK and had asked that it be split up and a few letterheads posted to us urgently. On completion of the job, our printer decided to send the whole consignment by courier. But he had not realised that Alombada did not appear on ordinary maps and continues to be an elusive backwater.

He advised us that he had despatched it on an overnight normal delivery so it should be with us by the following Monday or Tuesday. Returning home on the Monday we found nothing: the same non-appearance greeted us over the next few days. Eventually we phoned the printer to say it hadn't arrived.

"You'd better try the local courier office. It might be best to enter the package details on their website because my information is that it has been delivered."

We went on to the tracking site and entered the Airway bill number and found a litany of excuses. Apparently on the Monday it had been delivered – sort of. On the Tuesday, the receiver was not in. On Wednesday, it had been left at Reception and signed for. On Friday, the receiver had moved.

"What a lot of to-ing and fro-ing," sighed Sue. So with this information we contacted the courier's Portuguese Customer Services office in Maia, north of Porto.

"You must have moved. Our representatives have attempted to deliver the package three times."

"Well, I can tell you that no such parcel has arrived. It certainly hasn't been signed for at reception because there is no reception area. This is a private building and, what's more, it's still under construction. Furthermore, we have done some research in Alombada and no courier van has entered our village for some time."

This was true because we had asked our neighbours, Beatriz and Augusto, who knew everyone from God down to the lowliest peasant by name and sight. If they hadn't been seen, they didn't exist.

"Okay," the man from the courier company said reluctantly, "we'll track it down for you and call you straight back."

Five minutes later, the phone rang.

"I am now looking at the tracking – your package is on the van and will be delivered to you today."

But that wasn't the last of it. We spent another fruitless day waiting for the delivery. At 5.45 we phoned again with the same request, and spoke to another Customer Service person, only to be told by her:

"I don't know what my colleague said, I can only apologise, but it will be with you tomorrow."

It was turning into a farce. Nobody from the company was able to say whether they had the parcel or not.

"Can we have a delivery before 10 a.m. tomorrow?"

"Maybe. The delivery department will call you on this number with a delivery time. I apologise once again for the inconvenience to you." And she almost did sound sorry, too.

The next morning, the same ritual and another Customer Service operator advised us that it would be with us before 6 p.m. By now I had reached my breaking point – I believe I started jumping up and down as I harangued the unfortunate woman.

Sue told me afterwards: "You're certainly getting the hang of Portuguese. That was rather painful on the ears."

"What do you mean?"

"Hearing your explanation as to what that poor girl could do with the parcel – and that in your opinion their Customer Service department could close down and take up orienteering or some other such activity which would keep them well away from the general public."

"I suppose I could sense her quivering a little. Still, a man can only take so much."

After my diatribe, I was reassured (Portuguese style) that everything would be done to rectify the problem and that the despatch department would, once again, contact us within the hour. She would personally see to it. Well, we gave them the benefit of the doubt and left it two hours. There had still been no call.

So I phoned again and spoke to yet another Customer Services person. "I'm afraid I can't answer for what a colleague has said but..."

I cut her dead and demanded instant action. "If I have a chance of getting hold of your 'red book' I'll certainly enter a few pages in it. Probably a whole chapter."

All companies who deal with the general public, such as cafés, restaurants, cinemas and theatres, have to keep what was then called 'the red book.' If there was a complaint the customer concerned entered it in this book, a copy was sent to the Camara Municipal, and another given to the complainant, all numbered sequentially. Stern action could be taken by the licensing authorities if any criticism was upheld.

My mention of the book seemed to have magical powers, because within 10 minutes the Despatch Department phoned back to say the driver had our parcel on his van and it would definitely be delivered that day. We waited on tenterhooks for the next call from the driver to tell us when it was going to be delivered.

An hour later, a Customer Service man telephoned.

"I'm afraid our driver cannot find your village. Can you

meet him in Macinhata do Vouga outside the pharmacy at 7.00 p.m.? He's doing a special delivery just for you."
This was a village further down the mountain. Parking in the narrow street by the pharmacy would be awkward. "How about the Post Office?"
"Okay, he'll be able to find that."
"Do you think he'll really make it?" asked Sue.
"It's worse than Wells Fargo getting through the Indians," I responded.

A few minutes after our conversation with the courier service representative, we had another telephone call, this time from Tony and Lydia. They had promised to take us to meet their friendly market gardeners.
"Do you still want to buy some fruit trees?" asked Tony.
"Sure."
"Good. Let's meet up across the river from our house around 5 o'clock."
"How long will it take to drive to the market garden, buy the trees and return?" I explained about our rendezvous with the courier driver.
"Oh yes, that's no problem, it's not too far: you'll be back in plenty of time," he said.

It seemed the day for strange encounters so we agreed, parked on the opposite side of the bridge and waited for his arrival. Tony strode across the wobbling structure with practised ease.
"We'll have to take both cars because I have some extra business afterwards. I don't want to delay you for your meeting." He grinned.

The journey turned out to be a country mile because his 'not too far' took us 35 minutes up narrow mountain passes, driving through a host of tiny villages high above the River Vouga.
"It's the best place to buy your fruit trees because they've been grown in roughly the same soil type and at the same altitude as Alombada," said Tony.

It was an odd experience negotiating as novices to buy fruit trees whilst standing on the top of a mountain with such magnificent views. We were able to sample the fruits on some of the trees so knew we were purchasing sweet oranges and tangerines.

"We've got both our Mums to thank for these," nudged Sue.

"Why?"

"Don't you remember, they both gave us some money last year as Christmas presents and we said we would put it towards some fruit trees when we moved here."

We bowed ceremoniously to the north.

Having walked around a couple of hectares of land and selected some trees, we concluded the deal and, although he didn't have much spare time that weekend, Jaime, the proprietor, promised he would deliver them to us early on Sunday morning. We shook hands with him and Tony, and dashed for our car.

By this time, we only had half an hour to return down the mountain and up the next one to meet the courier. We negotiated the riverside road as quickly as we could, but then were held up by a train on the bridge at Sernada. Just our luck, there are only two a day. We made it to the post office in Macinhata do Vouga with minutes to spare and, shortly afterwards, the courier arrived. With all the drama of the past week, when it came the delivery itself was a bit of an anti-climax. We really did expect another phone call to say the parcel would be with us the next day or some such message.

The driver though was very polite and apologetic: "Please tell me where your village is. Every day I had the parcel aboard I asked for directions in police stations and post offices in the local area including Águeda. Nobody has any idea where Alombada is. That's why you haven't received it earlier."

It was hard to disbelieve him and we gave him a brief explanation for future reference, whereupon he exclaimed:

"I wish I'd known it was the next village on from Chãs – an uncle of mine lives there and I go there quite often."

Bearing in mind our village is less than 4km past Chãs we

found this extraordinary, but were beginning to understand the unadventurous side of the Portuguese psyche. How Vasco da Gama discovered other continents is beyond us.

Business here isn't always as up to date as it could be. A few days ago an elderly gentleman complete with crash helmet, leathers and a pannier arrived in the village on his moped. He was delivering invoices and collecting payment for subscriptions to our local newspaper. We were asked if, in view of Lynne and Jeremy's absence in the UK, we would pay their invoice. Expecting something like five or six euros for the past month or so, we were staggered to discover that nobody had bothered invoicing for about two years, so the outstanding amount was 30 something euros. He looked so forlorn that we paid it.

He thanked us profusely: "It would have been at least another day's outing to find Alombada again." With that, he vanished back down the mountain, a happy man.

We went for a leisurely stroll in the early evening along the village and, passing Lynne and Jeremy's house, Sue noticed a movement in the window of the downstairs flat. On closer inspection, we discovered one of their cats had obviously been locked in during their absence. We had been given a spare key for emergencies and so let ourselves in.

One extremely slender but obviously starved moggie shot out through the door and went instantly in search of his regular food bowl. Even though he had obviously not eaten but found water from somewhere, after a good feed he was once again off on his travels down the mountain, apparently none the worse for wear – a true feral cat.

"Mice beware – he's back on the trail and about to make up for lost time," Sue laughed.

I felt a strange affinity with him after all our difficulties. There were a few rats I'd like to chase myself.

Chapter 14

Beatriz and Augusto had taken on the task of ensuring all our plants, fruit trees and vegetables would be placed where they (and in particular Beatriz) dictated. To combat their good intentions and to preserve our integrity, we had adopted our own cunning strategy by appearing to be stupid and uncomprehending when listening to their advice, a policy which seemed to be working surprisingly well. As a result we could then plant the seedlings, which she brought across to us in abundance, exactly where we wanted them.

It was a risk because the seedlings were not the only help she gave us. As they had owned the land beforehand, they had a battery of practical tips. Fortunately the never-ceasing flow of useful information did not dry up. Beatriz would explain how tall the trees and plants would grow, how to tend them and, when they were ready, how to cook them, besides dispensing other general handy hints.

"Do you think she realises what we're doing?" asked Sue anxiously, as we surreptitiously moved saplings one evening.

"Probably. Her eyesight is as keen as ever."

"She's being ever so kind. I don't want to hurt her feelings."

"I'm sure she'd let us know."

Perhaps, in her own way, she did. Often we would return to the house in the late afternoon to discover that Beatriz had decided to plant a row of dahlias and chrysanthemums in between the lettuces and other vegetables – because it looked as if there was spare soil going to waste. With our modifications to her well-meant help, we were very proud of our efforts and soon had a fine vegetable plot consisting of tomatoes, onions, garlic, potatoes, chilli peppers, lettuces – and, of course, flowers!

"We're attempting to be semi self-sufficient," Sue told Lynne as she showed her and Jeremy around our plot one morning.

"I really don't know why you bother," Lynne replied blithely. "The villagers always bring us more than enough for our needs."

I could hardly believe what I was hearing. A quick glance from Sue let me know I should keep my lip buttoned. "It's not worth an argument," she explained later. "If they don't understand by now that life is a two way street then they never will."

Later that day we drove into Macinhata do Vouga for a medical with our doctor, a mild-mannered local man in his mid-40's. These tests, for our driving licences, were hardly rigorous, consisting of a question and answer form which we filled in, having our blood pressure taken and undergoing a general check up to see if we were alive. He tried to keep the surprise out of his voice when we both passed.

From the surgery, we went hot foot to the Loja do Cidadão with our forms duly completed, clutching our passports, UK driving licences, certification from Junta de Freguesia (to say we lived in the area), numerous photographs and the usual bits and pieces. At the counter one of the officials checked all our paperwork. He was courteous at first but rapidly became unsmiling and perfunctory, shaking his head in despair. Apparently, we had once again committed grave errors.

My form had been completed with blue ink, a heinous crime, and Sue's signature (filled in correctly in black ink) had gone outside the box. He gave us back our forms and scribbled on a piece of paper.

"Go along the corridor to the stationery office," he pointed to his note, "and buy two new forms."

We felt like schoolchildren who had done poor homework as we went back to the office where we had originally purchased the forms. This cost us another handful of cents, which we paid and took the fresh documents back to the official. Under his watchful eye, we filled them in with black ink, keeping our signatures within the boxes, and passed them over. On inspecting them he smiled, relaxed and even enjoyed a joke or two with us before taking yet more photocopies. Returning everything, he told us to go to the next cubicle. This was on the same desktop but separated from his space by a low wooden partition. All we did was take both our chairs and shuffle along the desk to where another administrator sat, examining her nail varnish. She had obviously heard the conversation about our forms.

"It is my job to give you your temporary driving licence certificates and take your money," she informed us briskly.

In fact that last bit appeared to be everybody's job but I let it pass.

"How much do you want?"

"€22, please."

"What? Each? It's far less than that in Britain."

"That is no concern of mine."

"When will you return our UK driving licences?"

"Never. They will be sent back to the UK."

"So can we drive in the UK with Portuguese driving licences?"

"Yes, no problem. As you know, we're now all members of the same European Community and so they are valid wherever you drive."

"Well, why do we have to have Portuguese driving licences if EC member states' driving licences are valid anywhere?"

"Well, this is Portugal, and after six months living here you have to have a Portuguese driving licence."

"So you haven't changed your laws?"

Her blank stare could have frozen most of our fruit trees.

We didn't pursue the matter any further but presumed that there must be some logic somewhere.

Having spent the best part of the morning dealing with officialdom, we went to have a well-earned coffee at the small café inside the Loja do Cidadão. As soon as we ordered them, a laidback guy addressed us in English with a marked twang.

"Say, are you two English tourists?"

"No, we've moved over here. You sound like you're from Down Under."

"I guess you could say I'm half Australian and half Portuguese. I was born here but lived in Australia for 30 years. Where do you guys live?"

"You won't have heard of it. Alombada."

"Jeez, I know that place. Is it a British colony, or what?"

"There's another couple there called Lynne and Jeremy."

"Those are the ones. I helped them out when their car broke down in the multi-storey car park here about four weeks ago."

During the next ten minutes or so, he told us his complete medical history, his father's and mother's, along with that of the rest of his family.

"I reckon you Portuguese talk about your health in the same way that the British talk about the weather," observed Sue.

"I guess you could be right."

"For instance, since we first moved out here so many people have told us that they are 'constipado'."

"Yeah. What's so strange about that?"

"Isn't it a little intimate? I mean, do we really need to know?"

"Depends on what you think it means."

"Er, we translated it as constipation – obviously."

He laughed uproariously. "Hey, it's not only that. Check your dictionary. You'll soon realise 'constipado' means a cold in the nose."

We laughed to think how often we'd misinterpreted the word.

The building work was nearing completion. Adrio asked us to choose the tiles, colours for the interior walls, style of doors and bathroom fittings for our home. This was already an incredibly difficult task, made almost impossible when he phoned us at 10.00 in the morning and informed us he would pick us up half an hour later and suggested we were ready with our ideas.

Given how long we had agonised over the furnishings for the apartments, it was a tall order. Fortunately, we had already decided the basic colour schemes for each room with the help of Brenda, our Feng Shui consultant.

We spent another three and a half hours in the tile warehouse, looking through hundreds of different styles and again ended up punch drunk. Eventually we showed him our proposed choices.

"What do you think, Adrio? Quite traditional and yet fun."

He screwed up his face in concentration, picturing the scene. "Don't have those non-slip tiles on the veranda, Mister Ken," he said.

"Why not?"

"They won't blend in – go for another. The same goes for the balustrades and the main floor area in the lounge."

"What does he know about it?" Sue muttered.

"Well, he has had bit of experience," I calmed her. "Let's give it a try."

Later that evening, we tried out Adrio's revisions. Sue was grudgingly impressed. "On reflection, his ideas are very good," she admitted.

At six o'clock the following morning there was a clattering noise from the house. Poking our heads out of the office window in the apartments, we were relieved to see it was a gang of workmen complete with arc lights, cement mixer, wheelbarrows and tools. We rapidly dashed up to the house to enquire what they were doing today.

"We're putting apples on all the walls and by tomorrow they should be dry enough to smooth them out." Or so we understood.

We smiled in a bewildered fashion, shrugged and trudged through the mud back down to the apartments, leaving them to it. Once there, we rapidly consulted the dictionary to discover that for 'apple' (maçã) read 'plaster' (massa), pronounced almost the same but written differently, similar to our 'bough' and 'bow.' They were easily confused but, like 'constipado,' it just illustrated how much we had to learn, and how situations could become humorously mixed up.

So it was fortunately the plastering team rather than the greengrocers who were on hand. By 10 o'clock they had cleaned off the walls sufficiently to start plastering and, as the day progressed, the house took on a new dimension – it grew in stature (such was the optical illusion) and became our home. The pride these workmen took over making sure our walls were completely smooth had to be seen to be believed.

"Don't you agree there are two types of worker?" I asked Sue over lunch. "Either brilliant or shoddy – with nothing in between. The trick is to hire more of the former, and then everything's hunky dory."

Next morning, during one of the routine site meetings, one of the labourers limped down to the apartments and asked for a bucket of salt water into which he could to put his foot. He clearly had a bad sprain to his ankle.

Whilst Sue went to his aid, I was asking Adrio and Ricardo why we still hadn't received a quotation for the larger boiler, because our present system was not coping with our needs. They, in turn, were adamant that the two small gas boilers in each of the kitchens were sufficient for the showers and that the diesel boiler was solely for the central heating.

The workman with the sprained ankle was very reluctant to sit down in front of his two bosses but Sue was insistent and, to take his mind off the injury, I offered him a beer. This took all the Portuguese by surprise but he accepted it graciously although not without some misgivings because he did not wish to appear to be malingering. Sue then offered beers to Ricardo and Adrio to redress the balance before returning to help me in the task of convincing them that the heating systems and water pressure were inadequate.

All our arguments were meeting a solid brick wall so we organised a demonstration. I went into two of the bathrooms and turned on both showers whilst Sue went into the other apartment and followed suit. Adrio and Ricardo, being Portuguese, still a predominantly male orientated society, dutifully followed me. As luck would have it, the showers I had turned on were working pretty well.

Ricardo looked smugly at the jet of water and said, "No problem."

Sue yelled back from her bathroom in the other apartment: "You say there's no problem? Well, come here."

At her imperious call, they trooped off to see what she was referring to and discovered the merest trickle of water coming out of the shower. What's more, it was cold.

"Ah," said Ricardo, "but what happens if you turn the water off in here?" He proceeded to do so. We followed him to the next bathroom where he did the same, and back into the other apartment until only one shower was left running.

"You see, this is perfectly adequate. Just tell your clients to have showers at different times."

We could only laugh at his solution. It had all the overtones of one of the formidable landladies in the Giles cartoons, telling her 1950s boarding house guests exactly what they could and could not do. This was diametrically opposed to what we had in mind.

At this point even Adrio capitulated and agreed that it was woefully inadequate. Another debate followed, interspersed with various telephone calls to suppliers until finally a compromise was reached. A new and larger diesel boiler would be installed in place of the smaller one, this would cope with the heating, hot water and showers in the apartments, and the two gas boilers would be removed.

"At last, a result." Sue was cock-a-hoop when they had all departed.

"Considering we had this discussion last October and several times since, including a two hour session in Aldina's office in January, it's only taken them six months to come round to our way of thinking."

"In the meantime we have been severely inconvenienced and we're the ones who have to foot the bill for Ricardo's incompetence," she pointed out.

"Obviously we're just stupid amateurs and not engineers to be taken seriously."

The other good thing to come out of the meeting was less immediate. For weeks we had kept samples of our red rust filled water. We had fitted water filters and, on further 'expert' advice, had increased these to five a few weeks earlier to cope with the problem. But they hadn't solved it and we were now having the water analysed. The experts decreed that within days the problem of landslide soil in our bore hole would be resolved permanently.

"I'm looking out over the fields to the East," smiled Sue.

"Yes, I'm waiting for the three wise men to arrive as well."

The weather hadn't been helping. It had been raining heavily for at least three days, interspersed with thunder, lightning, hailstones and gales. Finally, it relented and the sun reappeared.

The workmen were now in our home tiling the bathrooms and floors, the underfloor heating having finally being installed. We were still waiting for doors and windows but because we'd ordered special non-reflective glass to keep it cool in summer and warm in winter, Adrio told us that it was taking a bit longer than anticipated. Naturally.

The new diesel boiler arrived next morning at 7.00 a.m. and was physically carried down the soil driveway to our apartments. We asked Mick and Montmorency why they hadn't let us know beforehand that they would be delivering it so early. Montmorency just shrugged and said:

"We only collected it this morning."

This seemed to suffice for them so that was the end of that conversation. They disconnected the smaller boiler leaving us bereft of any water, hot or cold, and manhandled it out on to the patio area whilst the new one was installed. This took most of the day and at the end of it we had a new hole cut into the wall and a pipe sticking out at right angles across the patio. It was fortunate we were around to notice this.

"We don't want the exhaust fumes coming straight out on to the patio," I insisted.

"Surely the flue should have gone straight up through the ceiling where it would be less smelly and unsightly," Sue reminded them. Whilst we had no water in the apartment we made use of the village fountain and over a cup of coffee she had read most of the 'Installation manual' which Mick and Montmorency had discarded on the floor.

"That's interesting," Sue said.

"What?"

"If a flue comes out at an angle instead of vertical, the boiler will be less efficient in burning the diesel." We showed this section to them.

"It's cheaper to install this way," said Montmorency, "and quicker – no roof slates to remove or lead flashing to worry about."

Sue politely pointed out they could stuff cheaper and quicker and get the job done properly. With much grumbling, they did as instructed. Two hours later they completed the flue installation to our satisfaction, although there was now a large hole in the boiler room wall. They departed, leaving the old boiler awaiting collection.

It was now dark and we both decided, having had a very long and tiring day working on the land whilst they had been installing the boiler, to have a shower. We childishly took great delight in turning on all four showers and the sink taps to test it to destruction. It didn't quite hold pressure for every tap and shower in the apartments (six taps, four showers) but that was the least of our worries.

"It's a great improvement on the old system," shouted Sue from one apartment. "It's unlikely that all showers and taps will be turned on at the same time."

"And it's good to have the radiators on," I shouted back.

"It also doesn't go cold half way through a shower." Well not yet, anyway.

Of course, we still had orange tinted water (an improvement on the dark brown of the previous weekend). This meant we had to pick a good day with clearish water to do a light wash and all our 'whites' were now a sort of dingy grey-brown colour. We were still waiting for Ricardo and Techniposse, the bore hole people, to come and resolve these frustrations.

The telephone rang that evening and a sales person asked if we would like to have broadband internet connection.

I laughed: "Yes, and I would also love to have a helipad installed in the next two days."

The sales girl, a very serious young lady, couldn't understand why we were laughing.

So I explained. "Less than a month ago your people in the Aveiro office said the situation of our house at the top of a mountain was too far away from the exchange for us to have broadband."

"Umm, what's your telephone number?" Even though she had obviously just rung it, I gave her the number, and she checked it out.

"There's no problem at all obtaining broadband on your line."

"Can you guarantee that?"

"Certainly. No connection, no payment."

Less than five minutes later a contract had been agreed, direct payments sorted out and the modem ordered.

A mere three days later, the postman was driving hell for leather up the mountain whilst we were heading down, almost running us off the road at the very sharp bend near the bridge. I saw him squeal to a halt in the mirror and pulled over to see what the problem was, and perhaps give him some trenchant driving advice.

"Are you the people I'm looking for?"

"Could be. Why?"

"I'm delivering a new broadband kit to a couple with an English name and noticed you had a right hand drive car."

He wanted €50 off us for cash on delivery. So there I was in the middle of nowhere writing out a cheque for our broadband router. I fervently hoped that none of the massive logging lorries chugging up and down the mountain would lumber into us as I did so.

When we returned home we set about installing the system. Although allegedly very simple, the technical details were obviously all in Portuguese and caused us great interpretation problems. No amount of translation seemed to get the box working. We tried their technical hotline number and spoke to a very pleasant assistant who went through the process with us again. At the end of this he tested our line and agreed that it wasn't working.

"This very evening I will write a report to the various departments concerned as a matter of urgency."

"What departments are these?"

"PT Telephone Linesmen, Sapo (part of PT but dedicated to broadband), the Head Office and Accounting Department. Unfortunately each of these operates independently."

"Let me guess how much will happen," said Sue. "Nothing." Spot on.

After five days, we called back to say we still hadn't been connected to broadband. Another assistant went through the same process and assured us that he personally would take charge of the matter and request a most immediate investigation into our problem, but if it wasn't rectified within another five days we must call him back… which we did and spoke the same person who said that although reports were sent to the appropriate departments, he could not do anything other than report it. But he would once again notify them of the situation and at the same time request a visit from one of their technicians.

A mere week later, we were hunkered down in conference with the builders, plumbers and electricians, when the technician from Sapo arrived to resolve the problem.

"It's not really the best time," I sighed resignedly.

"Come on," said Sue, "we might never see him again."

Just as well – he had rectified it within about two minutes. It appeared that an extra connector was required which hadn't been in the starter pack. Five weeks of frustration ended in the blink of an eye.

Moreover, we were amazed that, sitting here at the top of a mountain in a reputedly third world country, we could get broadband on a telephone line which was further away from the exchange than our own had been in the UK. And could we get broadband there? Fat chance.

However, when the internet connection goes down, it is nor usually restored for a week or more. Following one such breakdown, I was asked for my opinions over the telephone.

"Good morning Sir, we are conducting a survey into how our company dealt with your problem. On a scale of 0-10 did the system work?"

"About 4."

"What was the main problem with the service?"

"The people within the company were helpful, friendly and courteous. The problem is not the employees, the problem is the system."

"Could you explain?"

"Yes, when a complaint is made to the technical department, the complaint is logged and that is as far as that department can go, apart from checking the line and confirming that we have no internet. They then inform another department and tell them that we have no connection who in turn try to re-connect us internally. If unsuccessful they inform a third department who will then send out an engineer to see if they can rectify the fault. The problem is that at each stage the fault is not being repaired and each department has its own agenda. Because of this, repairs can take longer than necessary."

"I understand what you mean – it does appear a problem with the system. Can I help you with anything else whilst I'm on the telephone?"

"Yes, when our connection went down we were asked the type of modem we were using and we explained we were using a wireless connection. We had replaced the wireless modem with your model because we knew there was no back up for a modem we had bought independently. At this point the technical department informed us that the modem we had purchased from them was no longer supported. Can you tell me what I have to do to get my modem updated by your company?"

"I'm sorry, I cannot answer this question, I will have to report it to another department who deal with this sort of technical enquiry and they in turn will have to speak to the ADSL side of the company to see if they can do anything about it."

I explained that this was precisely the problem with their company. She should have been able to either put me straight through to the appropriate department or give me an answer.

"Thank you for your time. Your comments have been noted."

I wondered.

That evening, there was a huge forest fire on the other side of our mountain, which naturally caused great concern to everyone in the village. I was just fixing drinks when Natálio ran down the drive, gesticulating and urging us to come outside.

From the patio we could see a great pall of black smoke from behind the eucalyptus trees, even though it was several kilometres away. Further in the distance, an echoing column of white smoke towered into the evening sky. Natálio told us how much damage the nearer fire had caused. It had already destroyed about 2,500 hectares of pine and eucalyptus forest including areas owned by both his family and Adrio's, who lived where the fire was at its fiercest. I rang Adrio straightaway to check that he and his family were all right.

"Fortunately our home is not damaged, Mister Ken, but much of the surrounding land has been destroyed. There is also the sad part of forest fires which nobody seems to report, the devastation of the wild life, with squirrels, wild boar and other mammals killed through smoke and fire."

"It's all rather worrying," said Sue when I'd put the phone down. "We must check our building and contents insurance is adequate."

"I didn't realise the speed with which these fires can spread. It's frightening."

Next day we drove out to investigate the damage. It was incredible, terrifying. The fire had swept through the woods, stripping the leaves and the bark from the trees and consuming the oxygen until only black, smoking husks of trees remained on the charred mountainside, which a few short hours previously, had been lush, green forest.

These fires are often the bane of summer in Portugal.

As often happens, Isabela called in one Sunday afternoon: "I'm going to visit the market at Talhadas – would you like to join me?"

This was too good a chance to miss. We climbed into her truck and sped off. On the way, she gave us a guided tour of the area which proved to be as interesting and instructive as anything we had discovered hitherto. She showed us where Natálio had been born, his village and the family land, and where many of the local scandals had taken place. Eventually we arrived at the market.

"There is," she told us, "a market every Sunday at several villages. Each has its own designated Sunday in the month and not even Saints' days or national holidays will stop one occurring. The system works because everybody knows where a market is being held and those who do not have transport stock up locally once a month. It is also a great meeting forum and we can all catch up with the local gossip."

It was humming with activity. This had to be one of the longest markets we'd ever encountered. Starting at the main road it followed the mountain path up for about three quarters of a kilometre, with stalls all the way, until opening on to a large plateau where there were at least another 200-300. It resembled a vast medieval fair, with chickens roasting on the spit, plenty of booths with wine to drink, groups of men and women shooting the breeze and an atmosphere of relaxed conviviality.

"So why doesn't Natálio come as well?" asked Sue.

She laughed: "You see, being a man, he doesn't like going to markets because it costs money. He says he has better things to do with his time, but I'm not worried, it gives me all the fun of the fair and the freedom to buy all the things I like." As she said this, she rummaged through a stall, picked up a blouse and held it against herself. "What about this one?"

Sue agreed it suited her so she bought it. I made a mental note that I would continue to accompany Sue to markets.

The next morning Adrio turned up, his vehicle still dusty with the ash from the fire.

"Shouldn't you be working on your land?" I asked.

"I've done all I can there. Business must carry on."

He never ceased to amaze us with his patience and generosity. On hearing that we wanted to buy two gas barbecues, one for each apartment, he told us to clamber into his truck and he would show us where to buy them. After seeing the recent fires, we had decided to use gas barbecues instead of charcoal to avoid the obvious potential fire risks. Adrio drove for about 20 minutes and stopped outside a hardware shop in the middle of nowhere. It just looked like any other shop, dark and dingy with a low frontage, but, on entering, opened up into a huge Aladdin's cave selling everything from a single nut and bolt to agricultural implements. We bought two barbecues for the apartments – the display model and a flat pack for us to build.

This proved to be tough work.

"Remember the old DIY instructions, poorly translated from Polish or whatever into English which used to say something like 'put bar 1 into bracket 3D7 and turn upside down over Section 19 and tighten'?" I wheezed at Sue.

"I think I can."

"Well, imagine the same instructions in Portuguese."

"Oh, no. It's going to be the broadband saga all over again."

After about two hours of trying to translate whilst simultaneously looking at the diagram and putting one piece by the other, we discarded the instructions and just assembled it piece by piece copying the display model as best we could.

"There are still two nuts, a bar and a couple of washers left over and I have no idea where they go," I sighed as we grilled some chops and sausages that evening.

"So what," said Sue pragmatically. "It works fine and looks good."

Indeed, this had been one of our rare 'Days of Triumph.' On the very same day the deal had come through from Agualinda and we received an automatic swimming pool vacuum cleaner as compensation. Although I must confess that was a bit of a let down in reality, because when it arrived, it was the cheapest version and not the all singing, all dancing one we had been promised.

"Never mind," laughed Sue. "As a goodwill gesture for this disappointing compensation and as a thank you for buying the pool from her in the first place, I was given a water polo game by Catarina, the girl in the shop."

Living as we were in the apartments the outside and 'driveway' from the main road had become increasingly churned up and, without any sign of the rains abating, it became more urgent to pave the patio area and have the driveway 'blocked.' We approached Adrio, and asked him as a priority for a price to undertake the work. This was being treated as another extra and one we hadn't considered, but with hindsight wished we had. He came back with a reasonable price, so we authorised him to go ahead.

Monday morning, two workmen arrived on site, and by the end of Tuesday evening the patio outside the apartments had been laid. For the first time in months we were able to leave our shoes at the door and keep the entrance and the rest of the apartments clean and free from mud. The next morning we threw out all the cardboard off the floor, swept, mopped and felt content with life again wondering when the driveway would be completed to the same standard.

The following Saturday, we were expecting about ten people with earth moving machines, and were surprised when only five guys turned up with granite blocks, sand, hammers and string. We were equally astonished at the manner in which they chipped away at the 10cm square blocks to make them fit.

The system of laying the driveway was as follows: one of the workmen levelled the sand with a rake in advance of the other four who knelt on the ground and, working backwards to a string line, laid the blocks; so for the next few hours all we could hear was the tapping of hammers. The image came to our minds of the seven dwarfs working in the mine and singing to the sound of their work. By the end of the day this gang had completed the task – it had taken less than ten hours to lay a driveway approximately 120m long. We could now drive down to the apartments, park and remain mud-free at last.

That wasn't quite the end of the story: two weeks later there was a torrential downpour which washed away most of the sand from between the blocks and the edges of the driveway started to break up. We asked Adrio what sort of guarantee it had. Precious little, apparently.

"I'm afraid that's the way the driveway was produced, according to the quote. If you had paid an extra €1 per square metre the blocks would have been laid on cement."

"Well, you only gave us one quote so isn't that a little unfair?"

After some discussion he agreed that his workmen would make good our driveway, cement the edges and add a gutter.

Meanwhile the pine trees, which had been planted by a neighbour immediately adjacent to our apartments, were now growing at a great rate of knots. They were to cause us trouble soon enough.

Chapter 15

Returning from Aveiro one day we saw Augusto collapsed in the field with Beatriz fanning him. We immediately stopped the car and ran over to see what assistance we could give. He was clearly in a very poorly state. He was shaking and couldn't catch his breath properly. We explained to Beatriz that he must go immediately to hospital and we would take him there. Her worry over Augusto fought briefly with her fear of institutions and won.

We helped him to his feet and, although it wasn't very far to his house we sat him in the car and drove him round. Once indoors, Beatriz insisted he take off his old working clothes and put on his 'Sunday best.' This really was harking back to the 1920's when the mentality of the patient was that the doctor had to be treated with the utmost respect first and the fact that he, Augusto, was possibly suffering from a minor heart attack or similar condition, made no difference.

By the time he had changed Sue had contacted Isabela and Sandra to alert them that Augusto had been taken ill and we were driving him straight to the hospital.

It was a short journey thankfully with none of those frustrating hold-ups. I dashed in, grabbed a wheelchair from somewhere and sat Augusto in it. After the inevitable form-filling we were immediately summoned through to see the doctor. Sue stayed in the Reception in case Isabela and Sandra turned up and I went through to give Beatriz moral support. Within 15 minutes the doctor had given him tests and admitted him. Meanwhile, Beatriz was told that she should have brought the medicine he was currently taking. In all the confusion and panic poor old Beatriz had forgotten it.

So we returned to the house to collect it, only to be met by a worried Isabela. Probably out of fear, she shouted at her mother:

"Why did you forget to take along his medicine? You know how important it is for their diagnosis."

Beatriz could only sob wordlessly in reply.

"These things happen," said Sue. "It was all rather a rush."

"I'll go back with the medicine," I offered.

"Thank you," said Isabela, calming down, "but Natálio is on his way and we'll be ready to go over there soon. We can take it with us."

We really did fear for Augusto's life over the next week and although we made regular visits to see him there seemed to be little or no improvement. We were at a loss to know what to take him. He wanted for very little and because he had been diagnosed with diabetes and glaucoma along with several other ailments – this was the first time he had been in hospital for over 40 years – all sweets and chocolates were ruled out. There was no space for flowers in the tiny ward he shared with another three patients, but we offered moral support at least and slowly over the next three weeks he recovered sufficiently to come back home. It was certainly great to have him back in the village although it took a while before he was his old self again, teasing us with his characteristic sense of humour. At his age, it had obviously slowed him down.

There was a consequence to him being in hospital for so long. He was obviously unable to wind up the chapel clock so I offered to take over these duties until he was fit again. Beatriz agreed it would be a great help. At the same time I asked the other villagers if I could add a simple timer to the amplifier which would silence the bells from 11.30 at night until 8.00 in the morning.

Natalio said, "As far as I'm concerned you can turn them off completely."

"Noon would be a good time to start work." Beatriz added.

Everybody, it seemed, had his own ideas. A workable compromise was reached and I, as 'unpaid acting keeper of the bells,' now collect the key to the little capela every Sunday morning from Augusto, wind the clock, check that the timer is still set from 9.30 a.m. to 10.30 p.m. (it is affected by the village power cuts) and return the key.

This suited everyone; the villagers could hear it peeling in the fields and our tourists would now have a good night's sleep.

Shortly after Augusto returned from hospital we heard a wailing across the road and hurried outside. We found Beatriz sitting on the top steps of her house entrance crying her eyes out and repeating the name,

"Paulo."

We immediately went to her side, Sue put her arms round her asking what the problem was. Paulo, the apple of the family's eye and life of the village, had been rushed to Aveiro Hospital and then on to Coimbra with a medical condition which none of them understood. His body, it appeared, was shutting down, his kidneys and liver were malfunctioning, he had a high temperature and an extremely swollen face. He was evidently very ill and nobody knew the cause or cure.

The doctors in Coimbra tried him on several different antibiotics and treatments but nothing appeared to be working; they even packed his body in ice to try to bring the fever down, but that didn't do the trick either. After 48 hours he was still in a critical condition. Prayers were offered; it was a very quiet and mournful village. Everybody was dreading the apparent inevitability of the illness. I could almost hear a single bell tolling in my dreams.

But nobody gave up hope, on the fourth day the fever

broke and less than 24 hours later he returned from hospital, weak but able to eat soup and drink water. Everybody breathed a sigh of relief that the crisis was over, smiles were seen once more on faces which had been sad and drawn, especially those of Isabela, Natálio, Beatriz and Sandra. Unfortunately, such hopes were short-lived and at 2.00 the following morning he was taken back to Coimbra hospital – his fever had returned along with all the other symptoms.

The same cold hand took a grip on the village and remained there until Paulo finally turned the corner. Not until he returned once more to Alombada did anybody dare hope he had been saved. We still do not know what his illness was or why any of the treatments worked. Suffice it to say he was young, extremely fit and able to combat the sickness.

"My husband and my grandson have been spared," said Beatriz, "but these things come in threes. What next?"

A week later without warning, Natálio's father was taken into hospital where he quietly passed away the next morning whilst having breakfast.

Whether the hand of fate played a part in exchanging an old person's life for that of the young man, we'll never know; it just seemed so very much of a coincidence. Natálio had barely finished giving thanks for his son's deliverance and now he was mourning his father.

The next day his funeral began in Macida, the small mountain village where he had lived all his life. The open cask was placed in the chapel for his friends and family to pay their respects. With about 100 or so mourners the cortege finally left the village square, the hearse, followed by their cars, vying for pole position in the procession. The journey was about 8km along the mountain roads to the cemetery that had been recently opened in Talhadas. After parking, we followed the hearse on foot up the main high street to the church at the top of the town. Old and young walked behind the coffin in sombre mood.

The church was fully packed, so we 'onlookers' remained outside. Being a bitterly cold day, a group of us went into the café next door for a warming cup of coffee. At the end of the service we again followed the coffin down to the new cemetery (the old cemetery next to the church was full) where they re-opened the cask, laid it on a trestle where another service with last rites for the deceased was held, after which the coffin was closed, carried by Natálio and his brothers to its final resting place and lowered into the ground. We then returned to Alombada with Beatriz, Augusto still not being well enough to attend.

No funeral is ever fun. This was a sad day for our friend and the rest of his family but they are a pragmatic people and work recommenced the next day.

Back into the Portuguese banking system. As I mentioned earlier, it is a combination of 1930's etiquette crossed with modern technology. Strangely, outmoded etiquette was triumphant. Unfortunately, the modern technology was never allowed to succeed because their software programmes had been produced on the back of the old system. People who lived here and had to make transfers from outside the country often fell foul of its labyrinthine workings owing to the amount of time it took for a cheque transfer to find its way into their account. It might arrive at the Portuguese bank's head office (usually in Lisbon) within days, but it would then take three weeks to be cleared and paid into the local account.

This had serious and sometimes (as long as you weren't the person suffering) humorous results. Jeremy told us a salutary tale as he helped himself to another bottle of beer on our patio one evening.

"I was sitting watching television the other day when two electricity board people arrived and explained that payment hadn't been made so they were going to cut us off. I showed them the bills and the receipts to say that the previous two months had been paid, but no amount of proof would change their minds and we were promptly disconnected.

"When Lynne returned, you can imagine she wasn't too pleased. All hell broke loose. Down the mountain we went to their showroom and asked why we had been cut off, showing them the receipts. And do you know what their damn fool of an official said?"

We didn't.

"Ah yes, we know you have paid the last two months' bills, Sir, but we could not collect the direct debit in January, so that bill is still outstanding – weren't you informed by your bank?"

"No, this is the first we have heard of it," I told him, quite truthfully.

"To cut a long story short, three weeks earlier my direct debit which covers all living expenses had been transferred as normal but because of Christmas the banks took an extra two weeks to pay the money from Lisbon into my account, leaving us with insufficient funds. So we paid the outstanding bill, cancelled that month's direct debit and by the time we had returned to the village they had already reconnected us. But things don't always end so smoothly. Be warned, young Kenneth and Susan, of the pitfalls that lie ahead." He gulped hard on his beer, reaching for another.

We considered ourselves duly warned and I realised that this must have been the time that Jeremy had walked down with an extension lead in his hand and plugged it in to our outside electric point. He was wandering off back to his home when I saw him and asked what he was doing.

"Oh, just borrowing some electricity, dear boy. The damn fools have cut me off and I need it for my television."

I couldn't believe what I was hearing. The fridges, freezers and other essentials – maybe, but the television – surely not? It would also have been nice if he'd asked.

Having heard this story from Jeremy, we decided to renew our assault on the bank for plastic. Approaching the chief cashier, I asked:

"Because we now have a cheque book and are creditworthy, can we have a credit card?"

We filled in some application forms which he took away, and a high level conference ensued, lasting almost twenty minutes. Finally, the cashier slunk back towards us.

"Er, no, you don't yet use the account regularly enough for that."

"I know," I grumbled, "we aren't Portuguese, we don't have 62 children, or a pedigree dating back to Henry the Navigator. So it doesn't matter how much money is in our account. They expect us to re-apply a few years after we've died so they can see what the estate was worth."

"Ssshh," Sue calmed me. "The cashier is trying to say something else."

"I must also stress there is another reason you can't have a credit card."

"What's that?"

"Because it is credit – you must demonstrate your financial stability to us first."

I brandished my UK Visa and MasterCard in his face. "Do you know how long it took us to get these?"

"No."

"They came through the post almost as soon as we opened the account, within the week."

The cashier was speechless.

"I suggest you contact your head office and ask them to reconsider. Your information isn't good enough. As you know, statements from the credit card companies itemise all payments. We must have that as soon as possible."

Our needs were pressing. The bookings were starting to come in for our two letting apartments and people were paying us their deposits. At least so they said – we had no way of telling because transactions were never itemised and only included the date and amount. This was where the technology came to a dead end. There was no such thing as a detailed monthly statement. Our dilemma was that all payments were usually for the same amount, so we had no idea who had paid.

After a short confab with Sue, I approached the same cashier with our request. "We must know where this payment has come from."

"Don't worry, we'll phone up Lisbon and enquire for you."

After another ten to fifteen minutes wait, the cashier returned with the desired information. This particular payment had come from a client and had been paid into our bank some four weeks earlier. We hadn't been notified the name of the person by head office in all that time.

"Can we keep the print-out as a reference?"

"No, this is the bank's paper and, I'm sorry, it's confidential."

"Look, this isn't very helpful."

He was very sympathetic, but had no authority to do more.

"I'm afraid you have to wait until head office sends a letter with the relevant information each time a payment is made into your account."

"Is that really all you can do?"

"The only alternative is to keep coming into the bank and making the same request."

I was just about to give it up as a bad job, and Sue was ushering me away when, as an afterthought I turned back and asked him about internet banking.

"Oh yes, of course we have this facility and it is a good system. Very safe." He didn't offer any more information about it.

"Well, can we set up an internet banking account? It'll save your head office a fortune in stamps and avoid us having to come in and check."

Put like that, he had to consider it seriously.

"I suppose so. When do you want to start?"

"Now, please."

"Yes, certainly, I'll set up a contract for you straight away."

"All very easy, now that you've asked for it." Sue whispered to me.

Within minutes we left the bank armed with our secret passwords, the contract number and the firm assurance of the cashier that it was very, very easy to get online:

"All you have to do is enter the number – just the one – which you will find inside the sealed envelope."

We couldn't wait to try out our new-found freedom from the bank so beat a hasty retreat home.

"You must be keen, missing out your usual coffee, brandy and cake!" Sue neglected to mention that she enjoyed these as much as I did.

We set about entering the mysterious world of the Portuguese internet banking system. Like all magic kingdoms, it was hard to penetrate. After following the online instructions to the letter (as far as we could understand the Portuguese), the screen asked us for the security number. Sue tore open the sealed envelope only to discover there were two lines of numbers.

Since the contract number was obvious, we tried the other lines of numbers in every possible combination but to no avail. We had to turn away from the gates of the kingdom, temporarily rebuffed.

The next day we were due to go down to our local computer shop to pay a bill, so we took the banking details and information with us for Carlos.

Incidentally, he was the man we had once asked if all washing machines in Portugal were just cold fill and heated the water separately by electricity. This had baffled us.

He smiled. "No, my mother has a hot and cold fill washing machine."

"Fantastic! Where can we buy one?" Sue enquired. "Because the electricity here is very expensive."

He leaned forward conspiratorially. "We brought it back from America when we returned; we knew they didn't sell them here." So much for that one.

Anyway, Carlos sympathised with our banking predicament and promised to do the best he could. He couldn't get the numbers to work either, even though he was Portuguese and understood internet gobbledegook instructions, but he did discover one interesting piece of information which we had missed.

"It says here 'Select a password number between 10 and 12 digits which you can easily remember'." He raised his eyebrows.

"Sure, I've got trillions on the tip of my tongue," laughed Sue.

At the end of 10 or 15 minutes, Carlos had to admit defeat. He suggested we return to the bank and ask them for a demonstration.

"After all," he observed, "it's their system and they should be able to help."

It was a fair point. However, time was getting on and we had builders to see back in Alombada.

"I'm not sure I feel up to another bank visit just yet," I groaned.

So we returned home without any solution. Later that day, as we sat twiddling our thumbs waiting for the plumbers to arrive, we gritted our teeth, went back on the internet and tried again. Still no luck.

Sue noticed a telephone number for us to try because the 'Help' button just took us round in circles. We called this and pressed a sequence of buttons before being connected to the English speaking automaton. This might have made things superficially easier but we still couldn't get the package to work. Eventually, we decided we had to contact the customer service department.

"Before you can go online and enter your passwords, you first have to activate the telephone banking system."

"How do we do that?"

"You must give me a four digit access code and a different six digit security code."

"Which we must easily be able to remember..."

"Naturally."

Only then, after he had registered us for telephone banking, could we activate our account. At this point we had to give yet another two numbers, a six and an eight digit code, both of which we were supposed to remember. The Portuguese banking system, although laudable, takes security to the 'nth degree but we had finally succeeded in entering the inner sanctum sanctorum.

"Why couldn't we just use the same numbers for both telephone and internet banking?" asked Sue.

"I have absolutely no idea," I replied. "But at least, once entered, the system works wonderfully."

"It will save us hours going down to the bank."

"And it's only taken hours to sort out. We'll soon be even. Though I really can't understand why the cashier didn't tell us we had to register for telephone banking first."

So much for the wonderful world of finance.

Our swimming pool, which had given hours and hours of amusement to all and sundry in the village, including the sheep and dogs, had been operating quite happily when the pump suddenly stopped. There was an ominous grinding sound and a cloud of black smoke rising from the vent hole in the pump house. I hurried across, lifted the lid and saw the control panel had burned out. I quickly isolated this at the fuse box and phoned Agualinda.

"We have a problem."

"I see – someone will be there to deal with it in ten days."

"Not quite good enough, I'm afraid, because by the time your people get round here the pool will be going green with algae."

So, after much haggling, a compromise was reached.

"What did you agree with them?" asked Sue.

"Er, they'll get here when they can!" I confessed. "Best I could do."

Amazingly, we were just returning from one of our usual fruitless trips to the Loja do Cidadão a couple of days later when we saw an Agualinda van parked on our drive and spotted a different electrician dealing with the pump. He fitted a new control panel and told us what he thought the problem was.

"It has obviously been overworked: you should only put it on automatic for a maximum of one hour at a time."

"That's rather bizarre since the pump is designed to run continuously."

"Well, this is what I advise."

"Also, we told one of your colleagues that the panel had a faulty switch."

"What did he say?"

"He suggested we thump it and then it would no longer be a problem."

He smiled thinly. "Have you been doing that?"

"Yes, but we rather expected him to remove the panel and tighten the loose connections behind the box."

"That's what I have done." And off he went; happy in the knowledge that another good day's work had been completed. Or so we thought.

Two weeks later, we decided the evening was so perfect that we would put the pool lights on, only to discover they still didn't work. We reported this the next morning and waited another age for the lights to be reconnected. Eventually I'd had enough and called their offices. By sheer good fortune, I got hold of the head honcho himself.

"Ken from Alombada here. We're still waiting for our lights to be connected to the power," I began.

"Oh yes," he blustered. "Somebody will be with you either today or tomorrow at the latest."

I'd believe it when I saw it. I changed tack.

"Is there a timer switch for the pool lights which would save us going backwards and forwards when we want them on?"

"Yes, we do have such a timer."

"And what price might it be?"

He coughed. "Ahem, it's €200."

I told him very politely where to go and asked: "If we get a local electrician to fit a timer, would it invalidate the guarantee?"

"No, providing he doesn't touch the panel."

"Fantastic," I slammed down the phone and called our own electrician.

"I can't wait to tell our local newspaper about Agualinda, the wonderful swimming pool company," raged Sue. "Isn't it the one advertising 'Satisfaction Guaranteed – No Fuss Warranty – Professional Construction and Customer After-care'?"

Her memory was faultless.

About 6.30 one evening the oldest rust bucket of a van we had ever seen arrived at our house. Two workmen emerged complete with masks, compressor, spray gun and four tins of wood stain. These, they assured us despite our scepticism, would completely cover the whole of our timbered interior roof. By seven they had packed up, having only sprayed about a quarter of it.

"Where are you going?"

"We used the wood stain neat for a better job," explained one. "As a result we didn't quite have enough."

"So I see," I said, looking at the vast unvarnished spaces. "When will you finish it, then?"

"We'll be back tomorrow evening to complete the job, don't worry."

"And my name's Ronnie Ronseal," I muttered, as their van clattered off through the village.

Three weeks later the same rust bucket returned – as it was to do twice more. Their better job was certainly a slower one. The end result though was first class and people came flocking to admire it. Our house was now a bona fide tourist attraction.

"It makes me doubly pleased that we persevered and insisted Adrio removed that old concrete ceiling," murmured Sue.

One of the few luxuries we had allowed ourselves during our building project was dining out at lunch time. This was for two reasons: not only did we get to meet new people and gain some understanding of their culture and food, but we'd worked out it was almost as cheap as buying the produce ourselves and cooking it. Lord knows how they did it, but we reckoned the laws of mass production came into it, seeing how full most of the cafés were at lunch times.

Anyway, we enjoyed trying a variety of meals in different cafés where the food and ambience were always excellent and we soon had a network of eating places, although, on our first visit, there was invariably some difficulty at the end of any meal when we ordered coffee.

The culture of coffee is very different in Portugal to that of the UK – here, coffee is small, black, exceptionally strong and always comes with two packets of sugar (four teaspoons). There is also coffee with milk which comes either in a larger mug or glass with long teaspoon to stir the inevitable sugar, or café carioca which is a small coffee but weaker. We tried the different versions, but found them respectively too strong or too weak.

So we had to fall back on our preference, which it would appear from every café we entered was a complete mystery. This was for an ordinary UK sized coffee cup, consisting of half coffee, half hot water, making it a straightforward medium strength black coffee. Simple? Not so fast. We have variously been given a strong coffee in a small cup with a bottle of cold water, coffee in a small cup with a jug of hot water, coffee in a larger cup topped up with cold tonic water, and every other combination.

There was one café just by the old main road from Porto to Lisbon where we had an especially good meal, with cut after cut of delicious meat arriving on our table. When it came to coffee time, as usual our requests were met with incomprehension.

It was obvious the waitress concerned had absolutely no idea what on earth we were talking about. However, she was not fazed by this and strode back out with glasses, mugs, cups and jugs, all on a tray, pointed to each in turn and asked which we wanted. This was an open invitation for a debate, something the Portuguese rarely, if ever, pass up. All the other diners joined in the discussion and completely confused her and us for well over five minutes, by which time the participants were demanding coffees of their own. We were slipping rapidly down the pecking order. Eventually, one man stood up and, with an authoritative demeanour and a reassuring smile, walked over to the waitress, took her back into the bar area and showed her exactly what we required.

Bringing it to us, she said: "If only you'd asked for this in the first place, I would have done it straight away!" At this the whole café erupted in laughter. We had broken up their working day and given them something to smile and talk about for days to come.

This café became one of our regular haunts. She has never forgotten us and it was great to sit there at the end of the meal and ask for our usual coffee, knowing she'd do it just right.

"She is one of the better waitresses, but everyone's recall of what we like is remarkable," Sue pointed out.

In our experience, owners, waiters and waitresses alike are supremely professional.

We visited Aveiro for what used to be one of our day-long trips to the Loja do Cidadão. These were getting shorter and less involved because we tried to time our visits during the lunch hour when most other people were eating.

We left Alombada about half past eleven, sneaked onto the completely unused section of the old motorway by our special route and raced down towards the coast. As we zipped past Angeja and the road neared Aveiro, the mountains disappeared behind us and we cruised down onto the flattish coastal plain, where a few gentle hills rose like waves among the seaside levels. Another sign that we were closing on Aveiro was the pungent smell of the wood pulping mill at Cacia, which as usual I took as an urgent reminder to wind up the car windows for the next couple of minutes. Arriving at noon, we conducted our business with record speed, chuffed that we were getting to know the ropes.

Because we now had plenty of time to spare, we decided to go into the heart of Aveiro and have a coffee on the high street. It was a gloriously sunny afternoon and the historic part of the city was looking at its very best. Known as the Venice of Portugal, due to the lagoons that surround it and the canals that penetrate it, the houses fronting onto the main canal were gleaming. Aveiro appeared to have undergone a massive spring cleaning operation. In fact it was still going on.

Bearing in mind Aveiro remains one of the principal cities

in Portugal; it amazed us to see the centre and high street blocked to all traffic from 11 a.m. to 3 p.m. on this particular day. This, we discovered, was to allow the bombeiros to prune two offending branches off each of three trees. There was a wonderful carnival atmosphere with people standing outside in the street, sitting al fresco with beers and coffees or hanging out of shop and office windows watching some 20-30 firemen working with great deliberation, backed up by hordes of police.

"It's so much fun here," Sue remarked, as we waited for our coffees. "You'd never find this in England."

"You're right. In the UK the work would be carried out in the small hours of the morning. Of course that gives little or no inconvenience to the general public and trade. Here everybody shares in the experience, no other work is done and, hey presto, the cafés are full. So everybody wins."

"I expect the cafés sponsor the whole operation."

"You may be onto something."

"There are from time to time little frustrations because of the way they do things," she said, "but I don't regret moving over here for a single second."

I nodded, and when the coffees arrived, they were perfect.

Chapter 16

It was time to start drumming up trade. Our advertising for the holiday apartments hadn't started in earnest until April because we weren't confident the house would be finished in time. We also had issues with the water quality and had refused bookings. But with Adrio's blithe assurances ringing in our ears that it was a shoo-in, we finally started to advertise. Immediately we made every mistake in the book. I rang one Sunday paper (which should remain nameless, although it was actually the Sunday Telegraph) about the prospect of an advert.

"You're in luck," chirped the advertising space salesman. "I've got one place left in a definite high profile Portugal supplement in Sunday week's edition, and if you rush me copy and a cheque, I can squeeze you in."

Caught out by the old one place left line! In my defence, Sue and I were keen to make up for lost time, so we reluctantly agreed to pay the extortionate rate for a guaranteed advert in the supplement.

"One of their clients received 63,000 requests from one advert last year, according to their sales rep," I said, income dancing in my head.

"Well, it all depends on the day and we may get absolutely none," Sue warned.

"Fair enough, but let's at least hope for something in between," I conceded.

We picked up the newspaper the following Monday in Aveiro and turned expectantly to the supplement. After scouring it two or three times each, our advert was nowhere to be seen. Eventually we found it. It had been put in the small ads under the general heading 'holidays abroad.'

"What use was it there?" I questioned the rep. "Anyone remotely interested in Portugal would be looking at your supplement. It's not only cost us for the advert but also set us back precious time."

The man from the Telegraph admitted their error. "It's them down in typesetting again, but what can you do? They never listen, and they don't have to carry the can. I'll make it up to you. We can put the advert in again for another week free of charge."

"So everyone can ignore it again," scoffed Sue.

After much discussion, we agreed reluctantly we had nothing further to lose. The salesman also put our details on their holiday internet site which in our experience was a waste of time and predictably proved to be so.

"Why would anyone look on a newspaper internet site for a holiday?" asked Sue.

We also tried advertising in other Sunday papers, such as the Mail on Sunday, and a holiday magazine. Even good old Dalton's Weekly was given an airing. Success was limited. When we came to evaluate our campaign, the sum total of positive response from around £1,500 of advertising was two enquiries, one booking.

I'd had enough. "That was quite a loss. From now on we'll rely only on our own site and other holiday information websites."

"They're far more cost effective, people can book instantly and receive information the same day." Sue had put her finger on it – this was why the holiday advertising business was changing so fast.

However we also had a renewed enquiry from Sergio. Of course, we hadn't seen him in Alombada since his first visit, when the apartments were just brick walls. Nevertheless, we told him to go ahead because of the importance of the Euro

2004. It suited us both, because not only was he happy to have extra accommodation to let but we were more than pleased to have bookings.

"At least he's got us pointed in the right direction," said Sue.

"Right. You could say he kick-started the business."

She groaned at the pun, but she couldn't deny we were now full from 12th June right through till 3rd July.

The dogs in the village certainly had a wonderful life. None of this being kept indoors or tied up on a chain for them. This was in stark contrast to the large number of dogs we saw chained outside houses in the region. Many of them were being kept in unbelievably harsh conditions with little or no shade. Our village dogs, eight or so in total (we're never quite sure as to the exact number because the village seemed to gain one or two and lose some at various times), were no trouble at all to anybody. They just liked to lie down in the middle of the road and make people drive around them, an inconvenience at worst. If we were lucky, they would give us a filthy look and move slothfully out of our way – that was a red letter day.

The strangest habit of these dogs, one that we noted even after construction started on our apartments and home, was they would still, individually or collectively, wander down the driveway, across the patio, over our land and use it as a short cut to the other end of the village. This had obviously been their route for years and no amount of building was going to stop it.

In fact, when our home was still a shell and had no doors, the dogs used to go in the front entrance, down the stairs, out of the back, across the patio area and back onto their trail.

"I firmly believe they would still do that if the doors were left open!" Sue chuckled.

"You're right – and we mustn't encourage them."

The dogs had one routine that marginally interrupted their idyll of indolence. They enjoyed moving from one house to the next as the sun crossed the sky, so they could lie in the shade or the sun depending how they felt. We found an old stone sink and utilised it, refilling it with water every couple of days, and it became a favourite meeting place and watering hole, not just for the dogs, but the cats and the birds as well. This caused occasional squabbles if the predators could ever be bothered.

When we claimed the dogs were no trouble, there was an exception. One of them, which we had named Spotty Dog for obvious reasons, was a rather mischievous but beautiful Dalmatian, still young enough not to understand what he could and could not play with. He seemed to have taken a liking to, of all things, ladies' undergarments. Lynne unguardedly left her washing outside her house one day, and Spotty Dog was seen trotting merrily away with bras and panties dangling from his mouth.

"Without actually chaining him up it would be very difficult to stop him," Sue tried to appease her.

"Well, perhaps they should until he gets to know better."

"It's nothing personal. He also stole Isabela's leather gardening gloves and one of Beatriz's slippers."

We didn't know exactly what his owner said to Spotty Dog but after that episode there was a slight improvement. The outrages became less frequent.

"That should save his owner a small fortune in replacing clothes and toys," said Sue.

"And a few lawsuits," I added.

There was a great deal of second hand advice, full of half truths and misnomers, about the legal system, whether it concerned buying a car, a house, registering land, or whatever. However, one factor was always constant – there was absolutely no way of circumnavigating any of the processes. If a form was demanded in triplicate with photographs, then that is what it had to be. We had had more than our fair share of brushes with Portuguese bureaucracy, and we discovered this all over again when it came to drafting our wills.

Although we had both made wills in the UK, they were apparently invalid in Portugal. We had to make new ones. That much everyone was agreed upon.

Over here you might not like your family and want to leave the home or land to the equivalent of the Battersea Dogs' Home or Porto Football Club, but tough luck. Our children, grandchildren and, it appeared, anybody who had any part of our genes within them, however loosely related, all had a claim on the estate, irrespective of our wishes. It was what happened next that was the cause of debate.

The process on the face of it looked simple but ended up being very complex. In general terms, as far as we could gather, a will had to be drawn up by a solicitor and include all capital, belongings and property, to be assessed for probate purposes at that time. Aldina, delightfully vague about most other things, confirmed this.

"So everything's ready for the system to kick in when one kicks it!" I joked.

Aldina frowned at my levity in the face of mortality.

"That's good in a way," put in Sue hastily. "It saves an awful lot of time waiting for probate when somebody dies because everybody knows what they are getting before you pop your clogs."

"But the downside must be obvious," I said more seriously, glancing at Aldina.

She nodded.

When a senior member of the family dies there might be ten or twenty people who each had a claim on the estate. If the estate was worth, say €100,000, each individual person would only be entitled to €5,000 when the property was sold. However, the parties concerned might be spread all over the globe so nothing would ever be agreed. Equally, none of the parties would have sufficient funds to buy everybody else out, so, over a period of time the property would fall into disrepair, losing its value, until eventually it was abandoned and became only good for land value with planning permission.

"This is such a shame," lamented Aldina. "I've seen the

downfall of many beautiful houses around the area for exactly this reason."

"We've suffered from that inertia ourselves," Sue recalled, although our early attempts at buying the Quinta in Alombada now felt so far away.

Another legal complication within the framework was that on death two thirds of the estate instantly went to the benefactors and only a third to the surviving partner.

"This means that technically, when one of us dies, if there isn't sufficient cash left in the bank to buy the beneficiaries out then they can insist on taking over the house and land and push the surviving partner out," I mentioned to Sue.

"Hopefully we'll go together so we won't have to work out the nightmare scenario afterwards," she replied cheerfully.

Aldina looked as though she'd never quite fathom the English.

Whilst we were out seeking her advice on this cheerful issue, the external doors and windows people arrived, as normal without any prior notice, and proceeded to fit all the doors in the house. By the time we returned, they were in place and work on the windows had started.

"Are you sure this is the special glass?" I examined the panes suspiciously.

"Of course, this is exactly what you ordered."

"But it doesn't look or feel any different to the double glazing down in the apartments. Is this really the special non-reflective glass?"

"Yes it's definitely special," he replied non-commitally.

Because time was at a premium, there was nothing else for us to do but accept it for the moment. It only took two days for them to install everything. No longer open to the elements, our home could now dry out and the second fixings on the interior could commence.

"There's a hell of a lot of work left," I mused.

We got hold of Adrio by phone. "Look," Sue reminded him, "the house must be completed on time because we have tourists arriving in June."

"No problem."

"Well, can you pop over and we can discuss what still has to be done."

He came down, looked around the site, made a rapid list of the work outstanding, smiled and with an open-armed gesture, said: "Now the house has been built, I've got very little left to do. Everything will be completed on schedule."

We weren't convinced. Some of our outstanding queries needed to be addressed.

"Can you clear up this question about the glass in the windows? Is it special?"

He dismissed this: "Oh, no, it's not special glass, that would have taken much longer to deliver, and anyway it's not really worthwhile."

Sue showed him the schedule. "We had requested this after hearing about it from Aldina who has it in her home."

Adrio hastily closed the subject. "Oh all right, I'll get back to you on it."

A couple of days later, he brought Nuno to meet us.

He explained smoothly: "There really isn't any point in paying all that extra cash for the special glass because it only operates for about 5-10% benefit in financial terms. So you see, it's a waste of money. The most effective way of keeping the place cooler would be to keep the shutters closed."

Sue didn't wholly disagree. "I don't suppose Aldina will be too pleased if she realises the amount of extra cash she has paid out for very little return on her glass."

He looked somewhat sheepish.

We knew this was a typical bending of the truth. What had happened was that Adrio had clearly forgotten to give the windows company our instructions and thereafter quietly ignored them.

"And why do we have a green front door when we asked for a white one with a different design?"

"That's all right, we'll change it later on," came his rather subdued reply.

But we had even more pressing concerns. We were being thrown in at the deep end with our first visitors arriving all too soon. In a fit of realism, we knew there was no way the two of us could complete a changeover of up to 12 people in two apartments, cleaning them properly, changing the bedding, providing fresh towels, welcoming packs and all the other preparations in the short time available to us. So we enquired locally if anybody wanted to do four hours cleaning on a Saturday morning. This proved very difficult because life stopped here on the mountain between 12 and 2, apart from relaxing and eating. In desperation, we mentioned our problem to the owner of our local café.

Her answer was manna from heaven. "My sister is a cleaner and works at several large houses locally. If you like, I can arrange for her to meet you at the café tomorrow."

"That would be great."

"Come at lunchtime. You can drive her up to your place, show her the job and see what she thinks."

The next day we met up with her sister, Madeleine, and Sandra, Madeleine's daughter. They were both bright, bubbly and seemed ideal. There was, however, a snag about cleaning on our changeover day.

"Saturday mornings are not a possibility because I work elsewhere," said Madeleine.

"Oh."

"But if you are amenable, we can both come on Saturday afternoons at 2.00, and carry out the four hours together."

"That will halve the time spent doing the job," Sue said.

"Perfect!"

So we took them on. We soon realised we had two wonderful loyal workers with the ability to transform the residue of a week's occupation into an apartment good as new – the final result was remarkable. The fact that they chattered the whole time only spurred them on. Both our guests and ourselves were delighted at their efficiency.

At the same time we were looking at alternatives for the garden, again reluctantly acknowledging we couldn't do it all ourselves. One afternoon we visited a local garden centre where, amongst other things, they built arbours, decking and garden furniture.

"It's not what we want at the moment," Sue explained to the salesman, "but we could do with a good local gardener who could cut the grass for us until we've bought our own lawnmower."

The salesman pursed his lips thoughtfully.

Next evening, we were sitting on the veranda having our supper when we noticed two men wandering around our land. We were getting accustomed to inquisitive locals coming to have a look at our progress and greeted them in our usual friendly fashion. With broad smiles they came up to the veranda and we saw that one of them was the salesman from the garden centre, with another colleague in tow. He introduced his companion.

"This is Alberto. I hope you don't mind us dropping round but he is an expert, and you did mention you needed someone."

Close up, Alberto's winning smile and twinkling eyes, accompanied by an instant appraisal of our gardening requirements, endeared him to us instantly. He rapidly proved himself indispensable.

Not only did he cut the grass for us, but like Beatriz, he told us where we'd gone wrong, put it right and made us feel absolute idiots about all things horticultural. We didn't mind in the slightest. He, along with his wife, Fátima, instantly regarded our land as their own personal garden and he even brought us two banana trees in the back of his open truck.

"Where do you want these put? I have them left over from another job – what about here?"

"Thank you, Alberto. There will do nicely."

It would have been folly to contradict him. So we became the proud owners of two banana trees, and soon our fruit trees and plants were flourishing under his expert guidance.

Because my passport was expiring, we needed a postal order to send off to Porto, along with the forms. The reason I had to have a certified cheque or a postal order was because the mistrusting British government insisted on it.

You cannot send cash, obviously, and they wouldn't accept an ordinary cheque, so the only alternative was a certified cheque or postal order.

Soon after lunch, we entered the local post office in Arrancada and approached Teresa, the postmistress.

"I need a postal order – how do I go about buying one?"

"No problems, all you have to do is answer a few simple questions and provide me with the relevant information."

I fished out my bulging file and answered a fusillade of personal questions.

"I'd hate to hear the complicated version," breathed Sue.

A mere 25 minutes later, she put the finishing stamp on the documents. "Now, if you'll just give me the money and tell me the address where it is going."

"No, thank you, I'd like the individual postal order so I can put it in with my passport and application form. After that, I'll post it off."

"I'm afraid you can't do that. We only send the postal order. What you do with the forms is up to you, but it's our postal order and you cannot send anything else with it."

Once again, the Portuguese system may be extremely efficient but it was blinkered. They certainly did not treat postal orders like cheques.

"So, we've ended up wasting all that half hour," I groused.

"Well, wasted is perhaps too strong a word," said Sue sententiously. "Why not say it's more like we used up half an hour and gained another experience?"

"I'll give you another experience."

"Ooh, goody! Yes please."

We then went down to the bank and soon found out they didn't treat cheques as postal orders either.

"Can I have a certified cheque, please?" I asked the cashier.

"Certainly. That'll be €7!"

" Why?"

"Well, because it is the bank's cheque. We have to charge €7 or 2% of the value of the cheque, whichever is greater."

"Oh, my God." I'd forgotten all this palaver. "Great."

Anyway, armed with the certified cheque, I sent the documents off to the British Consul in Porto and received the new passport within the week. The office staff were really efficient.

Sadly, the UK Government, to save a few shillings, was on the verge of closing what was the oldest Consulate in the world. They moved some of the permanent staff to offices at Symingtons Port Wine Lodge Estate in Vila Nova de Gaia, admittedly with great views, but they downgraded the position to an honorary consul.

"Is there anything else that this damn Government wants to get rid of because it is historical, traditional and British?" I asked Sue.

Chapter 17

Amid all the worries about getting ready for the launch of our business, there was one major problem. Would our house be finished in time? It was vital.

Whatever else happened we had to be out of the apartments and living in our new home by the end of May at the very latest. This would only leave us eleven days to get the apartments emptied, cleaned, furnished and ready for our first paying guests.

Adrio had assured us that there were no problems. Indeed he was so confident that at the beginning of the month he stated that his job would be completed by the end of the second week of May. But, like many other times in Portugal when a seemingly clear statement was made, we were learning to read between the lines.

"Unfortunately, it doesn't appear we're singing from the same song sheet," I observed to Sue as we stared at the chaos of our house.

As a builder, he had indeed finished all his work by the second week of May. However, he had failed to tell us the remaining 'minor' jobs were the responsibility of other people and therefore didn't come under his brief.

"What does he mean by these 'minor' jobs?"

Sue scanned a list. "Building the cesspit, sorting out the electrics and a boiler, just for a start. Oh, yes, and a kitchen."

"I'd call those fairly major, wouldn't you?"

"I would."

So there we were, well into the third week of May, without any of these items. Equally, we had no fitted wardrobes, the granite stairway was still a concrete mass with no handrail, and the interior had still to be painted. This left us with very few days leeway.

"There's only one redeeming factor," mused Sue. "The floor's completely tiled and so the office can be transferred. It's not ideal, but we can work around it."

"Can't do it on our own."

"I know – Adrio," she exclaimed.

It was important to choose the right moment. We put him in a good mood by doling out the Aguardente one evening.

"Adrio, we know you've done all you can…" I wheedled.

"Yeeess," he conceded guardedly.

"But we do need an extra bit of help if we're going to be even nearly ready. There are less than two weeks to go."

Willingly, he agreed to 'lend' us four of his workmen one Saturday morning, along with his truck, to move everything out of the apartments. By now, we had at least got toilets, a cesspit and running water but still no hot (the boiler was not yet commissioned). Whilst shifting the furniture into our home we used the workmen to move stuff from storage.

Although the distance between the apartments and the house was less than 50 metres, the move took the whole day. The office alone, for instance, took three hours of backbreaking toil. The bedroom furnishings took much less time but transferring the remainder took the rest of the day. The trouble was, we didn't really have a clue where to put things. Consequently, boxes, pictures, standard lamps and spare crockery were dumped in the cellar and scattered all around the house as we tried to make sense of it all.

Eventually, the job was completed – of course we had several items of furniture left over.

"Listen, there are some things here which we'll never use," said Sue.

"We can take them away for you free of charge," volunteered the foreman with alacrity.

They vanished rapidly into the gathering dusk.

Sue was philosophical, but realistic. "I bet they'll still be gracing their homes for years to come."

For almost six months we had been relatively comfortable in the apartments. Yet, once again we were living out of boxes in the midst of disarray.

But it was exciting.

We spent our first night in our new home, knowing that all the furniture and fitments we had bought for the apartments back in January were going to be delivered at 9.00 a.m. sharp the next morning.

Among the constant flow of arrivals next day, we had the boiler people and the painters. Next, Adrio turned up so we asked him when we were getting our kitchen.

"Nothing to do with me. That is something you will have to sort out yourselves, it's not on the plans."

"But you gave us a 'key in the door' price and if you look carefully at the plans you will see the kitchen starts at that wall and finishes at that one over there."

Grudgingly, Adrio conceded the point, but emphasised the kitchen would have to be ordered by us as an extra.

"Why didn't you tell us this before, when we kept asking you when it was being installed?"

"It's common practice here; instead of just any old kitchen the client always chooses his own," Adrio shrugged. "I'll ask the carpenters to come and measure up for you. At the same time, they can put in your sink and cooker."

We seemed to be drowning in a whirlpool of people. However, one vital group was missing.

"Where are the furniture delivery men?" asked Sue.

"I'll call the company."

"They'll be with you at any minute," I was told.

Three further, increasingly exasperated phone calls to the company later, the van driver contacted us.

"Er, where exactly is Alombada?"

"Depends where you are."

The driver explained. I covered the mouthpiece as I hissed at Sue.

"God, they're 25 kilometres further away from us than when they started."

Patiently, I directed them back towards our home and told them to phone us again when they reached the bottom of the mountain. When at last they arrived, they did their best to make up for the delay.

What a fantastic trio of lads they were! All young – mid-20's – they couldn't have been more helpful. Not only did they put everything in the right place, they also built the beds for us and plumbed in the washing machines, at the same time advising us not to put the fridge freezers on for a good 24 hours until the gas had settled down.

"If there's a problem when you do put them on, we'll come back and check them out for you."

The only things they hadn't been able to get on board the van were our rather bulky pillows.

"I suppose we did order 24 of them," Sue looked at him plaintively.

The foreman of the gang thought for a moment: "Tell you what, I'll go back to Aveiro, collect them and return in a couple of hours."

"That's fantastic. Thank you."

"In the meantime, if you want, my two lads can put together the four chests of drawers and the bedside tables. After all this is the largest order the company has ever had."

"Really, and to think they were going to charge us delivery."

"But," he warned, "you can't say we've done it."

"Why's that?"

"Because we just deliver and don't install."

"Fair enough. We won't tell."

As we were finding out, the reality of life in Portugal was full of surprises.

With the exception of a really good clean through the apartments, the beds made and general tidying up, that side of our business was now complete. By the Friday night the two of us had cleared, cleaned, dusted and wiped everything that didn't move several times over. Fortunately, the local dogs kept away and Sue kept moving.

"Time to think about the welcome packs for our visitors," said Sue.

"What do we need again?"

"Cheese, salami, pate, bread, olives, milk, fresh fruit, a bottle of white wine in the fridge, and a bottle of red on the table."

"Aren't we also providing some staples?"

"Yup – coffee, tea, sugar, washing up liquid, loo rolls, kitchen rolls and all condiments and sauces."

"Blimey. Now I know how Christ felt feeding the five thousand."

She ignored my sacrilege.

Content that the apartments were looking great, we strolled hand in hand back up the hill to the house – it was not yet a home. The carpenter had been, measured up the kitchen area and taken our instructions for the style of worktop – black granite. He had also taken measurements for the wardrobes, explaining they would take a minimum of two weeks, maybe three. This was not a problem – our lifestyle had been evolving and we tended to go out at lunch time for our main meal. Instead of a kitchen sink, we just put a table by the taps and used a plastic bowl for our washing up.

The village remained a sleepy though quietly industrious backwater and we had made genuine friendships, not only with our immediate neighbours, but also elsewhere. Even now, after our Portuguese lessons were finally sinking in, we still had great difficulty sometimes making ourselves understood because Alombada has its own very distinct accent. When we were out and about we tended to use the local words and dialect, which were not always appreciated or understood by others. This was brought home to us when we accepted a dinner invitation.

One of the local cafés we visited regularly was in Beco, a nearby village. The proprietor and his wife very kindly invited us to their home one evening. We were, however, unsure of what to take with us.

"It would be like 'taking coals to Newcastle' if we took wine to a café owner," I said.

"What about a dessert?" Sue asked, mindful of local customs. We rang up to check.

"Please, nothing is required from you. You are our guests."

We arrived on time – at least 20 minutes early by Portuguese standards – and after a wait of about half an hour we were joined by a further 12 guests. This we discovered was about right for an impromptu gathering, but they had done us – and themselves – a good service by inviting friends of theirs who spoke English. However, we were accorded the courtesy of spending the entire evening talking Portuguese. Although this was tiring for us, it was very gratifying, and there were only a couple of times when we required a translation.

"I think they needed a translation more often," laughed Sue on the way home. "Some words seemed to be a complete mystery to them."

A couple of months later we were sitting in the same café with our guests, an ex-diplomat and his wife, when António, one of the gentlemen from the dinner party who spoke English, arrived in traditional 'scruff order' and joined us for a glass of wine. David was absolutely flabbergasted when he discovered that António was an international economist and had just returned from a month's visit to Angola advising their government on fiscal policies.

"I've been stationed all over the world in some really out-of-the-way places, and this area is as quiet and rural as I've ever seen," he commented later. "I'd never have believed that I'd be sitting in a café 12 million miles from anywhere, having an impromptu and detailed discussion with somebody whom I'd only just met about the life and works of Adam Smith."

We drank a toast to the Scottish eighteenth century founding father of international economics.

If nothing else, it illustrated the diversity and wealth of culture within our community. Not only were our new friends and neighbours generous both in spirit and deed, they also had a wealth of experiences and shared them willingly.

Bureaucracy was never far from intruding. Around this time Jeremy required some documentation for an extension project and had to travel to Águeda to sign a piece of paper and then another in Albergaria-a-Velha. These towns, about 18km apart, had very different views on what forms should leave their offices. Jeremy arrived at Águeda, asked what was required, and was told he had to sign here and there on dotted lines so he promptly did. He was then told he had to go to Albergaria-a-Velha and sign some more. He hot-footed it across there, managed to get in to see the official concerned after a wait of some 45 minutes and was promptly asked for the form.

"What form?"

"The form you need to sign in Águeda first before bringing it over to us here."

"But I've just signed it in Águeda and they never said anything about me bringing it to you. I was under the impression this one was going to be a different piece of paper."

"Oh, no, it refers to the same extension but we deal with a different aspect, so I'm afraid you will have to go back to Águeda, collect the paper and bring it back here for further action."

Jeremy, by now totally frustrated and fed up, returned to Águeda and enquired why he hadn't been given the paper to take with him.

"Ah," said the official, "if I'd given it to you, you wouldn't have had to come back for it!"

Of course some of this may have been due to the fact that Jeremy's Portuguese linguistic skills were limited.

The bank continued to give us wonderful and enlightened times. We enquired again about a credit card, filled out more forms, in triplicate, and waited.

Surprisingly, this time our application was approved. So we eagerly awaited the arrival of the cards, only to discover that our 'credit' was only €250 a month and for this privilege we had to pay an annual fee for each card. We took great delight in returning to the bank and cancelling the cards in front of the chief cashier, who couldn't understand why. Patiently we explained that the credit being offered was inadequate and, in our opinion, an insult.

He mumbled, "You have to start your credit rating somewhere."

This might have been so had we not already applied for and received a Visa card with much higher credit through ACP. It was the principle of the thing. Out of devilment, I produced these ACP Visa cards:

"Why is it we can get cards with decent credit from people we don't bank with?"

"Ah," he reiterated, "it's because it's credit and it's our credit." That old chestnut – there was just no arguing.

Our trials had become a constant source of amusement to our friends and neighbours and others in the area. We had, in their eyes, probably become minor celebrities. We could be sitting in a café some distance away and the proprietor or one of the waitresses would come over and enquire if we were the English from Alombada.

"The new ones," Sue would reply, careful to differentiate us from Lynne and Jeremy.

This fame was not always a good thing. We were asked if we could give an interview to a local newspaper. Being cynical about the accuracy of newspaper articles, we were worried what this might lead to, but felt we couldn't refuse. We did, however, insist on some conditions.

"Yes, but don't mention the apartments or the pool."

The journalist solemnly agreed. The interview for the newspaper was conducted in both Portuguese and French and seemed to pass off uncontroversially. However, we discovered to our horror two weeks later that the newspaper article had been embellished to suit one of our neighbours who had a vested interest in upsetting a local landowner.

The article started with a front page banner headline 'Alombada avoids being Deserted with the Investment of the new English in Holiday Homes.' Beneath that was a full colour picture of the apartments, the lawns and the swimming pool with our new home in the background. The article then went on to explain how a Portuguese landowner who lived in Venezuela was refusing to sell us a pocket sized piece of land so that we could cut down the pines. These had been planted after we had bought our land and would in time grow to block the sunlight from the apartments and swimming pool, threatening our tourist business (he had told us the pines would only grow between 3-5m, neglecting to mention this was per annum).

The journalist concluded the piece by saying that because of our investment the local villagers were totally and utterly impressed with the 'palacial' building which no adjectives could describe in detail, along with various other flattering but unhelpful comments. The most unfortunate part of this eulogy was that our building had 'evolved' during construction and a few minor additions had been made to the plans at our request. However, our obliging Adrio had carried out the alterations as he was building without reference to Leonardo.

This was all news to us. The first we heard about the article was after Adrio had attended a local builders' meeting with the heads of the various departments of the Camara Municipal. At the end, the head of the Licencing Department held up the newspaper and asked:

"Adrio, is this one of yours?"

An uncomfortable silence followed as Adrio read carefully through the piece.

"Er, yes, and very nice it is too, and I must say any alterations were really very minor!"

The head of the Licencing Department did not share this view.

A few days later Leonardo arrived in Alombada with Aldina and Adrio to sort out what had or hadn't happened in the intervening weeks since he had last been on site. He was unimpressed by our reasoning, for example, that the weather had been so atrocious that we had asked for our driveway to be paved urgently. Apparently, this contravened every Highways policy in Portugal. To add to this heinous crime, a small retaining wall had been built that, according to Leonardo, had to be demolished, because it was less than 10m from the centre of the road (even though the offending road was only a bridle path).

"So what must we do?" Sue asked.

Leonardo coughed. "We must submit some revised plans to be approved and the authorities will make a final inspection on your home."

"What's the worst that can happen?" I glanced at our solicitor.

Aldina laughed. "I don't think we need to consider that just yet. You'll probably be fined, possibly have to demolish all the extras, or maybe get a slap over the wrists and told what living in Portugal is really about."

It was becoming more confusing by the day.

Chapter 18

We were starting to get nervous, as the time for receiving our first guests was drawing ever closer. Progress had been made on all fronts – of a sort. Meanwhile, we had one last bureaucratic hoop to jump through.

The re-registration for our car had alternately come on in leaps and bounds and then stagnated. Hardly to our surprise, we were told we had yet more paperwork to furnish before we could have our Portuguese number plates. We hurried down to the Alfândega, and filled in yet more forms.

"Is that everything now?" Sue asked the cheerful official.

"Oh yes," she said brightly. "There's no problem and your registration documents should come through within 20 days or so."

She stamped our temporary papers for a further month.

It wasn't, though, the end of the matter. Two weeks later we received a letter from the Alfândega requesting that we supply a further certificate from the Águeda Finance Department stating that we were not paying and had never paid Portuguese social security.

"For Heaven's sake," Sue uttered despairingly as she passed me the letter.

Later that day, we returned to the Alfândega office: "Why on earth do we need a certificate for re-registering a car here in Portugal stating that we have not been paying social

276

security? We are totally confused how the social security office comes into the equation."

Uncharacteristically Portuguese, nobody in the office seemed to have a clue. The Alfândega official told us with a laugh even she couldn't understand some of the requests: "I've never heard of this one before, but somebody in another office has asked for it and so, unfortunately, I can only advise you to do as they say."

We took the letter to Aldina who was equally bemused. She phoned the Alfândega direct to make sure that there hadn't been some mistake.

"No," she passed on the message to us, "it's another trip to the council offices for you two, I'm afraid."

We were now pretty conversant with the Camara Municipal in Águeda and in fact every other official building locally. I approached a rather bored-looking man on the Information Desk.

"Er, do you have a certificate saying we're not paying social security?"

"Of course," replied the man, as though it were the most natural procedure in the world.

Once again, we handed over all our documents and he photocopied them – possibly in triplicate but we weren't absolutely sure – and returned them to us.

"We'll be able to sort it out within a couple of weeks."

"That means we'll have to pay another visit to the Alfândega," exclaimed Sue.

The man nodded vacantly.

When we finally received the paperwork, we called in to see how long it would be before our Portuguese registration plates came through.

"I will be checking every few days to find out where they are," our friendly Alfândega girl assured us.

"It's a never-ending circuit," Sue said as we chugged homeward.

About this time, we called Nuno and asked him if we could have our front door re-designed so that the top half opened rather like a stable door.

"Our idea is that this would give us a rather good cooling effect with a through-draught in the height of the summer," Sue explained.

She didn't bother to mention that at the same time it would keep the local dogs outside.

He was dumbfounded. "In 30 years of making doors I've never been asked to produce one like this."

"Haven't your customers seen any Westerns?" Sue was equally incredulous.

Nuno considered this for a moment. "We'll have to research it in the factory but now you've mentioned it, it is rather a good idea."

"Also can the plastic catches for the shutters be replaced with metal ones? They're not man enough for the job."

"Okay."

True to his word, a couple of men from his company arrived on site the following day whilst we were down at the apartments, took off our door without any reference to us and put it in the back of their truck. They were just about to drive off when we heard them, hurried up the hill and managed to stop them:

"So where's our temporary replacement door?"

"Oh, we're just taking this one, it'll be back tomorrow or the day after!"

"Look, this is our front door and we need something to replace it with. If you do that, you can take the other door for a week if necessary. But whatever you do, we can't be without one."

This confused them. "We've never been asked to put a temporary door in – people normally just accept it."

"Maybe they do. There is a difference, though," Sue explained, "those people probably weren't living in the premises at the time."

The chatty one scratched his head and nodded.

So, they got out of the truck, replaced the door and went off muttering they would come back another time. A week later, we were down on the bottom field, when the same van pulled up with the same two workmen. We dashed up rapidly to see what was happening. They had once again removed the door and were attacking it with circular saws and drills.

"Have you seen what they're doing?" Sue exclaimed. "They're cutting it in two on our dining room table!"

"At least they took the tablecloth off first and put some paper down!"

We gritted our teeth, and waited for the sound of our table collapsing. It never came. In less than four hours they had completed the job and it looked exactly as we had in mind. The downside was that they were still trying to source suitable metal catches, which slightly spoiled the effect.

"Whoever heard of stable doors with plastic catches?" Sue asked, not unreasonably.

Our local dogs hadn't, for sure, and regarded them with disdain.

Over winter we had noted with a twinge of sadness that although the skies were clear and there was plenty of forestry around us, there was not much sight or sound from the wild life and birds. It was about the only feature lacking in our surroundings. After spring arrived, things changed – we sat on our patio and watched with interest how many birds there were around us.

Birdsong accompanied their return. When we listened closely, we could hear the dawn chorus and its counterpart at night. Alombada was now home to an amazing range of birds from the green and spotted woodpecker, robins, blackbirds, sparrows, finches – some we recognised and others we didn't – through to vast swoops of swallows diving for insects all around our home and pool in the evenings. Locally, the storks made their homes at the top of electricity pylons where the electrical company, EDP, had thoughtfully provided circular metal platforms to assist their nesting. We had also seen many eagles and hawks on our travels round the area.

There was even a hoopoe quite happily walking around the swimming pool one morning, digging in the lawn wheedling out insects with its long pointed bill. Having a striking white and black tipped crest, pinkish coloured plumage and black and white barred back, the hoopoe, competing with the very proud cockerel from the neighbouring hen house, took to waking us up daily.

"It is a misnomer that cockerels only crow first thing in the morning," groaned Sue. "That particular one appears to crow incessantly. Does it never shut up?"

The answer was no, although I was secretly thinking how lucky he was, if crowing meant what I thought it meant!

One afternoon I saw Beatriz shuffling down the street and thought I'd get the benefit of her wisdom. "Why are we only just starting to hear the birds sing?" I asked.

"Maybe they were getting to know you properly first," was her enigmatic reply.

Unusually for a rural community, education about the local fauna and flora did not include any useful knowledge about the different species of snake – such as which ones were poisonous. There is, as in England, only one we needed to be wary about, the common viper. One of these had bitten Augusto some 45 years previously which partially excused his own phobia and that of Beatriz. To the Portuguese every snake presented a problem and had to be killed. In our limited experience, unless someone actually trod on one (highly unlikely as the snakes were none too keen) there was more chance of being run over by a tractor than seeing a snake, let alone being bitten by one.

Even more than the local populace, the builders were all absolutely terrified of anything moving in the grass. One morning after breakfast, we were given a battered and deceased snake by a workman with almost child-like pride. We looked at the sad corpse and asked him why he had killed it.

He shuddered: "It was either him or me."

The snake in question was a ladder snake, about 60cm long. Like other grass snakes and lizards, it was a gardener's friend and devoured insects and small mammals. The ladder snake's fangs were at the back of its mouth, which was so small it made it virtually impossible to bite and injure a human being. We were furious it had been killed and told all the workmen that in future, rather than killing any snakes or other wildlife on our land, we would prefer it if they ignored them and we were sure the wildlife would do likewise. This was met with silence but we were pleased to notice they respected our wishes.

Meanwhile, the problems over our water supply were becoming acute. Our protestations about the quality of the water from the bore hole eventually got through.

Ricardo had sagely announced: "I know what the problem is – the stop cock to the new tank is turning the pump on and off too quickly. It's stirring up all the sediment at the bottom of the bore hole and causing the water to become tainted."

He neglected to mention he had installed two 500 litre tanks earlier that month, saying it was definitely going to cure the problem.

"What do you recommend?"

"Fit an electric stop cock which will be much smoother."

What with two 500 litre water tanks, as well as all these electric pumps, pressure vessels and filters, our cellar was beginning to look more like an industrial bottling plant.

People from Techniposse, the company who had originally drilled our bore hole, turned up a couple of days later with a huge lorry complete with compressor, hoses and goodness knows what else on the back of it. They proceeded to disconnect the pipes and tubes from the top of the bore hole and dismantle the seal, then removed the 175 metres of piping, hose, electrical cable and the end pump.

Their specialist decided one of the biggest problems was the pressure of the pump at the end of the tube that had been fed into the bore hole.

"It needs a smaller pump fitted so the water doesn't rush back up the tube and we must raise it by ten metres from the bottom."

He poked another tube back down and turned on the

mighty compressor. This created what can only be described as a mini Vesuvius with muddy brown, contaminated water shooting 15m up into the air. It was unfit even for irrigation without some filtration and quite disgusting.

This was not the opinion of the assembled onlookers, who 'oohed' and 'aahed' appreciatively. By now a sizeable crowd had gathered – not only the cats, dogs and people of the village, but from others all around. Sue and I looked at each other in askance as we noticed our plumber loitering behind a tree, and of course our workmen downed tools and enjoyed the sideshow.

Thirty minutes after forcing air down into the bore hole, these so-called experts considered the job done. They replaced everything and the specialist declared:

"You need a sand filter. This will filter all the rubbish completely and leave you with pure clean water."

Two days later they turned up with a cylinder about 2m high resembling a scud missile. This necessitated our builders digging a hole in the cellar so it could stand upright. We were losing more and more confidence in Techniposse and the system.

"It all seems to be second hand material," said Sue.

"Not only that, it's old technology," I agreed.

However, we decided we ought to give it a try and allow them to complete their modifications. Because we had ourselves expressed doubts about the water ever being clean without a filter, we didn't at that time have any real fears about the sand filter not working.

In any case there was no alternative as we didn't have much time to spare before our first visitors arrived. We had already had some guests staying with us who loved the apartments and the area, but had also had to endure the changeable quality of our water. As such we were still using the village fountain for drinking water.

Two days later we noticed that the tap water was once again going brown. In frustration I rang Techniposse.

"You know that sand filter?"

"Yes, we want €1,000 for installing that."

"Forget it. Just give us a new bore hole which, under the guarantee, we're entitled to. We've had to endure this filthy water for over six months now. Get it sorted quickly."

There was a large intake of breath at the other end of the phone. We now only had ten days before our first guests arrived.

To make matters worse, our swimming pool, which had been crystal clear, had now started to turn green, then brown and finally jet black with froth over the entire surface. Sue phoned up Techniposse and demanded that something was done immediately.

"We'll see what we can do."

It wasn't the reassurance we craved. We watched as our dreams of a successful holiday business faded into the mire of a black swimming pool.

Nothing happened for two days and we were getting desperate when one evening, out of the blue, we received a phone call from a water treatment company in Aveiro who said they had been approached by Techniposse to resolve our problems at Casa Sulo by any means. They explained over the phone that because they had a wealth of experience in the area, they felt confident that they could purify our water and made an appointment to visit us the next day. We readily agreed and waited expectantly for their arrival.

The owner of Limpagua, the water company, and his brother in law – who spoke excellent English and was there to act as interpreter for the technical content – duly arrived, looked at the installation, water and all other aspects, then approached the problem in a professional manner. They revived our dwindling confidence.

"I can resolve your water situation but it won't be cheap. You'll have to pay us for our work and then reclaim it from Techniposse. Oh, and I can't start work for two to three weeks because of commitments to other projects."

"That's fine, except for not being able to start for two weeks." We explained the situation about our tourists and the business.

He promptly made several phone calls, the first one to his

technician at home and asked if he could start work the following week.

The solution was three new filters and a drip feed chlorine tank (he wouldn't work with any of the existing installation). Apart from anything else the sand filter Techniposse had put in had been sold to them by Limpagua five years earlier and had been used in a kindergarten until recently.

To add insult to injury a new sand filter was going to cost us a mere €25 more than we had been quoted for the second hand one. They finally agreed that work could start the following Tuesday and everything would be completed by Thursday, just two days before our guests arrived. Meantime, we were asked to empty the swimming pool prior to their arrival.

That Tuesday, a clean white van arrived. On first inspection, it looked too small and we didn't think they had all the equipment with them. However, when we looked inside it was rather like the Tardis – there were tubes, copper pipes, motors, three huge filters, tools and everything necessary to complete the job. The technician and his assistant were extremely efficient, working diligently and by Thursday evening the new system was commissioned.

"Fill the swimming pool up and we'll return with the necessary chemicals to keep it healthy."

On Friday afternoon the technicians from Limpagua arrived complete with an array of different pool chemicals, chlorine blocks, flocculent and anti algae which they added to our pool. "This is a 'shock' treatment for the water so it will be crystal clear for your guests tomorrow."

"Thank God, the job's been completed on time," Sue sighed that evening.

"Have you tried the water? It tastes sweet and looks absolutely fantastic."

Some shock treatment. On Saturday morning, we woke up early, walked out on to the veranda and gazed with horror at a green swimming pool. A few hours later, it was going brown. I finally got hold of the owner of Limpagua on his mobile and told him to come over immediately.

"We'll get to you as soon as possible, probably on Monday, but not to worry – at least it's not like last time when the pool went black."

By 3.00 the pool had gone black. Our guests were due in less than an hour.

Our first nine guests arrived in absolutely perfect weather, the apartments spotless and shining.

"One question though. Is it usual to have a black pool?"

"No," Sue replied, "the problem's just arisen this morning."

"It's something to do with a reaction between the pool chemicals and the water," I added.

"Oh." They put away their towels.

I explained to Sue that I had discovered what was happening with the water.

"When it is under ground without any air, it remains crystal clear, but when it's pumped to the surface and mixes with the oxygen, within hours the iron in the water erodes and rusts, rather like an old nail in a puddle."

"At least we can tell people that it is perfectly safe."

But that was exactly what was happening and Techniposse, although they had drilled numerous bore holes in the region, had failed to diagnose the problem. Instead of drilling a new one, they had passed the buck on to somebody else.

On the Monday, the manager from Limpagua arrived, took more samples and concluded that the problem with the swimming pool was we had added far too much chlorine and this had caused the reaction.

We both looked at each other, knowing full well that it wasn't us. It wasn't worth the discussion. The manager pledged: "I'll get the local Camara Municipal to deliver fresh, clean water to your pool via the bombeiros."

I remembered the streets being closed in Aveiro as the firemen attacked the trees. "Are you sure they won't have any branches to cut down?"

He looked blank. "I'll pay for this myself and then invoice you – but only at cost."

I thanked him for this, tongue in cheek, considering it was his people who had messed up. Unfortunately the irony was lost on him.

He accepted my thanks graciously: "Don't mention it, any time."

The swimming pool was once more drained and cleaned out by us (the last 10cms. of water take an awful lot of sweeping down a plughole). Anyway, after about three hours' hard work in the hot midday sun, watched by our appreciative and amused guests on their patios drinking the obligatory pre-lunch gin and tonics, we had it emptied to await the arrival of the bombeiros.

Half an hour later an agent from Agualinda, the original botchers, arrived to see what he could do about cleaning the pool and analysing the water. This was becoming a farce.

Sue pounced on their ill-fated representative. "Didn't we phone you more than two weeks ago to ask you to come out urgently and give us some advice on the water in the pool?"

"Er, I don't know. I'd better check with head office."

So his visit was, like everything else they had done since installing the swimming pool, a complete and utter waste of time. It didn't stop him from presenting us with an invoice for €47 for a one hour call out to clean an empty pool.

I tore it up. "We're still waiting for you to install the second electrical panel and timer for the lights. You promised to come out in April and it's now June."

The guests had been most understanding about everything and agreed we had done all in our power to make their stay as welcome as possible. They went off to their football matches and on their return were having a few glasses of wine on the patio at 10.30 at night when a huge tanker rolled into the village. It was the bombeiros, with the first load of municipal water from Águeda.

"Why are you coming at this time of night?" Sue asked the chief fireman.

"Umm, we're all part timers and this particular crew has

just finished a shift fighting a forest fire. Turns out a crew member's the only person in the Águeda fire service who knows where Alombada is."

We recognised him instantly as Luis, who had installed our satellite dish. Soon enough we had our first tanker load of water in the pool and it was a beautiful sight.

Over the next day we had three more deliveries, filling the pool. It was a wonderful moment that afternoon when our visitors jumped in and christened it with an hour long game of water polo.

This was the end of all our pool problems – or so we thought. A couple of months later we thought it would be a good idea for Limpagua to do an analysis check on the water. The technician announced that it was almost perfect but would require a small amount of chemical to raise the pH level to perfection. He added about 200gms of powder to the pool and was flabbergasted that within 10 seconds the whole pool had turned brown, and five minutes later black. His face was a picture of dismay.

"What happened?" he moaned. "I have never, ever witnessed such a transformation in all my life." It was clear he had absolutely no idea what to do next.

We were getting used to it. There was no doubt in our minds that we had to pump out the pool again. After discussions with Limpagua, we decided it was best to change the pool from a chemical to a salt-water system. This would also make swimming healthier for our visitors by eliminating all chemicals other than salt, be less work and less expensive in the long run.

Of course it cost us an extra chunk of money to convert but we were pleased we did it. There was no adverse reaction other than, when we added fresh water, the pool still turned a delicate shade of green, then olive green, light green and back to crystal clear over a period of 24 hours. It was a phenomenon we had to live with.

"I must say, when we don't have visitors I find it quite endearing!" said Sue. It is, in its way, our own bit of magic.

Chapter 19

We decided to hold our house warming party on the first available weekend in July, inviting our neighbours and friends to come along and celebrate with us in the early afternoon.

Oh, how naive we were!

They say ignorance is bliss. Nobody intimated what might happen. We estimated that, if we were fortunate, between 25-30 people might turn up. So, on the day we borrowed trestle tables from Natálio and Isabela, along with extra crockery, glasses and jugs. By one o'clock we still didn't have a clue how many people were going to turn up.

"It's a bit hot," Sue said, "we'll probably only get 15 or so."

"What'll we do with all this food?" I asked.

We had organised a roast suckling pig, which Isabela showed us how to cut properly, barbecued 15 chickens, poached a whole salmon and prepared a large vat of chilli con carne, along with enough rice, salads and cheeses to feed a small army, plus a few desserts – we obviously didn't worry too much about these, knowing they would be forthcoming. We also provided enormous quantities of wine and beers – oh yes, and some soft drinks and water for those who didn't imbibe.

There should have been no worries about a surplus – but we'd forgotten that the Portuguese don't do small…

By 1.15 more than 40 people had arrived, milled around and sat down, knives and forks in hands, waiting to be fed! Fifteen minutes later we had 55 and were beginning to panic that we were in serious danger of the food running out. Although dashing backwards and forwards serving everybody without a breather, the two of us still couldn't keep up with the demand, as our guests thoroughly enjoyed themselves.

"Calm down," called out Beatriz, "sit here with me and eat something."

"No chance" we chorused.

Not until everybody had eaten their fill did we sit down with them and have a bite to eat ourselves. On the plus side, there were plenty of puddings.

Whilst we were munching on the last of the suckling pig, Sue and I took in the scene. Just about everyone we'd met in Portugal was there and it presented us with a microcosm of our new life.

There were Lynne and Jeremy, who had been our first contacts in Alombada. If we hadn't booked our first holiday together with them, we wouldn't have moved to the village. Carlos from the computer shop was explaining some new product to them but it was well over Lynne's head and although Jeremy was nodding agreeably, he had a glazed expression that showed he'd been enjoying himself considerably.

On a bench sat Beatriz and Augusto, chattering earnestly, probably about how much the bash had cost us. Along with Natálio, they had sold us the land, making our dream a reality. Augusto was still not totally recovered from his illness but this showed us he was on the mend.

Nearby were Natálio and Isabela, chasing away some of the village dogs, who'd rolled up to see if chicken was on the menu. We would always be eternally grateful to Natálio, Isabela and family for their selfless help and patience at all times as well as their willingness to share their knowledge and time with us. Natálio turned, saw us, raised his glass and smiled broadly.

"Do you remember a conversation we had all those years ago?" he said.

"There've been so many, Natálio."

"No, but this was very specific, relating to us selling you the plot of land."

I did, as a matter of fact. So did Sue.

"What do you want to do with the land?" Natálio had asked us.

"We want to build on it," I'd said.

"Okay. What do you want to build?"

"We're going to build a house."

He thought for a moment. "What type of house, a holiday home or what?"

"A home, to live in," replied Sue.

"Do you mean a permanent residence?"

"Yes, is there another kind?"

"In that case I will sell you the land at an agricultural price – we want Alombada to grow." He had spread his arms and then clapped his massive hands together. "It is no good for the village to have only weekenders here."

"We always remember that," said Sue. "It was helpful to us in so many ways."

"And you told me that you wanted to build two holiday apartments," Natálio went on.

"That's right," I recalled.

"You had a vision." He paused to sweep his eyes over our property. "Both Isabela and I are very pleased that you've pursued it and achieved what you set out to do. Not only us – but all the family."

Sandra was sitting nearby with her boyfriend, who was home for the weekend from his military service. They were deep in conversation – we suspected that they had plans for when he returned to his permanent job – but she looked up and smiled amiably.

Paulo sauntered over from the drinks table, arm around his girlfriend. His complexion was rapidly returning to its former olive glow from its near deathly pallor.

"Can I take your strimmer out? I've seen a few brambles."

I fell for it, hook, line and sinker. "I don't think so." My mind was on the near disasters he had caused.

"Only joking," he laughed and wandered off. He had inherited his sense of humour from his mother and grandfather. Isabela winked at us, pleased, as we all were, to see her son better.

Further down the room Adrio was standing with his feet apart and surveying the buildings with a proprietorial air. Earlier, on his arrival, he had asked if he could quietly 'walk the house' on his own and, on returning to the party, had thanked us for insisting on sticking to our plans for the interior and – to him – our outlandish colour scheme. It had all worked and he was proud to call it one of his builds.

"Do you think, Mister Ken," he murmured, "that it might be all right to bring future clients here to show them what I can do?"

"I'm sure it will," I said, "but I'll have to check that it's okay with Sue."

Sue smiled. "Just give us some notice so that I'm not in the shower."

"And don't turn up too early. We've never known anyone so punctual," I added.

It was his turn to smile. He knew about my morbid fears of lateness.

Aldina and her husband were unwinding from a hard week. She was looking beautiful in a white summer dress, laughing in her delightfully scatty manner. They were talking to Rui and Cláudia, who seemed to take almost as much pride as we did in the transformation of the land.

Elena and João wandered past. We had seldom seen her so animated.

"Now if you'd taken the trouble to build me a house like this, I might think differently about Alombada," she said. This was praise indeed from such a confirmed townswoman.

"Humph," he replied.

"Instead, you spend all your time with your animals."

"Yes."

"I sometimes suspect you prefer it that way."

He neither confirmed nor denied this.

Thinking himself unobserved, Leonardo had removed a tape measure from his pocket and was surreptitiously recording the height of the wall at the side of our little road.

A group of café owners had huddled together and were comparing notes on business whilst they knocked back a few glasses of wine before hurrying back to work. It was strange to see them outside their natural habitats, almost as odd as if one of João's sheep was lurching through the party.

Hang on, that was one of João's sheep lurching through the party...

Madeleine and Sandra were jabbering away excitedly, for all the world as if they hadn't met for a month or more. For once without their overalls, they appeared even more relaxed and animated than usual, a feat that I'd have declared impossible, had I not seen it with my own eyes.

Alberto, chicken leg in hand, was making some infinitesimal (but in his view necessary) adjustments to the layout of the garden by the swimming pool, while Fatima and Vitória, his young daughter, looked on. Was he aware that Beatriz was watching him as he did so? Or was it her twin sister?

Tony was checking how some of the fruit trees he had helped us buy were growing, pleased that his advice about the market garden had been so propitious, and Lydia, one of the most outstanding cooks we knew, was going round to everybody exalting the virtues of our chilli con carne.

Ricardo, however, was nowhere to be seen. He'd either refused or couldn't be bothered (we weren't sure which) to sign off the electrical wiring and plumbing; this had resulted in Adrio having to find another electrician in a hurry to approve the work.

"I feel as though Ricardo's the ghost at the feast," I said to Sue.

"That's true. We've had our differences with him, but we still like him."

The swimming pool water glittered in the sun, innocently unaware of the battles fought in its name.

It was just too inviting, and one of our visitors dived in and broke his nose on the bottom – drunk as a skunk, he had blood everywhere, with his wife and mother both putting wet towels over his nose to soak up the blood and stop the swelling.

His wife was furious with him. "Why on earth did you dive into the swimming pool, you idiot? Didn't you see the signs saying the pool is only 1.2m deep?"

His reply was enigmatic, as he struggled to open another bottle of wine: "But our swimming pool at home is 1.75m deep and I can dive in there!" His wife ushered him away, blood still dripping from his nose.

Augusto sidled up to me shortly afterwards. "It's a good omen."

"What?"

"Blood spilled at the opening means a calm house."

I was fairly sure he was pulling my leg, seeing the twinkle in his eye.

One of our other guests had brought along his accordion and a friend a clarinet, so immediately after the meal had finished the music started and more fun followed, with dancing and singing.

Around 7 o'clock most people drifted off and we were left exhausted but contented. Various people offered to help clear up but we felt this time we would like to do everything ourselves. It was obviously the right thing to do because those who had asked if they could help, promptly rinsed a glass, opened more wine and sat relaxing on our veranda until dark.

It was only later we discovered our mistake, though nobody was critical about it.

"We just understood that you didn't understand," Rui enlightened us whilst pouring us a well-earned glass of wine.

Apparently if a meal is organised at lunch time, then another meal of equal importance and size is generally provided in the evening. Obviously the people who drifted off earlier had realised they weren't going to be fed again, and had returned to their own homes or back to neighbours' houses for the evening meal.

"In future, any parties we organise we'll go the whole hog," Sue decided.

"Or, if it's a more intimate gathering, ask people for early evening," I said, more conservatively.

Cláudia then reminded us why our numbers had swelled significantly from the original headcount – if someone was invited for a meal, drink or party, it was not uncommon for him to bring his wife, children, parents, grandparents and anybody else who would normally be with the family on that day, for the meal. Even though it made predicting numbers tricky, we found it to be an infallible system for making new friends.

Now, as our party wound down, the ancient local reporter who had written the unfortunate article about us and our home, saw us unattended and came over. "Is everything all right and do you now have your licence?"

"Not really. That article has created a lot of problems and raised issues with the local council about planning permission." I tried to be as civil as I could.

"Don't worry, just leave it with me. If you wish, I'll have a word, because the president is a close personal friend of mine. It will all be sorted out soon."

"That's good of you, but please say nothing and let it rest."

"You see, I heard about your difficulties with the pine trees. I can see how they might obstruct the sun for your visitors. They should be hewn down, or at least a few rows of them."

"Nevertheless, we'd appreciate it if you left well alone."

But he wouldn't give up. "I feel that Alombada is the perfect setting for your tourist trade – in my opinion more people will want to come here than go to larger cities like Aveiro. Are you thinking of expanding and building more apartments?"

My God, he was a persistent old bugger.

"No," Sue said emphatically.

I elaborated: "Look, Andy Warhol once said 'everybody has 15 minutes of fame' and I'm afraid ours has been a bit longer than that. Now we just want everything to cool down."

He wandered off to refill his glass.

Of course, we couldn't disagree with his conclusions. We had built our home in a small corner of paradise and were now sharing it with our visitors. As the day started to fade and people continued to drift away, the setting sun reminded us of how much we now had to lose. More headlines were the last thing we desired.

"We rather need the council to succumb to Alombaditus," asserted Sue.

Alombaditus – a benign sleeping sickness affecting all who arrive here. The air is so pure and fresh that within a few days our visitors relax and, as their stay here progresses, their lie-ins become later and later.

After everybody left and we had finished clearing up, we went outside and sat on our veranda. It had been a risk, coming out here at our time of life to undertake a substantial building project and set up a new business. We might never have done it if we'd delayed for even a couple of years. But it had been worth it and we'd both fulfilled our cherished dream.

We looked up at the canopy of sparkling stars. Far away, a comet or perhaps a shooting star blazed swiftly through the heavens. Nearer at hand, the eucalyptus trees were dancing a graceful pavane in the soft late evening breeze. Sue turned to me, chinked her glass against mine, and said: "I could, what about you?"

"I think I know what you mean."

So we stayed.

Casa Sulo

For further information on the Beiras and Costa de Prata regions of Portugal, visit our website at www.casasulo.com. We live in a quiet, rural, working village that offers a peaceful, safe and relaxing environment.

Although we are located at the top of a mountain with no through traffic, it is only a short drive to the Costa Nova with miles and miles of generally deserted golden, sandy beaches.

We have a saying here in Alombada, 'we are forty minutes from Porto, Viseu and Coimbra and only twenty minutes from Aveiro. Where else is there in the world?'

We consider Casa Sulo and Alombada to be the perfect location with the best of both worlds.

ISBN 1425156940